Beyond Tithing

Beyond Tithing

Stuart Murray

Wipf and Stock Publishers
199 W 8th Ave, Suite 3
Eugene, OR 97401

Beyond Tithing
By Murray, Stuart
Copyright©2002 by Murray, Stuart
ISBN 13: 978-1-61097-747-0
Publication date 1/3/2012
Previously published by Paternoster, 2002

To Sian

Contents

Contents ix

Foreword

What's wrong with tithing? Many Christians would say that nothing's wrong with tithing! Some pastors would agree: ever since their churches introduced tithing they have had more than enough money for salaries and buildings, with money left over for missions, local and global. Other pastors, eyeing the former enviously, wish that their people would be willing to tithe – or at least give five per cent. To some Christians in an age of downsizing and cost-cutting, tithing has seemed to be a spiritual and practical cure-all.

Stuart Murray disagrees. In this learned but accessible book he recognises that tithing has elicited sacrificial giving from some Christians and has brought some benefits to churches where it has been practised. But Murray's gaze is penetrating. He examines contemporary practice in light of the Bible and in light of church history. And he comes to some surprising conclusions. He contends that tithing is 'biblical, but not Christian'; that Jesus didn't affirm it; that the early Christians for three hundred years didn't practise it; and that tithing came into full flower among Christians only well after the conversion of Constantine in the civilisation that we have come to call Christendom. Thereafter, throughout the history of Christendom, tithing became a source of contention and dispute, poisoning the relationships of clergy and laity. In England, tithing eventually expired as a system in the 1930s. Just as Christendom was disintegrating, some Christians began to laud tithing as the Christian way to structure personal giving and church finances!

As I read this history of tithing, I was struck by how characteristic this is of the methodology of Christendom in general. Christendom thinkers and institution-builders, finding Christ and the Early Church dangerous and unsettling, leap back to the Old Testament for comfortable clues to ethics and the ordering of society. They do this on numerous issues – on war, priesthood and oath-taking as well as on tithing and wealth. Then, without consulting Jesus or the Early Christians for their views, they apply selected Old Testament motifs to society and call the result Christian. On issue after issue, this method has produced a church that has justified 'the powerful on their thrones'; it has been risk-averse and devoid of surprise; at its worst it has led to oppression and an all-pervasive joylessness.

Murray's approach is different. It profits from the lucidity of his legally trained mind. Murray is brilliant at figuring out how things such as the tithe worked in the Old Testament and in Christian history – or didn't work. And he explains things with great clarity; in his prose complicated things make sense! Murray's approach is further rooted in his Christocentrism. For him Jesus Christ is the triangulation point from which to view all of life. This leads to a probing and radical questioning of assumptions and practices that have been common among Christians. If tithing is so central, why did Jesus talk about Jubilee and an extravagant sharing in response to God's grace – and not tithing? Why did Paul urge koinonia and equality and the global redistribution of wealth – and not tithing? If tithing is so central, why didn't the early Church get the message? Looking at church history and at tithing churches today, Murray asks: does tithing perhaps function as a kind of regressive tax, burdening the poor while the rich get richer? Does it lead to legalism and a 'don't rock the boat' approach that are alienated from Jesus?

Above all, Murray writes as a hands-on missiologist. An experienced church-planter in urban England, Murray is aware of the crisis that Christianity is facing at the turn of the millennium. He suspects that a lot of the disinterest in Jesus and the church comes from people's deep memories of Christendom Christianity that was oppressive, uncreative and after their money. His question is, 'What kind of a church will intrigue and meet the deep needs of people in a post-Christendom society marked by a consumerism that can never satisfy?' His conclusion: it will be churches that are communities of justice and generosity, filled with the Spirit of Jesus. These will not be churches that legalistically tithe; they will be churches that discover freedom to respond to need and to share their weaknesses and wealth; that learn not to calculate percentages but to love God and others with heart, soul, mind and strength. Murray concludes his book by asking 'what if' about a plethora of practices that could transform the way Christians live and think. These practices, unlike the tithe, are creative and gracious, psychologically profound and Jesus-scented. And I find my mind racing and my spirit leaping with longing and hope.

Alan Kreider,
25 September 1999

Preface

I am grateful to a number of friends, colleagues and students who have helped me in various ways as I have studied the subject of tithing. Conversations with Mark Bonington several years ago helped to convince me that this was a subject worth exploring and Mark kindly supplied me with his own bibliography on the subject. Alan Kreider has been a valued friend and conversation partner on this subject (and many other subjects), and I am grateful to him for his helpful and incisive comments on the first draft of this book and for agreeing to write the foreword.

Responses from students at Spurgeon's College and elsewhere to two short papers on the subject I wrote some years ago have helped to refine my thinking. Judy Powles, librarian at Spurgeon's College, has helped me to track down numerous obscure books and articles on the subject. Anne Wilkinson-Hayes has read and commented on some sections of the book, as have Debra Reid and Arthur Rowe. Elaine Newey, my secretary, has helped in various ways with the preparation of the manuscript. Errors of fact or interpretation are, of course, my responsibility.

Chapter 1

Tithing: The Legacy

'The Church is Always After Our Money!'

This statement represents a remarkably familiar complaint among those who are not church members, but who come into contact with the church through occasional attendance, participation in one of the rites of passage, or conversation with a minister or church member. This judgement is common especially – but by no means exclusively – in inner-city areas where the population is relatively poor and alienated from the churches. The church is perceived as an institution that expects financial support, not only from its own members, but also from the community at large. This perception results in a degree of resentment, in the frequent characterisation of the church as being concerned about its own interests rather than those of the wider community, and in suspicion that the church, whatever it claims about its aims and priorities, is primarily interested in attracting financial support for its clergy, programmes and buildings.

It is tempting to dismiss this perception as a serious misunderstanding of the church's relationship with the wider community; to blame it on such tasteless stunts as the use of giant promotional thermometers outside church buildings to encourage gradual progress towards the goal of the organ restoration fund; to bewail the increasing influence in the cable and satellite television age of banal, exploitative and apparently money-obsessed tele-evangelists; or to respond merely by reminding visitors to church services that they are not expected to contribute as the offering plate is passed around (unless, of course, they have 'come prepared').

But this view of the church is surprisingly deep-rooted. The church is regarded as an institution that is not only mercenary in its ethos but grasping in its approach to those who are not personally associated with this institution. It is difficult to explain the strength and persistence of this perception solely on the basis of personal experiences, negative media images or insensitive church leaders. Some critics will be aware of and offended by the wealth of the church as a major landowner, the hard-nosed financial policies of certain church administrators, the unscrupulous or unwise financial dealings of denominational committees, and the general identification of the church with the well-to-do. But most of those who express the conviction that 'the church is always after our money' would be hard-pressed to substantiate their claim.

Nevertheless, there appears to be within our culture, perhaps operating primarily at a subconscious level, a deep suspicion that the church is in need of financial support and expects this to be provided, not only by its own members, but by the whole of society. From where does this suspicion come? What are the roots of such a persistent and widespread perception of the church?

There is reason to conclude that the primary source of this attitude towards the church is the practice of tithing that permeated European society throughout the many centuries of what has become known to historians as the era of Christendom. Christendom was the political and religious system that developed gradually between the fourth and seventh centuries, following the conversion of the Roman emperor Constantine I to Christianity.[1] The 'Christian Europe' that emerged from the Dark Ages was built on a close relationship between the state and the church and on the assumption that all members of society were automatically also members of the church. The tithe was introduced, initially as a voluntary offering and then as a legal requirement, in order to fund the state church.

Although Christendom has been fading over recent centuries, weakened by the cumulative influence of such social and philosophical developments as the Reformation, the Enlightenment, secularisation, pluralisation and postmodernity, many vestiges of it

---

[1] We will examine the concept of Christendom in more detail in chapter 5.

live on. These have been part of the culture of church and society for so many centuries that they are often hard to detect and harder still to challenge. Some are positive legacies that remain valuable in a changing culture, others may be neutral, but some are serious hindrances to the church and its mission in contemporary post-Christendom society. Tithing, despite the surprising enthusiasm for this practice in many churches today, is one of these vestiges; in my view, it falls into the category of vestiges that hinder the church and its mission.

Throughout Europe, tithing was for many centuries a fundamentally important but often deeply resented means of supporting the established churches, their buildings, programmes and clergy, and of making some provision for the poorer members of the community. The support of the state church by all members of society, of course, made sense in a Christendom culture, where membership of society was coterminous with church membership. Under the Christendom system, everyone benefited from and participated in the activities of the church (at least in theory) and so everyone could legitimately be expected to contribute to its upkeep.

But the fact that tithing may have made sense does not mean that the tithing system was ever popular. As we will see when we chart the history of this system of taxation from its origins in the early centuries of the newly Christianised Roman Empire to its final demise in the middle of the twentieth century, this is a history of conflict, misery and mutual recrimination between churches and their parishioners.

As Christendom has lost first its coherence and then its legitimacy over the past two or three centuries, many of its institutions have disappeared. After a long and painful struggle, tithing too – at least as a legal requirement – has been abolished, although this took place much more recently than many today may be aware. Despite the fact that the tithe had been for many decades widely regarded as anachronistic and unjust, and despite the damage done to the reputation of the church by its insistence that it should still receive tithes from those who were no longer remotely interested in the church, let alone active members, it was not until the 1930s that the tithe was finally prised away from the church in England.

This history – and the church's desperate but unsuccessful struggle to hold on to its financial support base – may be entirely unknown to the vast majority of those who regard the church as 'after our money', but it seems that its legacy lives on. What else can explain these persistent perceptions and suspicions, which are passed on in families and communities without apparent scrutiny or challenge, and which continue to alienate people from the church? The church to which you belong is not after the money of non-members, is it? You are doing nothing to suggest that people in your community should support your church financially, are you? In fact, you are doing all you can to make people feel welcome in your church, aren't you? So why do they still suspect that you are 'after their money'? And what can you do about this?

The first aim of this study, then, is to examine the practice and impact of tithing in the Christendom era and to explore ways in which Christians in post-Christendom can deal with its legacy.

Tithing: A Chequered History

In 1936, after long and vigorous campaigning by politicians, tithe-payers, reformers, free-church leaders and several of the more enlightened ministers of the established church, tithing was finally abolished as a legally enforceable payment under English law. One of the more irksome vestiges of the Christendom era had at long last been removed.

Or has it? Sixty years or more after the demise of tithing as the system whereby the established church was supported, tithing is still familiar as a method of funding numerous free churches across the country. This would surely come as quite a shock to the founding members of these churches and their denominations, many of whom were implacably opposed to tithing as a means of supporting the established churches and very wary of using the principle of the tithe to fund their own churches. Just as the established churches were finally letting go of the support system that had sustained them, albeit at the cost of alienating generations of their parishioners, many of the descendants of those who had protested against this system, sometimes at the cost of fines and imprisonment, were beginning to urge the members of their own churches to tithe their income as a sign of obedience to God and commitment to their church.

Indeed, interest in tithing appears to have increased markedly in recent years. A spate of books, booklets, tracts and sermons on the importance of tithing and the benefits accruing from this system appeared in the middle years of the twentieth century. The impact of this teaching about tithing and the exhortations to tithe that accompanied it have been considerable. With surprisingly little resistance, congregations, church leaders and whole denominations have embraced the system of tithing and have taught it as the norm to new members and to the next generation. Emerging networks of churches, especially those with an evangelical and charismatic theology, have enthusiastically adopted tithing as a sign of faithful discipleship and have raised very large amounts of money from those who give generously to causes in which they believe. Tithing continues to be advocated vigorously in many free-church circles, especially those that have been growing in numbers and influence in the past two decades.

This transmuted form of tithing is, of course, voluntary and mainly local – quite unlike the statutory requirement of tithing to support a national church, which had only recently been abolished when the early books and sermons on tithing began to appear. But it does seem surprising that so many free churches were willing so quickly to adopt a model of giving that had been so deeply unpopular for so long and against which their own forebears had fought so vigorously. Furthermore, it is striking that arguments used to endorse the practice of voluntary tithing are remarkably similar to those used through preceding centuries to justify the system of legal tithing. More worrying still is what is missing. Almost absent from this smooth and rapid transition of tithing from the established churches to the free churches[2] is any careful examination of the history of tithing, any reflection on the persistent complaints about the injustice of the tithing system within that history, and any critical engagement with historical attempts to interpret the biblical and theological foundations upon which tithing supposedly rests.

---

[2] In recent years, Catholic and Anglican churches have also begun to advocate tithing, but it is in the free churches that this practice is more prevalent.

The history of tithing is rarely mentioned in most of the sermons and books on tithing which have appeared in recent decades. Perhaps the advocates of voluntary tithing have assumed that it was the framework within which tithing had operated for so many centuries that was the problem, rather than tithing itself, and so did not dwell on this history but concentrated on biblical references to tithing and their contemporary application. This is the more charitable view of such a surprising silence on so many years of experience with tithing. A classic example of this is R. T. Kendall's claim that tithing, 'though not a twentieth century innovation (!) . . . has spread more widely in the last hundred years than in previous generations of the Christian church.'[3]

It may be that Kendall and many other advocates of tithing are simply ignorant of the history of tithing. Or perhaps they have not recognised that there is an issue here and have fallen into the familiar practice of jumping straight from biblical texts to the contemporary context without reference to the hundreds of years of intervening history, experience and reflection. This intervening history is not determinative and certainly does not preclude new interpretations or applications of the texts, but some knowledge of how tithing has operated in past centuries might be of relevance in assessing whether this is an appropriate model for churches today.

So the second aim of this study is to reflect on the history of tithing and on arguments used in previous generations to endorse this practice, with a view to assessing whether tithing, even in its transmuted form, is a helpful model for Christians today.

Tithing: What Does the Bible Really Teach?

If most twentieth-century advocates of tithing have given little attention to historical perspectives, their awareness of issues of biblical interpretation in relation to the subject of the tithe also seems limited. Tithing is generally presented as *the* biblical model for dealing with questions of giving and sharing among the people of God, as a direct and clear scriptural command that is binding on Christians in all times and places, and as the biblical basis for guaranteed divine blessing.

---

[3] R. T. Kendall, *Tithing* (London: Hodder & Stoughton, 1982), 38.

Although explicit biblical references to tithing are relatively limited, especially in the New Testament, these references are often ascribed paradigmatic significance within biblical teaching on financial matters. The principle of the tithe is then used as the interpretative framework for dealing with the extensive biblical teaching on how rich and poor people relate, on patterns of consumption and giving, on social structures, and on issues of lifestyle and justice. Although tithing is not even mentioned in the vast majority of these passages, which reflect the various theological and sociological perspectives of their authors, the principle of the tithe is placed as a grid over these texts and their contents are understood by reference to this.

No persuasive argument is advanced for employing the principle of the tithe in this controlling way. Relatively little thought appears to have been given to contextual differences between the cultures within which tithing was practised in biblical times and the cultures within which tithing is advocated today. Furthermore, there are substantial difficulties involved in determining how the system of tithing operated in biblical times, how it related to other economic dimensions of society, whether the tithe meant the same thing in different eras, and even what percentage of income was required. The result of this methodology is not only a crass and monochrome exegesis which fails to appreciate the richness and diversity of biblical teaching on economic issues, but a blinkered approach that seriously hinders proper engagement with some of the most liberating and challenging dimensions of the biblical story. Much recent advocacy of tithing is very disappointing in the way it handles the Bible. It appears to be based on naive and literalistic biblical interpretation, which no amount of proof-texts, enthusiastic exhortation, and glowing testimony to the benefits of tithing will offset.

Such testimonies abound within the literature and make heart-warming reading. Many fine Christians have expressed their devotion to Christ, their faith in God's promises and their commitment to the advance of God's kingdom through tithing. They testify to diverse spiritual and material blessings, which they associate confidently with the practice of tithing. It is not the intention of this study to dismiss such testimonies or to minimise the love, faith and generosity of those for whom tithing has been a powerful aid to discipleship.

However, testimonies can be interpreted in various ways. For God is gracious and God sees the heart's intention. God's blessing on those who tithe does not require us to conclude without further question that this implies God's blessing on the system of tithing. Our assessment of tithing should not exclude such testimonies (or, of course, the other testimonies, not normally included in books on tithing, of those whose experience of tithing has been negative and who have found it discouraging and even oppressive). But it cannot rest on these – or even on a combination of testimonies and biblical proof-texts.

The third aim of this study is to look carefully at biblical references to tithing in both Testaments, to set these in their contexts and, in conversation with other interpreters through the centuries, to offer an alternative way of interpreting and applying these references.

Tithing: 'Bad news to the poor'

A less than positive testimony about tithing was one of the factors that prompted me to study the subject and eventually to write this book. Several years ago, I was approached by a friend at the end of a church meeting during which nothing had been said about tithing or giving. She was in a very poorly paid job and could only just manage to make ends meet. She was worried and wanted to ask for advice. She had calculated that, if she tithed her income after paying tax, she could still just about cover her weekly expenses; but if she tithed before paying tax she would start to get into debt. She was convinced she should be tithing – and had had no difficulty with the calculations – but she had heard someone teaching that God must come first and so the tithe had to be paid before deducting tax. She didn't want to 'rob God', but she couldn't see how she could cope financially if she did this.

For me, this conversation was a defining moment in my thinking about the issue of tithing. Tithing for my friend was oppressive rather than liberating, a source of anxiety rather than joy, an expression of legalism rather than grace. No doubt some would have counselled her to pay her whole pre-tax tithe and trust God to provide for her needs. Others might have encouraged her to choose the more manageable option of tithing after tax and have assured her that this is a perfectly legitimate way of interpreting the tithing system. My own reaction was to determine to research the whole subject of tithing thoroughly. If the gospel is meant to be 'good news to the poor',[4] something seemed to be wrong here.

So the fourth aim of this study is to investigate the way that tithing has had impact on both the poor and the rich throughout the many centuries it has been practised, and to assess to what extent the practice of tithing today is good or bad news to the poor.

What's Wrong with Tithing?

In this study, then, we will examine the model of tithing, with a view to assessing whether it is an appropriate principle to guide Christians and churches in handling their finances today. We will explore questions of biblical interpretation, consider historical precedents, and investigate the pastoral and missiological significance of this practice. Some of what follows will necessarily be quite detailed – since tithing is not the simple 10% principle most advocates claim but a complex set of regulations that has varied enormously over the centuries – but it will not be technical or unduly complicated. Underlying questions, which we will keep asking in relation to tithing, are:

- Tithing is undoubtedly biblical, but is it Christian?
- Can tithing be extracted from its biblical context without becoming an unjust and oppressive practice?
- Tithing has been a source of misery and conflict for centuries – can it be redeemed?
- What do we fail to see in the teaching of Jesus and the rest of the Bible if we read it with 'tithing blinkers' on?
- What attitudes, practices and reflexes are associated with tithing, and what kind of community life is fostered by tithing?

We will attempt to focus on the issue of tithing and resist the constant temptation to broaden the scope of our investigation to

---

[4] Jesus identified this as a major component in his mission in Luke 4:18–20 and it recurs throughout the New Testament in various ways.

embrace a range of questions relating to economics, lifestyle and discipleship. This temptation is especially strong because it is just such questions that are so often marginalised when tithing becomes dominant. But our intention here is deliberately more limited: to examine as thoroughly as space allows the biblical and historical foundations upon which the principle of tithing rests and the implications of adopting this practice in churches today.

The conclusion towards which we will argue may already be evident from this introduction, but to avoid any uncertainty (and to save those readers who thought this book might endorse tithing both time and money), let me be clear about my position. While I respect and honour the convictions and motives of many who tithe, I do not agree with tithing and I believe there is much that is wrong with this practice and the way it is advocated. My firm conviction is that tithing has been a pernicious and unjust system through many centuries; that it is based on a deeply flawed interpretation of biblical teaching; that it hinders thoughtful engagement with the much broader scope of biblical teaching on the issue of handling resources; that it fosters unhelpful practices among Christians; that it is good news to the rich rather than good news to the poor; and that those who have in recent decades eagerly but uncritically embraced tithing would do well to reconsider this decision.

Alternatives to Tithing

Although we will resist broadening the scope of this study as we argue towards this uncompromising conclusion, it would be unfair simply to leave things at that point. Not only would a book entirely given over to the deconstruction of tithing be rather negative, it might also be thought pastorally irresponsible. Those who challenge the practice of tithing are often accused of advocating a soft option or of jeopardising the well-being of the church by threatening its support base. So, in the final part of the book, we will consider some alternative principles and models. How can we handle our resources if we do not tithe? What other biblical themes and practices have been marginalised by the dominance of tithing? What positive lessons can we learn from the long and miserable history of the tithe? What other paradigms might we discover once we have removed the 'tithing blinkers'?

What we will *not* do, however, is become prescriptive at this point. The last thing Christians need today is another programme or system. One of the main drawbacks of the tithing system is simply that it is a system. But we will reflect briefly on a number of biblical themes and practices. We will listen to the witness of Christians in other times and places who did not practise tithing but found other ways to deal with their resources – especially the Christians of the first three centuries and the members of dissident movements who were not as affected by Christendom assumptions as their contemporaries. And we will ask some 'what if?' questions as we encourage one another to be creative, to listen to the Spirit, to talk together about our resources and to dare to question our priorities and values.

Why Bother about Tithing?

But is it worth writing (or, for that matter, reading) a study of tithing through the centuries? Does it really matter whether Christians and churches use the tithe as a model for their giving and receiving of resources? Is this a significant issue or a case of splitting hairs?

You will need to decide for yourself about this – either now as you decide whether to read on or later as you review what you have read. Let me explain why I chose to invest time researching and writing about tithing.

First, if this is a minor issue, it is surprising how many Christians and especially church leaders are interested in it[5] and intrigued by the suggestion that there are problems with the tithing model – especially if this is in the context of suggesting that this model is not

---

[5] A recent search for references to tithing on the Internet revealed nearly 10,000 entries from a wide range of perspectives, some advocating and others challenging the practice. Sermons on Christian cable television channels frequently advocate tithing. 35% of evangelical churchgoers informed a recent survey that they were taught by their church leaders that every Christian should tithe their income.

radical enough. This interest has been mainly in evangelical and
charismatic churches, no doubt because it is in these churches that
tithing has been most energetically advocated in recent decades. It
seems that many in these churches have assumed that the only
available options are tithing or a return to the paltry and undisciplined giving which has characterised many churches where tithing
is not advocated. The idea that tithing itself is deficient because it is
not sufficiently radical is not one that most have previously
considered.

I have not often addressed meetings on this precise subject –
after all, debunking the tithe does not sound an exciting topic!
And one or two church leaders, knowing my stance on tithing,
have banned me from speaking about this in their churches! But I
have taken many opportunities in various contexts to mention in
passing my concerns about tithing, raising questions about its
biblical basis and whether it is a just and useful way of dealing with
financial issues. I have almost always had a queue of people waiting
to speak to me afterwards about this (rather than the main point of
the lecture or sermon). Most of these have been eager to hear
more; many have expressed for the first time their own reserva-
tions about tithing and their disquiet that their church teaches and
expects this; some have spoken of being liberated by what they
have heard.

Second, the presenting issue may be tithing, but challenging this
practice is a helpful way to encourage a fresh look at a range of other
issues about lifestyle, discipleship, the nature of the church, social
justice and mission. Once the 'tithing blinkers' are removed, all
kinds of new ideas and possibilities can be explored. Deconstructing
the tithing paradigm clears the ground and invites creativity and
conversation rather than compliance with a fixed standard.

Third, the way in which the Bible has been used (I would say
abused) to advocate tithing, unless challenged, can easily become a
model for interpreting biblical teaching on other issues. Indeed,
advocacy of tithing is often accompanied by teaching on a range of
subjects that evinces similar and equally deficient principles of interpretation. Challenging the hermeneutics of tithing is a useful
starting point for challenging the illegitimate ways in which the
Bible is used to justify all kinds of 'biblical' but non-Christian
practices.

Fourth, as mentioned earlier, tithing is but one of many vestiges of the Christendom era that remain alive within our churches. Christendom as a political arrangement may be defunct, but the structures, models, mindset and reflexes that developed during this period are still surprisingly influential. We may be tempted to hold on to these ideas and practices, partly because they are very familiar, partly because we associate them with an era when the church was supposedly healthier and more central to society. But we are wiser if we reject such nostalgia, embrace the new opportunities and challenges of post-Christendom and apply ourselves to developing new patterns of discipleship that will equip us for mission and ministry in this environment. Letting go of tithing and thinking creatively and contextually about appropriate principles for giving and sharing in the twenty-first-century church might encourage a similar response as other vestiges of Christendom are identified.

Fifth, the ways in which we handle our resources and particularly the principles that govern how we use our money are of considerable significance in contemporary culture. Christians have commented extensively on the materialism that permeates our society (although we must bear in mind that some aspects of postmodernity represent dissatisfaction with materialistic attitudes), but it is important that we do not fail to engage with a closely related phenomenon that is even more dominant and probably a greater challenge to spirituality and community values – the culture of consumerism.

Colin Campbell, a social historian, identifies as the key factor in consumerism 'the want to want' and traces the development of this imperative over several centuries.[6] Campbell's work is referred to in a collection of perceptive essays, edited by Rodney Clapp, entitled: *The Consuming Passion: Christianity and the Consumer Culture.*[7] Among the components of consumerism identified by contributors are: the stimulation of insatiable desires; the implication that

---

[6] Colin Campbell, 'Romanticism and the Consumer Ethic: Intimations of a Weber-Style Thesis', *Sociological Analysis* 44 (Winter 1983), 279–296.
[7] Rodney Clapp, *The Consuming Passion: Christianity and the Consumer Culture* (Downers Grove, Ill.: IVP, 1998). For a more accessible popular introduction to consumerism, see Mike Starkey, *Born to Shop* (Eastbourne: Monarch, 1989).

happiness and meaning are obtained through seeking and obtaining certain possessions; the influence of advertising and peer pressure; the enjoyment of the *process* of obtaining goods; shopping as a social and cultural pursuit rather than a merely functional activity; and an emphasis on individualism and appeal to individual choice in the context of the severe limitations imposed on such choice by mass production.

In the context of a consumerist culture, giving, sharing and community discussions of lifestyle issues become crucial but counter-cultural practices for churches to explore and model. Some advocates of tithing seem blissfully unaware that their advocacy of tithing not only fails to identify and challenge the culture of consumerism but depends upon consumerist values and perspectives (especially individualism). Many more who teach tithing present it as an effective way of resisting the influence of materialism and consumerism – of conquering Mammon – but it is extremely doubtful whether tithing was intended to accomplish this or has the weapons to win this particular battle. We need to look again at how we give and share resources without making the dangerous and unfounded assumption that tithing can release us from Mammon's clutches.

Finally, we do need to have something authentic to say in response to those who claim: 'The church is after our money.' If the tithing system of previous centuries has been a major factor in the church being perceived in this way, it seems rather unlikely that a transmuted form of tithing, however voluntary, will do much to change this damaging image which seriously hinders the church's mission. Of course, stopping tithing will not by itself achieve this change of image: tithing as a legal requirement in England was abolished over sixty years ago, but the suspicion that the church wants money from others still persists. The only legitimate and effective way to change the church's image is to change the church.

Only when congregations up and down the land are known as communities of justice, simplicity, giving and sharing will we be able to say in response to those who think the church is after their money: 'That was certainly true sometimes in the past, but things have changed. Come and see how we operate now.' Only when local churches recover their divine vocation to be 'good news to the poor' will they have anything that sounds or looks remotely like good news in a post-Christendom world that is sure that Christianity is obsolete, boring and irrelevant. Only when we develop counter-cultural reflexes and practices in the area of resources will our churches have anything useful to offer to a consumerist society that is being consumed by consumption but does not know where to look for alternatives. Tithing will not produce these kinds of churches – indeed it will almost certainly hinder this process. Abolishing tithing might just be the stimulus we need to engage in fresh ways with both our culture and biblical teaching and to rediscover what it means for our churches to become 'good news to the poor'.

But those who advocate and practise tithing will not easily be persuaded to let go of this. Tithing does, after all, offer some significant benefits to both tithers and local churches. In the next chapter, before exploring biblical teaching on tithing, we will examine some of these benefits. But we must also discuss some of the problems and drawbacks associated with tithing, which are less often considered by its advocates.

Chapter 2

Tithing: Costs and Benefits

Arguments for Tithing

1. Tithing is simple

A flat rate of 10% has the important merit of being simple to understand and apply. Not only is the concept easy to grasp but the mathematics are also straightforward. Indeed, it has been suggested that the concept of the tithe, which was common in many ancient societies as well as Old Testament Israel, derived from the primitive use of fingers and thumbs to effect calculations. Whether one receives an annual salary, a weekly wage, casual earnings, or some form of state benefit, it is a simple matter to work out what 10% of this income comprises and to set this aside as one's tithe. Similarly, whether one earns £6,000, £60,000 or £600,000 a year, calculating the tithe of this income is simply a matter of adjusting to the number of noughts in the figure. However high or low one's income, a tithe of this can be calculated and paid. Because tithing is based on a proportion of income rather than on the amount given, nobody who has any income at all is deprived of the privilege and responsibility of giving.

Whether this simplicity obscures certain problems with tithing – such as the apparent inequality of sacrifice required of those earning £6,000 and those earning £600,000 – we will explore in due course. It is worth noting immediately, however, that there are some complications involved in attempting to apply the principle of tithing, especially if the biblical model is one's intended guide rather than a bald 10% of income. One such complication prompted my friend to initiate the conversation I mentioned in the previous chapter: is the tithe paid on gross or net income? This is a far from academic issue for people at both ends of the income scale. For those like my friend on a very low income, it may make the difference between just managing and going into debt. For those on a very high salary in an economy that taxes such earners punitively, tithing their gross income might conceivably require them to give away more than they actually earn once they have also paid tax. But the Bible does not seem to indicate whether the tithe should be paid on gross or net income. Nor does it give any guidelines about how to treat expenses that are allowable against tax, or whether certain kinds of state benefits are subject to the tithe.

The root of the problem, of course, is that the biblical tithe was designed for a very different context, where such questions did not arise and so were not addressed. In primitive societies, especially those operating without a money economy or income tax system, it may be relatively straightforward to apply a 10% rule. But in modern societies, where economic transactions are complex and where all kinds of taxes and exemptions apply, it may be far from simple to work out what income should or should not be tithed and at what point. Indeed, the history of tithing indicates that the system has been fraught with practical difficulties over many centuries, even when the economic system was far less complicated. English case law on tithing is extensive. It evolved century by century as those from whom tithes were due and those responsible for collecting tithes have argued in court over all kinds of questions. Which kinds of crops were subject to tithe? When was the tithe to be paid? In what form was it to be paid? Could the tithe be commuted into a cash payment? On what basis was this to be calculated? The history of tithing is a history of constant disputes, and laws relating to the tithe are characterised by hair-splitting and bewildering complexity.

Giving 10% of one's income sounds simple, but careful examination of the financial dealings of an average family reveals a range of questions if one is wanting to achieve precision. Of course, one response to this is to argue that such calculations are legalistic and that tithing should be seen as a matter of principle rather than detail, a biblical norm rather than an amount to be worked out by accountants. But it is doubtful whether this will satisfy those who are concerned to ensure that they are being fully obedient to what they see as a biblical requirement. Perhaps this is being uncharitable, but it also seems likely that those who are richer and whose finances are more complex will, given the freedom to do so, choose an interpretation of the principle that will ease the burden of tithing on them. Furthermore, if working out what it means to tithe today is not as straightforward as it appears, the same can be said of tithing in the Old Testament. Biblical legislation about tithing, as we will see in a later chapter, appears to be much more complicated than simply giving away 10% of income, so even attempting to apply 'the biblical principle' is fraught with difficulties. However careful we are, we may simply not be comparing like with like.

2. *Tithing is ancient*

Part of the appeal of tithing is that it is such an ancient and long-established principle. No other approach to giving can claim such antiquity or widespread usage. For many advocates of tithing, it is the references to tithing in some of the oldest strata of Old Testament documents that authenticate this practice as a divine requirement from earliest times. As Clarence Lee writes:

> Perhaps the most widely employed law of stewardship in the history of the church has been the law of the tithe . . . The wide acceptance which this particular system has enjoyed is undoubtedly due to the fact that it supposedly rests upon the authority of the Bible. No other system or technique for raising money has been able to rival the tithe as a way of meeting one's responsibilities vis-à-vis God, simply because no other system has managed to find such an impressive sanction in the Scriptures.[1]

But tithing, as mentioned above, was not invented by the Israelites or unique to their economic system. There may be distinctive elements of the Israelite tithing system, but some form of tithing was practised throughout the Middle East and in many ancient cultures. The fact that tithing was so common in ancient societies can be interpreted as either challenging or endorsing the view that this is a divinely instituted economic provision. If tithing developed from

---

[1] Quoted in Lukas Vischer, *Tithing in the Early Church* (Philadelphia: Fortress Press, 1966), ix.

the use of fingers and thumbs to make simple calculations, this might be thought to undercut its supposed divine authority. It might also bring in question the relevance of tithing in a society that no longer relies on such computational aids (although working in tenths is still helpful in everyday mental arithmetic).

Some have suggested, though, that the widespread use of tithing is evidence rather of its divine origin. Thus, Herschel Hobbs writes:

> The survival of this practice [tithing] among all ancient peoples, plus the biblical record, would indicate a common denominator which God set forth in the beginning. As he hallowed one day out of seven, so did he make holy unto himself one tenth of the whole as a reminder of his creative work and continuing ownership.[2]

Tithing would thus be based not just on Old Testament texts but on a creation ordinance applicable to all societies. Hobbs insists: 'the tithe was not a scheme invented by the Levites, but is a basic law of God's universe.'[3] The teaching of the Old Testament on tithing could, on this basis, be understood as an adaptation (by Yahweh or by Israel) of a familiar cultural element and its incorporation, together with a new theological and ethical interpretation, into the worship and civil law of the covenant people. Tithing would certainly not be the only example of such a process.

The origins of tithing, however, are obscure and it is a question of conjecture as to how tithing began and what status it should be accorded. Although tithing is undoubtedly an ancient practice, it remains an open question whether it can be translated unchanged from cultures – biblical or pagan – where it was part of an integrated economic and religious system into contemporary societies that are very different. If tithing was a divine ordinance for all humanity, as some claim, then some application of this principle should surely still be attempted today, although there is no particular reason why a contemporary application should have much in common with the application of this principle in Old Testament Israel. But there is no way to validate this claim.

---

[2] Herschel Hobbs, *The Gospel of Giving* (Nashville: Broadman Press, 1954), 14.

[3] Hobbs, *Gospel*, 18.

If tithing was a widespread – but not divinely mandated – cultural norm that was subsequently taken up into Israelite law and religion, it may (like much else in the Old Testament) be instructive and challenging for contemporary Christians, but it cannot be regarded as binding on non-Israelites. As we reflect on what the tithe meant in Old Testament Israel, we may find clues as to how we deal with our financial resources. This could be helpful, provided we recognise two things: first, that this was a culturally specific adaptation of a common practice; and second, that it was but one element in the much more complex economic system described in the Old Testament. Simply giving away 10% of our income fails to take seriously enough the Old Testament teaching on tithing and its context.

3. Tithing is systematic

By comparison with spontaneous responses to appeals, the emptying of small change into offering bags, and other forms of occasional giving, tithing has the significant advantage of being systematic and regular. This has benefits for both givers and those who administer the gifts.

For givers, tithing ensures that they are dealing responsibly with their financial resources, that they are giving consistently and in an organised manner. Although those who present their tithe in the form of cash or cheques still need to remember to make the appropriate calculations and regular payments, they are relieved of having to make and review decisions about how much to give. Those who pay their tithe by standing order are relieved even of the need to remember what they are giving and when – provided they remember to adjust the amount they give as their income increases. Tithing enables a decision to be made at a single point in time and then to be implemented without further consideration.

There is much to commend in this systematic approach to giving. Tithing represents for most givers a serious and disciplined approach to financial discipleship. Being proportionate to income, the tithing system ensures that as income rises giving keeps pace. Without this safeguard it is all too easy to continue giving the same amount as one gave when one's income was substantially less – especially when giving by standing order. Keith Tondeur rightly reminds us: 'when Christians do not plan their giving they usually have nothing to give.

All of us tend to allow our standard of living to drift upwards in line with our income.'[4] Furthermore, in a culture which has been described as 'resources-rich but time-poor', establishing and maintaining a systematic approach to giving may be seen as sensible stewardship of time, involving a single decision rather than a drawn-out series of decisions.

Churches in which a substantial proportion of members tithe also benefit from this systematic approach. Knowing that they will receive regular and predictable amounts of income from their members enables those who administer church finances to plan with confidence in relation to staffing, premises and projects. There will, of course, be some degree of variation, as members join or leave and as incomes of members rise or fall, but such churches are in a much stronger financial position than those who rely upon special gift days, appeals and erratic amounts in the weekly offerings.

Two further factors enhance the benefits enjoyed by churches that teach and practise tithing. First, members of these churches generally tithe most or all of their income to their local church, whereas in many other churches giving is split between support of the local church and support of other people and causes – missionary societies, individual Christian workers, charities, campaigning groups and other organisations. The charge given by the prophet Malachi to 'bring the whole tithe into the storehouse, that there may be food in my house' (Mal. 3:10) is interpreted in many tithe-oriented churches as requiring tithes to be brought into the local church for administration and disbursement rather than being distributed by the giver. Hobbs urges: 'The church, your church, is the bride of Christ. Let the bride have both the credit and the glory as you lay by in store your tithes and offerings in the storehouse of God – your local church.'[5] There are other ways of interpreting this verse and other ways of tithing than directing the

---

[4] Keith Tondeur, *Your Money and Your Life* (London: SPCK, 1996), 102.

[5] Hobbs, *Gospel*, 45. The earliest example of this interpretation I have found is in James Hensey, *Storehouse Tithing: or, Stewardship Up-to-Date* (New York: Fleming H. Revell, 1922). This approach is taught widely in the House Church Movement and is also strongly advocated in R. T. Kendall, *Tithing* (London: Hodder & Stoughton, 1982), 70.

entire amount into the local church, but the stronger the emphasis
on tithing, the more likely church members are to tithe mainly or
exclusively to their own church. Once the tithe has been paid in this
way, further 'offerings' can, of course, be given to other people and
agencies.

Second, those who tithe tend to be deeply committed to their
local church in other than financial ways. Tithing is both an
expression of this multifaceted commitment (and is taught as one
dimension of this) and an enhancement of it. Those who tithe are
more likely than occasional givers to support the work of their local
church in other ways – through regular participation in meetings
and programmes, through active recruitment of new members,
through prayer and encouragement. Giving regularly to the church
increases the sense of ownership a church member feels towards the
church and its mission.

Beneficial though tithing is as a systematic approach to giving,
there are a number of factors that may need to be taken into account
in assessing whether this feature of tithing is an unmitigated
blessing. Several of these are related to the tendency of any systema-
tised form of giving to separate the giver from the gift and from the
act of giving. At its worst, systematic tithing can degenerate into a
subscription mentality – tithers can be inhibited from spontaneous
and extravagant acts of generosity, and giving can become divorced
from the context of worship. In some situations, tithing to the local
church represents an abnegation of personal responsibility for
administering one's giving. Although this may be presented as an
expression of commitment to the vision of the church and an
indication of trust in the church leaders to administer gifts wisely,
the system may foster inadequate accountability of those who
administer the gifts and limited ownership by givers of the objects to
which their gifts are applied. If things go wrong in such a context,
they can go badly wrong.

Tithing need not operate in this way, of course, and those who
administer tithes can both be held accountable by tithers and take
care to ensure that tithing is set within the context of worship and a
high level of ownership. But there are many churches which are
well endowed financially through the consistent tithing of wealthy
members but which fail to engage with these tithers on issues of
discipleship. Tithing may be for some a relatively cheap way of

ensuring themselves a place of honour in a local church without having their lifestyle disturbed, their priorities challenged, or their time and privacy invaded.

The point is not that tithing always or even usually results in such distorted views of church membership and discipleship. As we have already commented, many tithers are deeply committed and wholehearted church members. The point is that tithing in itself is no guarantee of such commitment and that tithing may serve to insulate those who tithe from facing challenges relating to lifestyle and discipleship.

There are other disadvantages with systematic tithing. Having established 10% of income as the proportion one gives away, it is easy to become complacent and insensitive to opportunities and challenges to give beyond this limit. Tithing can hinder one's responsiveness and function as a cap on generosity. Lee comments:

> The tithe, when adopted as a divinely appointed measure of Christian giving, leads almost inevitably to the belief that it represents a fulfilment of what God expects from us. The tithe which commits a tenth part of our wealth to God makes it possible for us – but allegedly with divine approval – to retain personal control over the greater portion of our possessions.[6]

Of course, this need not be so, and many churches that teach tithing insist that the tithe represents a baseline for giving, a starting point, a minimum, and that 'offerings' can and should be given on top of the tithe. But a recent research project into patterns of giving among evangelical donors reports:

> We also noted that with regard to giving to church and Christian charities giving 10% of monthly household income was the 'upper limit' of giving . . . In a world becoming increasingly wealthy compared to that of our parents and grandparents, we find it very difficult to give away our money to Christian work.[7]

---

[6] Quoted in Vischer, *Tithing*, x–xi.
[7] 'Who Gives to What and Why? . . . Getting to Know Evangelical Donors' (a survey carried out by Redina Kolaneci under the auspices of the Whitefield Institute, 1998), 13.

Commitment to tithing ensures systematic giving, but this may be at the expense of both spontaneity and generosity. Giving away 10% of income may represent a generous and even sacrificial response for someone on a low income, but for a high-earner tithing may represent a paltry sum and may deflect the challenge of submitting one's lifestyle and finances to the lordship of Christ.

Problems with Tithing

We have already indicated some of the problems associated with tithing and have suggested that even some of the recognisable advantages of tithing may carry with them unforeseen and unwanted consequences. There are other problems that we have yet to discuss.

1. Tithing tends towards legalism

The enthusiasm for tithing evident in many charismatic churches seems anomalous within a movement that has emphasised grace rather than law and has encouraged reliance on the Holy Spirit rather than submission to rules. That tithing is also taught within Pentecostal churches is less surprising given the tendency to legalism that has characterised this older renewal movement, but tithing and charismatic spirituality do not fit together that comfortably. No doubt tithing can be presented as a free response to the grace of God and as a mark of the Spirit's work in individuals and churches, but this is not wholly convincing. For the tithe was part of the Old Testament law and the very few references to the tithe in the New Testament are all set in the context of either the law or legalism.

Furthermore, the long and troubled history of tithing suggests that it is especially vulnerable to legalism. Not only were tithes legally enforced for many centuries, but arguments over tithes were often characterised by wearying negotiations over details that were good news only for the lawyers paid to resolve these disputes. Richard Nelson, a Lutheran writer, reminds us: 'it would be well to remember how vulnerable the tithe has been to legalism . . . the

Reformation was triggered by a stewardship program which obscured the gospel!'[8]

Contemporary advocates of tithing might protest that they are interested in voluntary rather than legal tithes and might wish to disassociate themselves from this depressing history, but a survey of books on voluntary tithing written in the past century indicates that the tendency to legalism is alive and well long after statutory tithing was abolished. Not many contain statements as blatant as those of Hobbs, whose book, *The Gospel of Giving*, begins with the assertion: 'Our God is a God of law – and grace – but basically of law.'[9] But several commend tithing along similar lines to popular Bible teacher Stephen Olford who insists: 'the responsibility to bring *all* the tithes and offerings to the local church is plainly illustrated in the Old Testament and definitely taught in the New Testament . . . Now this is scripturally binding upon all who desire to see the blessing of God'.[10]

Robert Hastings quotes an unnamed American professor whose survey of teaching on tithing among American Baptists led him to the following conclusion:

> I am deeply concerned about the tendency . . . to refuse the responsibility of freedom in Christ under grace. We seem to be afraid of freedom and therefore we are inclined to put ourselves under law. To teach our people that tithing is the Christian way of stewardship is to deny our people the right to be full-grown, mature people in the kingdom of God . . . we must challenge them to accept the responsibilities of grace and freedom and teach them full, all-encompassing stewardship in the kingdom of God.[11]

It is surely not accidental that Jesus mentioned tithing only in the context of legalism. There may be ways to advocate and practise tithing that are not legalistic, and some who teach tithing mount a

---

[8] Richard Nelson, 'Biblical Perspectives on Stewardship', *Lutheran Theological Seminary Bulletin*, 70(4) (1990), 3–11.

[9] Hobbs, *Gospel*, 12.

[10] Stephen Olford, *The Grace of Giving* (London: Lakeland, 1972), 26.

[11] Robert Hastings, *My Money and God* (Nashville: Broadman, 1961), 67.

vigorous defence of tithing against this charge,[12] but it does seem
that this methodology is especially prone to become legalistic.

2. Tithing relies on inadequate hermeneutics

Most advocates of tithing are concerned to establish a clear biblical
basis for this practice from texts that refer to the tithe. This is not
strictly necessary: church members can be encouraged to give a
tenth of their income to God or to the church on the grounds that
this will enable the church to cover its costs or that this is a
reasonable percentage to give away in order to display a
commitment to the church and its mission. Or a more general
biblical basis for tithing might be sought that does not rely as heavily
on texts where tithing is explicitly mentioned. Christians can be
urged to reflect on the extensive teaching in the New Testament on
possessions and how to handle these and to consider whether giving
away a tenth of their income is an appropriate response to this
teaching.

But advocates of tithing are generally interested in demonstrating that there is a more substantial biblical basis for the tithe. Thus,
Kendall insists: 'There is ultimately only one reason why every
Christian should be a tither: because it is biblical. All other reasons,
whatever their advantages may be, would not have any weight
behind them at all if what we are talking about was not utterly
biblical.'[13] Sermons and books on tithing draw heavily on the
references in both Testaments to the tithe and argue from these that
tithing is a divine requirement. The lines of argument vary a little
among writers and preachers, but the small number of biblical
references to tithing tends to limit the scope for different
approaches.

What is apparent – and disturbing – in much of this advocacy of
tithing is the minimal attention paid to principles of biblical
interpretation. Literalism and proof-texting seem to dominate the

---

[12] By claiming that the tithe predates the Law, by challenging the
meaning of 'legalism', by using other words like 'duty', or by differentiating between 'legally required' and 'legalistic'. Several of these arguments
are employed, not wholly convincingly, in Kendall, *Tithing*, passim.
[13] Kendall, *Tithing*, 25.

discussion. Tithing is read off the pages of Scripture and into contemporary church life with little interest in the biblical context within which these texts occur and little apparent awareness of the difficulties involved in discerning the significance of these texts for a very different context. Those who challenge this naive literalism or raise concerns about contextual issues are sometimes accused of wanting to evade the challenge of Scripture or of introducing unnecessary complications. It is certainly true that some theological and hermeneutical discussion can function in such ways, bringing confusion rather than clarity. But there are real issues of interpretation here that need to be faced if we are not to end up with a simplistic reading of Scripture which itself evades the biblical challenge.

Among the issues of interpretation relating to tithing are the following: What role did tithing play in the Old Testament law? How did it relate to other economic provisions? What theological, liturgical and ethical implications did tithing have? How many tithes were there in Israel? How did tithing develop over the centuries covered by the Old Testament and during the inter-testamental period? What understanding of tithing was current in first-century Judaism as the background to the New Testament references to tithing? Why are there so few references to tithing in the New Testament? What do these few references actually teach or imply? How have the biblical texts that relate to tithing been interpreted through the past twenty centuries? What are the contextual differences between contemporary culture and the cultures within which tithing was practised in the Old and New Testaments? How then, in the light of these considerations, should biblical references to tithing be understood and applied today?

A particular weakness in much writing on tithing is the inconsistent treatment of the diverse biblical material on steward-ship and economic matters. Why is this one aspect of biblical teaching taken literally when so much else is either ignored or treated very differently? Texts about tithing comprise a very small proportion of what biblical authors have to say about financial issues. On what basis are they given paradigmatic significance? What other biblical principles or practices do we fail to grapple with when we prioritise the tithing texts in this way?

Adrian Mann warns:

> Money is the subject which shows most clearly the difficulty of
> drawing codes for living in simplistic fashion from the Bible. Those
> who desire to proclaim the Bible as a literal source of direct authority
> often stop short of taking on board the full implications of Jesus'
> strictures on wealth. Instead they find in the Old Testament guidance
> more congenial to their circumstances – the decalogue or the tithe.[14]

Far from being an expression of radical obedience to biblical
teaching, adopting tithing as the model may be (and there is
historical evidence that it has been) a way of evading more
demanding standards and failing to embrace the more liberating
practices taught by Jesus and the New Testament authors.

3. *Tithing is often promoted through dubious means*

One of the most frequently quoted texts on tithing is the passage in
Malachi 3, which contains both a warning and a promise in relation
to tithing. The warning to those who withhold the full tithe is that
they are under a curse because they are robbing God. The promise
to those who tithe is that God will open the windows of heaven and
pour out blessing. The conjunction of warnings and promises,
curses and blessings, is familiar in the Old Testament and is carried
over, though with some very significant changes of emphasis, into
the New. The issue of tithing in Malachi's prophecy, although
important in itself, was related to a range of other issues which
together indicated that Israel was failing to live up to its covenant
obligations and so was risking judgement and forgoing God's
intended blessing.

Advocates of tithing have taken up both elements in this passage
– the warning and the promise – and have employed them
effectively to encourage tithing. Those who tithe can claim the
promise of God's blessing in this passage; those who do not tithe are
not only deprived of such blessing but risk the judgement about
which the prophet warns.

---

[14] Adrian Mann, *No Small Change* (Norwich: The Canterbury Press,
1992), 99.

The fundamental problem with this approach is the widespread assumption among advocates of tithing today that the kind of tithing about which Malachi was writing applies to their hearers and readers. The verses about tithing are quoted and lessons are drawn from these, but the context within which these verses are set receives little attention. That these verses apply in a modern context is asserted rather than demonstrated. The challenge of tithing is presented, along with warnings and promises, without allowing an opportunity to explore the legitimacy of this application. The problem with this approach is exacerbated by the pastorally unwise and ethically dubious way in which such warnings and promises are sometimes phrased. It is not easy to stop and ask questions about the applicability of tithing to the contemporary context when one is being offered wonderful rewards for tithing or being threatened with dire consequences for failing to tithe.

Some of the worst instances come from books written many years ago. A particularly unpleasant example of this genre can be found in the writings of P. W. Thompson, a chartered accountant, who insists: 'failure to tithe means God is robbed . . . If he [a Christian] does not [tithe], he loses that blessing, loses also an enormous part of his usefulness, but does not, one believes, lose his Christianity. He loses on earth, and he will have lost in heaven, but he himself is not lost.'[15] Although it may come as a relief to readers to discover that failure to tithe does not constitute an unforgivable sin, the threat inherent in this line of argument is considerable. Milo Kauffman compares failure to tithe with the original sin rather than the unforgivable sin: 'Adam and Eve . . . were dishonest and appropriated to themselves what God had reserved for himself . . . they committed the same sin that any man commits when he keeps the whole pay check without honoring God with His tenth.'[16]

But there are enough more recent examples of this genre to suggest that it is far from defunct. Those who have encountered the writings of Gary North, one of the more extreme proponents of

---

[15] P. W. Thompson, *The Whole Tithe* (London: Marshall, Morgan & Scott, 1929), 107, 122.

[16] Milo Kauffman, *The Challenge of Christian Stewardship* (Scottdale, Pa.: Herald Press, 1955), 19.

Christian Reconstruction, will not be surprised to find in his book on tithing statements accusing non-tithers of being thieves and assuring them that they are under a curse.[17] Even Kendall, whose approach is generally more measured, warns that withholding the tithe is robbing God and so not to tithe is 'to our spiritual impoverishment, perhaps even to our peril'. He makes it very clear that he regards those who do not tithe as refusing to obey God (rather than disagreeing with his interpretation of Scripture) and concludes with an encouragement to non-tithing readers to 'confess your sin of not tithing'.[18]

Others concentrate on the blessings that will accrue to tithers, with many offering assurances that such blessings are material as well as spiritual and are guaranteed. This line of teaching is associated especially with prosperity teachers, who encourage tithing in order to receive much greater blessings from God. Their promise, backed up by persuasive personal testimonies, is that those who tithe will receive back from God a hundredfold return on what they gave.[19] Less extravagant expectations are to be found in the writings of other advocates of tithing, but there is still a strong emphasis on those who tithe receiving, as a matter of course, both spiritual and material rewards. 'You can't out-give the Lord' seems to be a favourite sentiment.[20]

Many use both warnings and promises to encourage tithing. Thompson, having issued warnings to those who resist the obligation of tithing, turns next to consider the benefits of tithing: 'Tithing is a system under which you have all to gain and nothing to lose . . . If you pay your tithe, this means definite increase for you which you would not have received without such payment . . . for your material tithe there is material prosperity.'[21] His banal recipe for a happy life is: 'Tithe, work, take a proper amount of bodily exercise, sleep with your bedroom window open, and don't

---

[17] Gary North, *Tithing and the Church* (Tyler, Tex.: Institute for Christian Economics, 1994).

[18] Kendall, *Tithing*, 22, 69, 90.

[19] See, for example, Gloria Copeland, *God's Will Is Prosperity* (Tulsa, Okla.: Harrison House, 1978).

[20] See, for example, Kendall, *Tithing*, 76.

[21] Thompson, *Whole*, 124, 134, 153.

worry'!²² Olford, too, employs language that invites his readers to tithe in order to avoid two dangers – incurring guilt and missing out on God's blessing: 'One of the great sins of our time is the robbing and defrauding of the local church by its membership. And until such restitution is made, God will not bless.'²³

The language of insurance policies is employed with relish by some writers. Frank Leavell, having promised his readers that 'tithing, if conscientiously practiced, absolutely guarantees material blessings', concludes quaintly but confidently that 'these promises (Mal. 3:10) constitute nothing less than a holy insurance policy with heavenly security. There is insurance against disaster, misfortunes, poverty, drouth, boll weevil and any other adversity to man.'²⁴

Those who advocate tithing in these ways may entice or frighten people into paying their tithe. But this is an illegitimate and simplistic approach that risks distorting the image of God in the minds of those who are persuaded, lacks ethical justification, and is storing up all kinds of pastoral problems. It is to be hoped that those who listen to such advocacy of tithing will be as discerning as Eileen Flynn, whose perceptive letter to a Jesuit weekly not only provides evidence that Catholics also are being encouraged to adopt tithing but reveals that here, too, tithing is being commended in dubious ways. Her letter is worth quoting at length:

> I recently listened to the pastor and four laymen speak at Mass from the pulpit in my church about 'Tithing: God's plan for giving' . . . The men to whom I listened on two 'tithing Sundays' presented a fundamentalistic, proof-text biblicalism and said that as the Hebrews gave the first ten percent of their crops to God a few thousand years ago, so should Catholics today give the first ten percent of their gross income (no attempt was made to explain why the contribution should be from gross rather than net earnings or why a literal reading of the Bible in this case was warranted). Two speakers alluded to semi-miraculous cures that God had granted in order to reward their tithing. The other two speakers stressed how their families had been

---

²² Thompson, *Whole*, 145.

²³ Olford, *Grace*, 26.

²⁴ Frank Leavell, *Training in Stewardship* (Nashville: Sunday School Board of the Southern Baptist Convention, 1920), 79, 81.

providentially blessed because of the fact that God was given a rightful
share . . . I was alarmed by the tithing appeal I heard because God was
presented as a puppeteer who pulls strings to reward generosity (and,
implicitly, punish stinginess), the Scripture was misused, the large
questions of parish financial decision-making and economic social
justice were ignored, and the most vulnerable members of the congregation (the sick, anxious, superstitious, and ignorant) were exploited.
Beware the theology of the tithing team which wants to present its
message from your pulpit.[25]

4. Tithing often accompanies a compartmentalised view of stewardship

A serious problem with the adoption of tithing is that it frequently
hinders engagement with a broader range of issues. Sermons on
stewardship become sermons on the much more limited topic of
tithing. Clyde Tilley writes: 'It is an unfortunate impoverishment of
our understanding of stewardship which changes its more
life-embracing sweep to a narrower focus upon financial matters, or
even to an equation with tithing.'[26]

It may be assumed by those who tithe that tithing is all that God
requires in the area of stewardship and that a faithful tither is also a
faithful steward. Questions about how money is earned; about how
the 90% which is not tithed is saved, invested or spent; about how
the earth's limited resources are being used; about how to partici-
pate in wider economic and social debates; about the stewardship of
other resources than money – too often, such questions are not
asked on the assumption that a tithe has been paid and so God is
satisfied. Tithing can lead to an unwarranted complacency about
whether one is living justly and generously in a world of need and
injustice.

One of the disadvantages of tithing is that we can be lulled into a
false sense of security, feeling that money no longer has control over
our lives. Lukas Vischer warns: 'the demand that the Christian tithe

---

[25] Eileen Flynn, 'Beware the Tithing Team', *Theology Today*, 40
(1983/84), 195–196 (reprinted from *America*, 6 November 1982, 262).
[26] W. Clyde Tilley, 'A Biblical Approach to Stewardship', *Review and
Expositor*, 84(3) (1987), 434.

can even become a dangerous thing, for it permits the false conclusion that the problem of Mammon has been met and conquered.'[27] This conclusion may be far from the truth. For rich Christians (and that includes most Western church members when wealth is measured, as it must be, on an international scale), tithing may be a very cheap way of avoiding hard questions about our life-style, expenditure, where we choose to live, what we possess, who we identify with, and why we vote as we do.

We referred earlier to the designation of our culture as 'resources-rich and time-poor.' It is also increasingly the case that time itself is becoming a commodity as time costs are factored into negotiations. Perhaps it is significant that Old Testament teaching on tithing is closely connected with provisions about Sabbath days and years, which represent a proportional approach to time rather than material goods. Those who have few material resources may be able to offer large amounts of time; those who have more money may prefer to tithe this rather than facing questions about their use of time and their priorities. Writing cheques to charities may be a lot less demanding than giving an evening a week to working as a volunteer. Could tithing sometimes be a way of inoculating the tither from such challenges? Perhaps a more comprehensive review of time and possessions would be more effective.

5. Tithing is individualistic

Running through literature and sermons on tithing is an insistence that tithing is an individual matter between the tither and God alone (although usually involving the tither's spouse). This is sometimes presented as a safeguard against undue legalism or unwise pastoral pressure – however strongly tithing is advocated, a decision to tithe must be left to the conscience of the individual. Michael Wilson writes: 'Be a little wary . . . of people who want to dictate a rigid system to you; the matter is between you and God.'[28] Similarly, Tondeur, having stated that 'everyone who is working should tithe', follows this with the caution that 'our giving should be . . .

---

[27] Vischer, *Tithing*, 10.
[28] Michael Wilson, *Managing Your Money* (Leicester: IVP, 1994), 51–52.

private . . . as a rule the only people who know how much you give should be you, your partner and the recipient'.[29]

This insistence is essential if undue pressure is not to be brought to bear, but it often seems rather disingenuous, especially in the hands of the more dogmatic advocates of tithing. Readers are urged to give 10%, are warned of the consequences of 'robbing God' by giving less than this, are promised wonderful rewards if they tithe – and are then reminded that their finances are their own business and they should decide in conversation with God alone how much to give to God! Thompson, despite his dire warnings directed to non-tithers, nevertheless insists: 'your tithe is a matter solely between yourself and your Maker.'[30] So the standard is 10%. No other options are presented. You will suffer the consequences if you do not tithe. But, of course, the choice is yours!

This emphasis on individualism is, however, not just a safeguard against the imposition of tithing or a doffing of the preacher's hat to grace at the end of a sermon based on law. For many who are opposed to the system of tithing also insist that giving is a matter for the individual and God. Rather than assuming that 10% should be given, each individual should settle the amount or proportion prayerfully and in private. Thus Gordon Clinard, rejecting detailed calculations of the tithe, urges: 'All the details of working must be left to the individual conscience.'[31]

Such individualism and privacy in relation to money is deeply rooted in our culture, although such attitudes are not uniform throughout our society. But, certainly in a middle-class church, money is a taboo subject. The most influential biblical text used (or misused) to undergird our reticence to talk openly about our finances is Jesus' counsel in the Sermon on the Mount to give in secret so that our left hand does not know what our right hand is doing (Mt. 6:3f.). There are numerous indications of this culture of secrecy. It is remarkable how tiny a £10 note can be made by multiple folding before insertion into an offering bag – just in case anyone else sees what you are giving! If you doubt the power of this

---

[29] Tondeur, *Money*, 92.

[30] Thompson, *Whole*, 123.

[31] H. Gordon Clinard, 'Preaching on Stewardship Themes', *Review and Expositor* 70(2) (1973), 201.

taboo, try asking the members of your congregation next Sunday morning to turn to their neighbour, share with them how much they earn, and pray together about how much they should give away. I have tried this, and the shocked expressions on faces all over the hall were ample evidence of the power of individualism in this area.

One of the questions we will need to take with us into our examination of biblical teaching on tithing is whether such privatising of this subject is biblically justified. For the moment, we want to insist that the alternative to systematic tithing is not haphazard giving where the issue is left entirely to the individual conscience.

6. Tithing is unjust

Perhaps the strongest argument against tithing is that, as it is applied today, it is an unjust approach to giving and stewardship. A perceived advantage of tithing is that, because it is proportional rather than based on fixed amounts, it enables everyone to give something. However, this fails to address the inequality in the worldwide church, where the amount tithed by a wealthy Christian each month may be many times the annual income of a poor Christian. While advocates of tithing may be right in their insistence that even the poorest Christian should not be deprived of the privilege and dignity of giving, biblical texts on tithing seem to focus primarily on the poor as recipients of the tithe rather than tithers. Furthermore, in a world where resources are distributed so unevenly, rich Christians surely should not be content merely to tithe. Tithing, far from being good news to the poor, really does nothing to challenge the fundamental injustice of the global economic system that perpetuates poverty. The truth is that tithing is actually good news to the rich – a way of satisfying conscience and apparently obeying God that has only a minor impact on one's lifestyle.

Various writers have recognised this problem. Mann, whose aim seems to be to encourage members of Anglican churches to consider even half a tithe, acknowledges that tithing or any other fixed percentage will affect those on higher and lower incomes differently. He writes: 'a particular standard will leave the wealthy unchallenged and risk placing an unnecessary burden of guilt upon the less well off. Five per cent is almost certainly too low for a highly paid executive or professional person, and almost certainly too high for someone on a low income supporting a family.'[32] Likewise, American Mennonite, Donald Kraybill writes:

> The inadequacy of tithing as a rule for giving is obvious. A person earning $10,000 a year gives $1,000 and retains $9,000. The person earning $100,000 gives $10,000 and can live extravagantly on $90,000 . . . It's not important that one family gives $1,000 and another gives $10,000. What is important is that one family struggles along to make ends meet with $9,000, while another family self-righteously spends $90,000 lavishly because, after all, 'they have tithed'.[33]

Tithing is simply not radical enough for the kingdom of God – especially where tithes are used primarily to support church staff, premises and programmes. Costly decisions are needed that may involve living more simply, moving into smaller houses and into run-down neighbourhoods, redistributing resources across the world church, investing capital as well as income in kingdom projects, and much else. Becoming rich honestly is no barrier to following Jesus, but retaining wealth in a world of poverty, hunger and suffering surely is. Andrew Kirk concludes: 'as long as there are people suffering without the basic necessities of existence, to hold onto riches displays an attitude of disobedience to God'.[34] The problem with tithing is that it does not engage effectively with such wider issues and tends to shortcut discussion of them. As Franklin Pascall warns: 'Tithe paying is dangerous if it becomes the end of stewardship.'[35] Discipleship that is truly Jesus-centred cannot be content with tithing.

Douglas Johnson sums up several related problems with tithing:

---

[32] Mann, *No*, 141.

[33] Donald Kraybill, *The Upside Down Kingdom* (London: Marshalls, 1978), 147.

[34] Andrew Kirk, *A New World Coming* (Basingstoke: Marshall, Morgan & Scott, 1983), 74.

[35] Quoted in Clinard, 'Preaching', 202.

The tithe is not an appropriate standard for giving in an affluent society. The tithe is a rather easy rule to follow and, by following it, the more stringent demands of giving are ignored . . . Second, God's demands are far greater than the tithe, a 10% token of one's possessions. Third, the tithe, for an affluent Christian, holds no opportunity for sacrifice . . . The tithe in an affluent society is no more than a charitable deduction . . . Fourth, the tithe talks only about money. Giving should not be tied only to money.[36]

Are we saying, then, that tithing was unjust in Old Testament days? No. The problem is not with tithing itself, but with the way in which it has been extracted from its context and applied without proper recognition of its role within a different and more complex economic framework. Tithing – as part of a system involving the principles of jubilee, Sabbath years, gleaning, firstfruits, care for the poor and many other components – made sense and aided in the more just distribution of resources within society. But tithing played only a relatively minor role in this system and was not designed to function as a stand-alone institution. Tithing by itself, transported into a culture and economy that operate quite differently, is neither just nor sensible. It may well fall under the judgement that Jesus applied to the Pharisees, who tithed their spices and herbs but ignored issues of mercy, justice and faithfulness (Mt. 23:23). Those who tithe diligently may at the same time be supporting unjust economic, political and social (and ecclesiastical?) structures, because they are concentrating on certain issues of personal finance rather than setting these in the broader framework of an unjust world system.

Sri Lankan theologian, Vinoth Ramachandra brings a perspective from the two-thirds world to this issue:

Most sermons on stewardship are simply appeals to rich members to contribute their 'tithe' towards financing church projects in the neighbourhood and abroad. They rarely, if ever, raise disturbing questions about the way people acquire their wealth or what they do with the wealth that is left over from tithing. Least of all do modern

---

[36] Quoted in Richard Rusbuldt, *A Workbook on Biblical Stewardship* (Grand Rapids: Eerdmans, 1994), 61.

Christians give time to explore how their professional work and their church 'programmes' may actually be reinforcing structures of exploitation in their world and thereby contradicting the very message they are eager to proclaim.[37]

How to respond to this important challenge is something to which those advocating tithing need to give attention.

Tithing: Pragmatic or Biblical?

There are, then, undoubtedly advantages and benefits associated with the practice of tithing, to which numerous individuals and churches will testify. But there are also, as we have indicated, serious problems involved at the level of principle as well as in relation to the practical application of these principles. On what basis can we decide whether to abandon tithing and search for alternative principles for faithful financial discipleship, or to retain tithing and work for a more just, liberating and pastorally sensitive application of this system of giving? For many people, the underlying question is whether tithing is biblical. If it is, they would insist, then we must be committed to this practice and find ways of making it work effectively.

We will examine this issue in detail in the next two chapters, looking first at the New Testament evidence and then at the Old Testament references. The order is deliberate, for there are many Old Testament practices that are no longer appropriate under the new covenant or that need to be radically reinterpreted in the light of the Christ event. Many things are 'biblical' which are not 'Christian'. Some of these are recorded by the biblical authors simply because they happened rather than as models to imitate. Others were commanded or at least commended in the Old Testament, but seem no longer to be appropriate in the New Testament, as Jesus made clear when he shocked his disciples by saying repeatedly: 'You have heard that it was said . . . but I tell you . . .' (Mt. 5). It is important, then, that we recognise what we are asking when we enquire whether tithing is biblical.

---

[37] Vinoth Ramachandra, *Gods That Fail* (Carlisle: Paternoster, 1996), 47.

Tithing is certainly biblical if by this we mean that there are various references to this practice in both Testaments (although substantially more in the Old Testament than in the New). But we may want to establish more than this. Was tithing something that God required of his covenant people, or was it an aspect of their culture that he adopted? Was tithing a practice that had independent status and so can be extracted as a principle without detailed reference to its context and applied in a different cultural setting, or was it a component in an integrated system and incapable of appropriate application without the other components in this system? For example, can tithing be extracted from legislation about the annual feasts, the Sabbath and Jubilee years and gleaning practices, without distorting its meaning and impact?

We may also want to ask whether tithing is essentially an Old Testament practice that was not carried over into the New Testament, or whether it is a principle that applies equally under old and new covenants. We will need to examine the paucity of references to tithing in the New Testament and decide whether this implies a lack of interest in tithing or that tithing was taken for granted as an established principle that the new covenant did not challenge.

On the basis of our investigation in the following pages, we may hope to reach some conclusion as to whether and in what sense tithing is biblical. However, it may not be illegitimate to ask again at this point a question we raised earlier in this chapter: does it matter whether or not tithing is biblical? There are many practices with which churches have become comfortable for which there is no explicit biblical basis. Among these are the appointment of church secretaries, the announcing of notices in church meetings, deacons' meetings, locating baptisteries in church buildings, the use of pipe organs, church car parks restricted to members only, the use of overhead projectors . . . and the list goes on and on. It is legitimate – and important – to keep such developments under review and to ask whether they are consistent with biblical principles, but they are generally accepted without explicit textual support.

Might it be worth considering tithing as a pragmatic rather than a biblical issue? Even if we discover that there is little biblical support for the way in which tithing has been practised through the centuries and continues to be practised today, we might choose to argue that it is a sensible way of funding local churches and a simple and systematic way of helping individuals to give regularly and substantially. We might even suggest that church members pay a 10% levy on income as a subscription to their local church in order to fund its staff, premises and projects. This need not be regarded as 'giving', but simply as payment for services rendered (and as such it really ought not to attract tax relief through being covenanted as if it were charitable giving!). This situation is akin to members of a golf club contributing towards the upkeep of the course and clubhouse and the salary of club staff. Giving only begins once these necessary expenses have been met and is directed to charitable causes rather than the maintenance of the institution to which the givers belong.

Of course, we will still want to examine such pragmatic tithing in light of biblical principles, and it may be that such a system would contravene some of these. But at least such a pragmatic approach would enable us to continue to fund staff, premises and projects in which we believe without suggesting that tithing was a divine mandate or that our 10% levy was all that the Bible requires in the area of financial discipleship.

On balance, however, it may be preferable to dare to remove the 'tithing blinkers' altogether and to look afresh at the question of giving without them. Even pragmatic tithing may tend to distract us from asking more radical questions about lifestyle, justice, good news to the poor and the nature of the church and its mission. It is disappointing to encounter several critiques of tithing that recognise the weaknesses and shortcomings of this system and the ways in which tithing has often been unwisely advocated – and yet still try to redeem and improve it.

Thus, Gordon Clinard complains: 'Sermons which deal at length with "how to figure the tithe" seem far too legalistic. Sermons which bring hearers under judgment for non-payment of the tithe, under all circumstances, are themselves under judgment as too severe. Sermons which major on "tithe and you will get ahead" retreat to an inadequate theology.' But, rather than searching for an alternative model, he attempts to rescue tithing by setting it in a different context: 'Tithing sermons should be based on the Christian doctrines of creation and salvation.'[38] This is certainly an improvement, but perhaps a more radical alternative is required.

---

[38] Clinard, 'Preaching', 203.

Richard Rusbuldt reflects on the frequent misunderstanding and misinterpretation of tithing in the churches:

> Many in the church view it as a legalistic requirement. Some consider it a burdensome duty rather than an opportunity for the joyful expression of praise. Some view tithing as an investment, assuming that the more they give, the more they'll get. Some see tithing as a requisite proof of redemption, as a sort of good work that is exacted as the price of salvation. For those who hold such views, either consciously or unconsciously, tithing can become very problematic; they experience guilt if they feel they may not have given enough, and they become complacent or even arrogant if they feel they have contributed lavishly. We pervert the concept of the tithe if we imagine ten percent to be a magic number that guarantees some kind of relationship with God. If we focus too narrowly on a specific percentage, we wind up tangled in all manner of details . . . if we are looking to cut our losses when it comes to tithing, then we have got it all wrong.

Despite identifying and carefully analysing all these problems, Rusbuldt does not feel able to move away from tithing, so he concludes: 'The progression of stewardship toward and beyond the tithe can be a discipline that frees us to comprehend the fullness of the gospel and the riches of God's grace. Properly handled, tithing is a vital step in Christian discipleship.'[39]

An article by Marvin Tate is another good example of this tendency. Tate argues that tithing has little biblical basis, that the early church saw tithing as a compromise, that its subsequent history was painful, that it is often wrongly motivated and legalistic, that the poor are hurt by it, that it hinders proper stewardship – but he then advocates its use as a benchmark! The problem seems to be that he cannot see an alternative except sloppy giving. He concludes:

> Despite the abominable nature of much tithing testimony and the dubious theology of the sermonic exhortations so often hurled at stoically defensive congregations, much may be said for tithing in the contemporary church. It does provide a definite plan for giving and

---

[39] Rusbuldt, *Workbook*, 61–62.

fosters discipline in the affairs of the tither. It is a constant reminder that the church is due the highest priority. The tither is made aware that the ministry and ministers of Christ deserve more than the haphazard and slothful giving which has characterized so much Christian steward-ship. Surely even legalistic tithing honors Christ more than the sorry and selfish giving of the tidbits of money and goods left over after church members have satisfied their own desires. Tithing has the capa-bility of producing liberality. It has been the experience of many that it is easier to give more when one begins with the tithe as a benchmark. Finally, the testimony of tithers must not be discounted too much. There is ample evidence for the genuine joy and spiritual strength that tithing has brought to faithful believers.[40]

This is an excellent summary of the benefits of tithing, but the conclusion sits very uncomfortably with the earlier part of his article. Is there no way to achieve these benefits without tithing? Is haphazard giving the only other option? Perhaps we need to go further than Tate will allow, abolish tithing (or at least suspend it for a while) and see whether there are preferable alternatives. But we are jumping ahead of ourselves. We must first examine the biblical references to tithing to see whether there is, after all, a firm foundation for the application of tithing to Christians today.

---

[40] Marvin Tate, 'Tithing: Legalism or Benchmark?', *Review and Expositor* 70(2) (1973), 161.

Chapter 3

Tithing in the New Testament

The Tithing Texts

There may have been serious problems associated with tithing in the history of the church in Europe. We may also have concerns about the contemporary application of tithing. But, provided we can find a sound basis for this practice in the New Testament, we can surely continue to use it with confidence. After all, many biblical practices have been misinterpreted and grossly abused at times in church history. The remedy for such problems is not to abandon biblical practices, but to recover the principles on which they were based and work towards their more appropriate implementation. This is the approach taken by those advocates of tithing who recognise that tithing has not always been helpful but nevertheless defend and promote it as an important biblical practice.

But it is when we examine the New Testament references to · tithing that we find ourselves in some difficulty. For there are very few references to tithing, and none of these applies the practice to Christians. Nowhere are followers of Jesus encouraged to tithe, nor is the Old Testament practice even used as an example to encourage a similar practice in the church.

There are only four passages in the New Testament that make explicit reference to tithing, two of which are simply different versions of the same saying in the accounts given by Matthew and Luke. We will consider each in turn.

Matthew 23:23: *Woe to you, teachers of the law and Pharisees, you hypocrites! You give a tenth of your spices – mint, dill and cumin. But you* *have neglected the more important matters of the law – justice, mercy and faithfulness. You should have practised the latter without neglecting the former.*

This verse has often been used to provide a New Testament basis for tithing, in that Jesus, while pronouncing a solemn 'woe' on the Pharisees and teachers of the law for their neglect of the more important matters of the law, nevertheless urges them not to refrain from tithing. Coming in a section of Matthew's Gospel where Jesus is presented as radical and scathing in his condemnation of many aspects of contemporary Judaism, it is significant, some would argue, that Jesus does not rescind the principle of tithing but appears to endorse its continued application. Kendall writes: 'It is striking that our Lord endorsed tithing in this verse . . . His approval and exhortation to tithe ought to be sufficient motivation for any Christian.'[1] This interpretation is widespread and has convinced many that Jesus approved of tithing and expected his followers to tithe, so we need to examine it carefully.

What Jesus speaks out against here, we are told, is the legalistic application of tithing and the associated dangers of complacency and self-righteousness – tendencies that we have already noted in relation to tithing today. The teachers of the law and the Pharisees have invested much more energy in ensuring that every herb and spice is properly tithed than in relating the practice of tithing to the underlying principles of the Mosaic law of which tithing formed a part. They are convinced of their righteousness under this law because they are tithing carefully, but Jesus accuses them of missing the point and of majoring on minor matters in such a way as to devalue the whole process. Tithing, it seems, makes sense only within the framework of a system that works for justice, mercy and faithfulness. Separated from this context, tithing brings those who tithe under condemnation.

But Jesus does not urge the abolition of tithing as a response to this situation. Rather, he calls for tithing to be set within its right context. The teachers of the law and the Pharisees are to stop neglecting justice, mercy and faithfulness – but they are also to continue tithing. So the problem Jesus identifies here, advocates of

---

[1] R. T. Kendall, *Tithing* (London: Hodder & Stoughton, 1982), 25–27.

tithing argue, is that those who tithe scrupulously and consistently can assume that by tithing they have fulfilled all that God requires. Clearly, then, Jesus is commending tithing, providing we also give attention to issues of justice, mercy and faithfulness. This proviso is certainly important and those who practise tithing would do well to view it as just a small part of their commitment to work for justice in society, to reach out in mercy to the poor and needy and to be faithful to the call of God. But nothing in this passage suggests that tithing itself is the problem or that this practice should no longer be endorsed.

But we need to be careful here – both that we do not read too much into this verse and that we do not minimise the impact of the proviso about the 'more important matters of the law.'

For, as Matthew presents this material, Jesus is challenging the inconsistency of the Pharisees and teachers of the law, not giving guidelines for his disciples. Matthew is certainly writing with the early churches in mind and giving guidance on a range of theological and ethical issues they were facing. But there is no suggestion in this passage that his Christian readers should understand that they were to operate within the same religious system as those with whom Jesus was discussing tithing.

They would know that tithing was taught in the Pentateuch and be aware that, within Judaism, it had a long history and served an important function. So they would not be negatively disposed towards tithing or assume that the Pharisees and teachers of the law were wrong to practise this. Indeed, as they had read Matthew's Gospel, they had found Jesus speaking positively about the Old Testament law, within which tithing was undoubtedly taught.[2] But they had also come across Jesus challenging several human traditions that the Pharisees and teachers of the law had added to the Old Testament law, especially where these traditions obscured the true meaning of the law and laid unnecessary burdens on people.[3] So they would no doubt have read this section of the Gospel with interest, as Jesus subjects more of the practices of the Pharisees and the teachers of the law to critical scrutiny.

---

[2] Most notably in Mt. 5:17–20.
[3] For example, Mt. 12:1–14; 15:1–20.

What would he affirm and what would he condemn? How would he deal with their tithing practices? The inclusion of spices and herbs was certainly a human tradition that had no basis in the Old Testament, but the fact remained that tithing itself was part of the Mosaic law. Thus it would not surprise them to read that Jesus had urged the Pharisees and teachers of the law to continue tithing – nor that he had challenged them to get their priorities straight and to set their tithing practices within the broader moral and religious framework of the 'more important matters of the law'.

But is there any reason why they should have interpreted this passage as requiring them to tithe? To deduce from this conversation between Jesus and representatives of the old order of Judaism that Christians should also tithe is surely to deduce too much from the text and to ignore the newness of the new covenant that fulfilled, but also in so many ways transcended, Judaism. Jesus evidently said a great deal about how his disciples were to handle financial issues – it has been calculated that sixteen out of his thirty-eight parables deal with the subject of possessions and that roughly one verse in seven in the Gospels is concerned with this subject.[4] But nowhere is it recorded that he taught or encouraged his disciples to practise tithing. In the absence of such teaching, it seems highly unlikely that readers in the early churches would have interpreted Jesus' words to the teachers of the law and the Pharisees as implying that tithing was an appropriate way for them to organise their finances. Nor is there any indication that Matthew intended them to draw such a conclusion.

This passage, which is concerned with a proper understanding of the principles on which the law was based, is simply not relevant to the issue of tithing among followers of Jesus. As Craig Blomberg comments:

> what is crucial to note in this context is that Jesus is appealing to the 'more important matters of the law', which is still in force until the establishment of God's new covenant at Pentecost, especially for the Jewish leaders who studied it so scrupulously. So long as the Old Testament era remains, tithing is mandatory for God's people.

---

[4] Milo Kauffman, *The Challenge of Christian Stewardship* (Scottdale, Pa.: Herald Press, 1955), 27.

Whether it continues to be required in the era of the new covenant must be determined on the basis of other passages.[5]

There is no evidence here that tithing is applicable under the new covenant – merely that those operating under the old covenant were liable to misinterpret the role of tithing. The tithing of herbs and spices to which Jesus refers, and which is nowhere advocated in the Old Testament, represents just the kind of legalistic application of Old Testament teaching that Jesus consistently refused to endorse in his dealings with the Pharisees.

Surely this passage is a very unsatisfactory basis upon which to argue that Jesus was commending tithing to his followers? For, if he is commending tithing here at all, he is commending its application to minutiae. Indeed, if there were any other passage that offered a more appropriate basis for the practice, it seems most unlikely that Jesus' comment here would be accorded the significance that it is by advocates of tithing struggling to find support for tithing in the New Testament. This passage, though, is the only place where there is even a remote possibility of enlisting Jesus' support for Christians' tithing. But it really does not seem that this passage can be interpreted as anything more than an ironic approval of such a practice within Judaism, let alone a basis for arguing that Christians should tithe.

But this passage does stand as a warning to any who plan to continue with the tithing system that it is a system that can be distorted through legalism, and through according to tithing a more significant function than is warranted. Even under the old covenant, tithing was but one provision within a more complex system; if tithing is extracted from this system in the way the Pharisees and teachers of the law had done, it becomes a hindrance to the pursuit of justice, mercy and faithfulness. There are reasons, some of which we have already indicated and others which we will consider in due course, why tithing should not form the basis of giving under the new covenant. But if tithing is to be practised still, this passage is an important warning against repeating the mistakes associated with tithing under first-century Judaism.

[5] Craig Blomberg, *Neither Poverty Nor Riches: A Biblical Theology of Material Possessions* (Leicester: Apollos, 1999), 136.

Luke 11:42: *Woe to you Pharisees, because you give God a tenth of your mint, rue and all other kinds of garden herbs, but you neglect justice and the love of God. You should have practised the latter without leaving the former undone.*

This is the parallel passage in Luke's Gospel. Apart from minor changes of detail, the two passages are identical and convey the same concerns.

Luke 18:12: *I fast twice a week and give a tenth of all I get.*

These words are put into the mouth of a Pharisee in Jesus' story of two men praying in the temple. They are part of the Pharisee's claim to be accepted by God. Luke records Jesus' comment that such self-exaltation does not lead to justification. This passage provides further evidence that tithing was practised rigorously by the Pharisees in the first century and that it was regarded by them as a sign of their obedience to the law. But, like the earlier passage in Luke and its parallel in Matthew, it gives no grounds for assuming that Christians should tithe. Indeed, as in the previous passages, tithing is again linked with legalism and self-righteousness rather than being held up for imitation.

These are the only references in the Gospels to tithing. It is surely significant that all three references concern the Pharisees, who were representatives of earnest Judaism rather than models for Christians to imitate. Their punctilious tithing was typical of the picture the Gospels paint of these men – men who were deeply committed to obeying the law but who had lost their way in terms of the real meaning of this law and were no longer reliable guides for the people of God. For the early Christians to accept this picture of the Pharisees but to adopt into their own communities one of the distinctive practices of the Pharisees – and one explicitly associated with the problem of legalism against which many early churches were struggling – seems rather unlikely. Whether or not they did so we will explore in a later chapter when we examine the ways in which these Gospel passages were actually understood and applied in the early churches.

Hebrews 7:1–10: *This Melchizedek was king of Salem and priest of God Most High. He met Abraham returning from the defeat of the kings*

*and blessed him, and Abraham gave him a tenth of everything . . . Just think
how great he was: Even the patriarch Abraham gave him a tenth of the
plunder! Now the law requires the descendants of Levi who become priests to
collect a tenth from the people – that is, from members of their own nation –
even though they are descended from Abraham. This man, however, did not
trace his descent from Levi, yet he collected a tenth from Abraham and blessed
him who had the promises. And without doubt the lesser person is blessed by
the greater. In the one case, the tenth is collected by those who die; but in the
other case, by him who is declared to be living. One might even say that
Levi, who collects the tenth, paid the tenth through Abraham, because when
Melchizedek met Abraham, Levi was still in the body of his ancestor.*

This passage in the anonymous letter to the Hebrews is part of a
sustained argument about the superiority of Christ and the new
covenant. Jesus, the eternal high priest, is compared with the
shadowy and enigmatic figure of Melchizedek, who appears both in
Genesis 14 and Psalm 110. The author contends that Jesus, being a
high priest in the line of Melchizedek, is superior to the old order of
priests who were descended from the tribe of Levi. The basis for this
conclusion is that Abraham, the patriarch of Israel and ancestor of
Levi, was blessed by Melchizedek and gave a tithe of his battle spoils
to him, demonstrating the superiority of Melchizedek. Since Levi,
although not yet born, was present during this transaction 'in the
body of his ancestor', the author argues that, in effect, Levi was
tithing to Melchizedek and so indicating the supremacy of the line
of priests from which Jesus came.

The sequence of steps in this argument may be less persuasive to a
Western reader in the twenty-first century than it presumably was to
a Jewish reader in the first century, but the important point for our
discussion is that, although tithing is mentioned several times in this
passage, it appears as a piece of supporting evidence in an argument
about quite a different subject. Tithing is mentioned in connection
with the incident recorded in Genesis 14:18–20, when Abraham was
blessed by Melchizedek, the king of Salem, and tithed to him booty
gained in a recent battle; and also in relation to the requirement under
the Mosaic law that the Levites should collect tithes from the people.
But the author makes no attempt to apply the comments about
tithing to the first-century context – this is not the subject with which
the passage is concerned.

As it stands, then, this passage, despite the fact that it contains more references to tithing than can be found in the rest of the New Testament, appears to be of no relevance to the question of whether Christians should tithe. It refers to a familiar Old Testament practice without any suggestion that this is applicable under the new covenant. It might, of course, legitimately be argued that there is also no reason from this passage to conclude that tithing has been abolished or superseded – although the whole thrust of the passage and its context is that all kinds of things have changed as a result of the coming of Christ and the new covenant. Tithing is not explicitly included among these changes, but the references here give no encouragement to those who are concerned to find a New Testament basis for tithing. As with the references in the Gospels, tithing is set within the context of the law and there is no indication at all that it is an appropriate practice under the new covenant.

It has been argued by advocates of tithing, however, that since tithing is here traced back to Abraham, the father of all who have faith (according to Romans 4:11), and to a period before the law was given, it is wrong to see tithing as only a principle of the Old Testament law or only applicable to Israel. If Abraham tithed, even though he was not under the law, it is claimed, so should we, his spiritual descendants, who are likewise free from the law. Although this line of argument is rooted in broader theological perspectives and will need to be considered more fully in the next chapter in relation to tithing in the Old Testament, it may be helpful to make a limited response to it here.

This argument sounds persuasive at first, and it certainly provides a more congenial basis for tithing in those churches where tithing as an aspect of law-keeping seems somewhat anomalous in the context of an emphasis on grace and spiritual freedom. But those who are drawn to this approach need to consider that the same argument could be used to urge all Christians to be circumcised, since that too predates the law and was practised by Abraham. The fundamental weakness in this line of argument is that this passage in Hebrews – and indeed the New Testament as a whole – does not support it. The issue in relation to circumcision, tithing or anything else is not how ancient a practice may be or whether it predated the law, but whether it is appropriate for followers of Jesus in the light of his life and teaching, death and resurrection, and of the coming of the Holy Spirit.

In so many ways these events made a radical difference. Circumcision, though still acceptable on occasions for tactical reasons,[6] is no longer required of Christians in the way that it was of Israelites in the Old Testament, and attempts to impose this require-ment on Gentile Christians were firmly resisted.[7] In the same way, there may conceivably be situations where individuals or churches find the principle of tithing to be tactically useful, but this is quite different from promoting tithing as a requirement on all Christians, as so many advocates of tithing insist. This requirement needs to be resisted as firmly as the Council of Jerusalem resisted the attempt to impose circumcision.

This is the only reference to tithing in the Epistles. Tithing is not mentioned by Peter, John, James, Jude or even by Paul – in spite of his extensive teaching on the subject of giving. Nor is there any mention of tithing in the book of Acts, even though economic matters are discussed in considerable detail in the early chapters of that book. There is evidence there (which we explore later) that the earliest church drew gratefully on Old Testament models of giving, but not on tithing. Far from tithing being 'mentioned throughout the Bible', as some claim,[8] there are only four passages containing explicit references to tithing in the entire New Testament, and not one of these is in any way related to Christians. This does not seem to provide a very solid biblical foundation for suggestions that tithing is an essential principle for Christians in their management of their finances.

Other References to Tithing?

Might there be any other references to tithing in the New Testament, where the term itself is not used? A number of possibilities have been identified.

---

[6] For example, in Acts 16:3.
[7] Acts 15:1–28. This is a major theme also in Galatians.
[8] Keith Tondeur, *Your Money or Your Life* (London: SPCK, 1996), 90.

Matthew 22:21: *Then Jesus said to them, 'Give to Caesar what is Caesar's, and to God what is God's.'*

The question addressed to Jesus was whether or not it was right to pay taxes to the Roman government. His response to what was an obvious trap amazed those who listened to him, according to Matthew. This response has been the subject of much debate and has been variously interpreted. It has been suggested, although without much scholarly support, that Jesus was endorsing tithing as well as paying taxes to Caesar. Milo Kauffman, for example, translates this text: 'render to Caesar the tax and to God the tithe'.[9] The requirement to pay taxes to an occupying power might, it is argued, have encouraged some Jews to default on their tithe on the grounds that they could not afford to pay both tax and tithe. Justo Gonzalez comments that, in Jesus' day, 'the burden of taxation was heavy . . . Foreign conquest had brought no relief from the traditional tithe and other such obligations and had added the further burden of secular taxation'.[10] Jesus might, therefore, be warning against a tendency to pay taxes rather than the tithe.

This interpretation would be more attractive if there were evidence either of such a withholding of tithes in the first century or of Jesus elsewhere endorsing tithing with rather more enthusiasm than in the passages we have already examined. But what evidence we have from this period indicates that tithing was deeply embedded in Jewish culture and was practised without question by pious Jews. Furthermore, it was to Pharisees whom Jesus was speaking in this incident. These were the same men who reappear in the following chapter as tithers of garden herbs. So it seems unlikely that Jesus is challenging such men to more wholehearted tithing here – or that such a challenge would have resulted in the amazement that Matthew reports.

---

[9] Kauffman, *Challenge*, 68. See also Jerome's comment on this verse, quoted in chapter 5.

[10] Justo Gonzalez, *Faith and Wealth* (San Francisco: Harper & Row, 1990), 72.

Did Jesus tithe?

Given that tithing was widely accepted and reasonably consistently practised in first-century Palestine, it seems likely that Jesus, his parents and relations, his friends and disciples all tithed. Although Jesus is represented in the Gospels as challenging various contemporary religious practices, we also read about him worshipping in the temple and in synagogues and in various ways living as a pious Jew. Given the scrupulosity of the Pharisees about tithing, it would be surprising if they had not criticised Jesus for failing to tithe if this were the case. But there is no hint of such a criticism. Questions were raised about whether Jesus paid the temple tax (Mt. 17:24–27), but Peter's impulsive certainty that Jesus did pay this charge suggests that Jesus was not in the habit of avoiding such payments – even if the source of the coins paid to the collectors was occasionally rather unusual.

This encounter may indicate that Jesus was less than enthusiastic about such payments, as may another more famous incident that has often been interpreted with insufficient attention to its context. Mark tells the story of Jesus watching people making donations in the temple and commenting on the generosity and sacrificial giving of a poor widow by comparison with the large amounts that many rich donors could so much more easily afford.[11] Used for generations as a model for Christian giving, often alongside teaching about tithing, this incident is quite problematic.

First, this widow was contributing far more than a tithe in her offering, whereas the rich donors were giving large amounts that cost them very little. One of the problems with the tithing system that we have identified is that rich Christians can tithe without any significant cost or challenge to their lifestyles. Poor Christians who tithe may not become utterly destitute like this widow, but they may find managing on nine-tenths of a low income very difficult. This incident, far from being an appropriate story with which to support the advocacy of tithing, actually highlights very clearly one of the problems with the tithing approach. Jesus seems interested here not in what is given by the rich donors but in what they are retaining, whereas tithing focuses only on what is given away.

---

[11] Mark 12:41–44.

Second, this incident involves not a gift from income but from
capital. The widow is not tithing what she has recently earned but
giving away 'everything – all she had to live on'. One of the
problems with tithing, as we will see later, is that it only relates to
income and does not provide guidelines for how Christians should
handle their capital resources. Yet in the Gospels, Jesus frequently
addresses the question of possessions rather than income. Here, he
commends the generosity of a poor widow. Elsewhere, he instructs
the rich young ruler not to tithe his income, but to give away all his
wealth to the poor.[12] Zacchaeus, too, is commended for disbursing
half of his possessions to the poor and offering to compensate generously those he has defrauded.[13] But Jesus shows no interest at all in
encouraging anyone to tithe.

Third, although Jesus is undoubtedly honouring the sacrificial
generosity of this poor but faithful widow, is he also by implication
castigating the religious system that would demand or welcome
such giving? It is here that we need to consider the context. In the
previous verse, Jesus has referred to the teachers of the law as those
who 'devour widows' houses'.[14] What would happen now to this
poor widow who had given away all she had to support the religious
institution run by these teachers of the law? How much pressure
had been exerted on her to give away her last mite? What responsibility would the religious leaders take for her now that she was
destitute? Simplistic sermons on this incident do not seem willing to
grapple with these issues.

Furthermore, in the next two verses,[15] Jesus predicts the
destruction of the very temple that the widow's donation was
supporting. However worthy her motives, her donation was
underwriting a system characterised by insensitivity, hypocrisy and
injustice; and her donation would actually be wasted, because the
temple that stood at its centre was already doomed to be destroyed.
In a provocative article, Addison Wright examines these contextual
difficulties and concludes that the only legitimate way to understand

---

[12] Luke 18:18–22.
[13] Luke 19:8–9.
[14] Mark 12:40 (cf. Matthew 23:4, where Jesus refers to the imposition of
'heavy loads').
[15] Mark 13:1–2.

this incident is 'to see Jesus' attitude to the widow's gift as a downright disapproval and not as an approbation'.[16] This may be too strong. The words of Jesus do seem to imply approval of the widow herself, even if he thoroughly disapproved of the system to which she was contributing.[17] But the context certainly does not suggest that Jesus was any more enthusiastic about these offerings and the whole financial system of first-century Judaism than he was about the temple tax. This was an oppressive system that especially hurt the poor.

These incidents perhaps provide part of the background to the passage we looked at earlier where Jesus criticises the Pharisees and teachers of the law for allowing their detailed attention to tithing to obscure more important issues of justice and mercy. Poor widows should not become penniless through donating all their money under such a system – any more than poor Christians today should be cajoled or induced into tithing within a system that does not address issues of injustice or offer good news to the poor.

So, did Jesus tithe? Almost certainly. That Joseph and Mary tithed is asserted in a section of *The Gospel of Nicodemus*, which reads:

> And on the Sabbath our teachers and the priests and Levites sat questioning each other, and saying: What is this wrath that has come upon us? For we know his father and mother. Levi, a teacher, says: 'I know that his parents fear God, and do not withdraw themselves from the prayers, and give the tithes thrice a year.'[18]

Whatever weight we ascribe to this document, it is more than likely that Jesus was raised in a family that tithed and that he adopted this

---

[16] Addison Wright, 'The Widow's Mites: Praise or Lament? – A Matter of Context', *Catholic Biblical Quarterly*, 44(2) (1982), 252.

[17] David Hilborn's comment seems more balanced when he concludes that the widow is 'commended for her generosity to God, even as the context suggests that she is pitied for having unwittingly subsidised a corrupt system'. See David Hilborn, 'Should EA Tithe?' (private paper, 1998), 2.

[18] *The Gospel of Nicodemus*, Part I: The Acts of Pilate (first Greek form), chapter 16. This anonymous document probably dates from the first half of the fifth century, although it draws on much earlier material.

practice himself. Hastings is surely correct when he writes: 'There can be no doubt that Jesus, along with Paul, Peter and his other followers obeyed the Hebrew tithing structure as prescribed by the Judaism in which they were raised.'[19]

Does this mean that tithing is mandatory for his followers? No. The New Testament evidence not only provides inadequate support for such a conclusion but suggests that a different approach is needed. We will look next at the teaching and practice of Paul, surely the most influential Christian teacher in the first generation, but it is important to set the lack of teaching about tithing in the Gospels in the context of the extensive teaching of Jesus on economic issues recorded by the Gospel writers. A number of scholars who have explored his teaching about money, giving and the poor have concluded not only that he did not endorse tithing, but that tithing is incompatible with what he did teach in this area.

Tate, for example, commenting on attempts to derive a mandate for Christians to tithe from Jesus' words in Matthew 23:23, writes:

> Such a conclusion is based on 'dubious exegesis which violates the context and misses the point of the verse'. The saying is directed towards Pharisees and scribes – not Christians – and seeks to emphasize the relative insignificance of careful tithing when compared with the deeper requirements of the Torah . . . the Christian approach to stewardship is based on presuppositions which preclude the simple adoption of the tithing practice of the Old Testament and Judaism. Christian stewardship is founded upon a much broader base than tithing and its scope is much greater. The revolutionary interpretation of possessions by Jesus is not adequately expressed through tithing.[20]

Blomberg, concluding his discussion of the same passage in Matthew, agrees: 'It seems significant that no other New Testament text explicitly commands [tithing], while the principles of generosity and sacrifice yet to be surveyed will suggest that different people should give varying percentages based on their varying

---

[19] Robert Hastings, *My Money and God* (Nashville: Broadman, 1961), 63.

[20] Marvin Tate, 'Tithing: Legalism or Benchmark?', *Review and Expositor* 70(2) (1973), 159, quoting Paul Stagg in Duke McCall (ed.), *What is the Church?* (Nashville: Broadman Press, 1958), 152.

circumstances.'[21] And Vischer is even more categorical: 'Everything that Christ has to say about possessing and giving is based on presuppositions which make it completely impossible for him to adopt the Old Testament commandment of the tithe.'[22]

It is these presuppositions that we will need to examine in a later chapter as we look at possible alternatives to tithing that have a more substantial New Testament foundation.

Paul and tithing

If Jesus and his disciples tithed, it is unthinkable that Saul the Pharisee would not have tithed – and he probably took at least as much care as the Pharisees whom Jesus knew to ensure that no spice or garden herb was omitted. But whether Paul the apostle either tithed himself or taught tithing to the churches for which he cared is a very different matter. Paul certainly writes a great deal about issues of finance, especially in his correspondence with the church in Corinth – about the right of those who serve the churches to be properly supported by the churches (1 Cor. 9:3–10); about the responsibility of individual Christians to set aside their gifts regularly and to give in proportion to their income (1 Cor. 16:2); about the importance of financial sharing and equality of resources between local churches (2 Cor. 8:1–15); about the proper administration of finances (2 Cor. 8:16–24); and about the attitudes that characterise true Christian giving – eagerness, enthusiasm, generosity, freedom, cheerfulness and concern for the poor (2 Cor. 9:1–15).

As a Jewish Christian immersed in the Old Testament, Paul draws on a number of Old Testament models of giving to encourage his readers in this area. In 1 Corinthians 9:9 he refers to Deuteronomy 25:4: *For it is written in the Law of Moses: 'Do not muzzle an ox while it is treading out the grain.'* In 2 Corinthians 8:15 he draws on the reference to manna in Exodus 16:18: *The person who gathered much did not have too much, and the one who gathered little did not have too little.* And in 2 Corinthians 9:9 he quotes Psalm 112:9: *They have scattered abroad their gifts to the poor; their*

---

[21] Blomberg, *Neither*, 136.

[22] Lukas Vischer, *Tithing in the Early Church* (Philadelphia: Fortress Press, 1966), 9.

righteousness endures for ever. Paul is not averse to using Old Testament examples and even specific commands from the Mosaic law to underscore his teaching. But he does not refer to tithing, even as an illustration, in spite of (or perhaps because of?) his experience of this system as a Pharisee, not even when he is writing about giving as proportional and regular.

The only plausible claim of any resonance with Old Testament tithing texts in Paul's teaching is based on the terminology used in 1 Corinthians 16:2. Kendall, struggling to explain why Paul never mentions tithing, argues that the phrase 'in keeping with his income' is 'about as clear a reference to tithing as one could get without actually using the word'.[23] This seems to beg the question as to why Paul did not use the word 'tithe' if this is what he meant. Olford focuses on another word in this verse in his search for a defensible New Testament basis for tithing: 'scholars have pointed out that the word "store" in that verse has an undoubted allusion to the storehouse tithing of Malachi's day'.[24] But it is hardly surprising that an author whose upbringing and education were so deeply immersed in the Old Testament should, consciously or unconsciously, employ familiar terminology in his writings. What is surely much more significant is that Paul did not use the tithing passages with which he was also so very familiar. This desperate hunt for indirect allusions to tithing in the New Testament really does seem to be clutching at straws.

Surveying Paul's teaching, G. F. Hawthorne concludes that his 'special vocabulary about giving . . . and his explicit teaching on the subject . . . indicate that for the Christian giving is voluntary . . . with no stipulated amount such as a tax or tithe demanded of him'.[25] Indeed, there are a number of indications in Paul's teaching that he is avoiding the tithing model and advocating a very different system of giving for the churches to which he writes. Among these indications (as well as his deliberate choice of other Old Testament models) are his insistence that giving is willing and not reluctant or under pressure (2 Cor. 9:5,7); his counsel that each individual

---

[23] Kendall, *Tithing*, 28.

[24] Stephen Olford, *The Grace of Giving* (London: Lakeland, 1972), 110.

[25] G. F. Hawthorne, 'Tithe', *New International Dictionary of New Testament Theology* (Carlisle: Paternoster Press, 1976/1986), 851.

should decide how much to give (2 Cor. 9:7); and his instruction to the church (1 Cor. 16:2) to set aside money each week (whereas the Old Testament tithe seems to have been an annual payment or at least a less frequent collection).

Even though neither Jesus nor Paul advocated tithing – and much in their teaching seems, at least by implication, to preclude this as the basis for giving among Christians – it is quite likely that some Jewish Christians in the New Testament period carried over into their new lives as Christians a practice that had been deeply rooted for many centuries in their Jewish culture. There were many such vestiges of Judaism in the early churches, for which there was no warrant in the teaching of Jesus and the apostles, and which only slowly disappeared as the churches sifted through their Jewish heritage and discarded what was no longer appropriate.

Tithing may well have been practised for some time and was probably dealt with in this gradual way, although there is insufficient evidence for definite conclusions. David Norrington may overstate the case slightly, but he is essentially correct that:

> there is no evidence in the New Testament that tithing was carried over from Judaism to the new community although some Jewish Christians may have continued the practice. There is, furthermore, little trace of it during the first few centuries of church life although views differ on its precise extent. In the New Testament, the emphasis was on voluntary and generous giving according to ability.[26]

Arguments from Silence

Some readers may object to the way we have argued in this chapter and the conclusion we have reached on the grounds that much of it is based on arguments from silence. Although the very few references to tithing we have found – and the complete absence in these references of any suggestion that tithing applies to Christians – are undoubtedly disturbing if we are wanting to authenticate the

---

[26] David Norrington, 'Fund-raising: The Methods Used in the Early Church Compared with Those Used in English Churches Today', *Evangelical Quarterly* 70(2) (1998), 124.

practice of tithing from the New Testament, there may be other ways of interpreting this lack of data. Arguments from silence are inherently dangerous. In fact, there seem to be two opposite conclusions that might be drawn from the data we have examined.

The conclusion I am suggesting is that there was a conscious and deliberate policy in the early churches of not adopting the tithing model. Why? Is it not likely that these churches refused to advocate or practise tithing because they were determined to break free from all forms of legalism and rule-based religion? Tithing, after all, was inextricably linked to Old Testament law-keeping and seemed prone to the kinds of legalistic attitudes and nit-picking practices that Jesus himself had identified in his conversations with those who did tithe. Generosity and mutual support would continue to be significant features of the community life of the new people of God, but tithing was not an appropriate model for their discipleship. Is it not also possible that the churches recognised in Jesus' teaching other paradigms for giving and sharing that were more radical than tithing (although equally strongly rooted in the Old Testament heritage) and more likely to be 'good news to the poor'?[27]

The only other conclusion that can be drawn from this silence on the subject of tithing in the New Testament is that, contrary to what I have argued, the ethos and practice of tithing was taken over from Judaism by the early churches so naturally and unanimously that it was simply assumed and did not have to be taught or encouraged, or even referred to. This is Kendall's argument: 'tithing was so deeply imbedded in the Jewish conscience . . . that it needed virtually no mention in the New Testament'.[28]

However, there are serious problems with this conclusion. While the supposition of a natural transition from tithing under Judaism to tithing under Christianity might be a reasonable assumption in a Jewish context, it seems less feasible in a mixed context such as the Corinthian church. Why should converted Greeks adopt tithing without needing at least some basic instruction on the subject? Thompson argues that Paul's teaching in 2 Corinthians about proportionate giving must have implied a tithe because both Jewish and pagan cultures used this model. He quotes from

[27] We will explore this suggestion in more detail in chapter 9.
[28] Kendall, *Tithing*, 25.

Didymus, in the first century BCE, who says: 'it was a general custom among the Grecians to give a tenth of the profits or revenues unto the gods.'[29] Socrates Scholasticus also gives an example of tithing in earlier Greek history:

> Chrysopolis is an ancient port situated at the head of the Bosphorus, and is mentioned by several of the early writers, especially Strabo, Nicolaus Damascenus, and the illustrious Xenophon in the sixth book of his Anabasis of Cyrus; and again in the first of his Hellenica he says concerning it, 'that Alcibiades having walled it round, established a toll in it; for all who sailed out of Pontus were accustomed to pay tithes there.'[30]

But even if this custom was still current in the first century (and this is not at all certain), it is not obvious why converts from paganism to Christianity would assume without further discussion that tithing was a transferable custom. Yet in the two detailed chapters on giving in Paul's second letter to the church in Corinth (2 Cor. 8–9), not only is tithing not mentioned, but Paul expressly urges the Corinthian Christians to make their own decisions about the level of their giving.

The second problem is how to square such a conclusion with the very limited interest in tithing in the churches and writers of the early centuries. Although the silence on the subject of tithing in the next three centuries is not quite as deafening as in the New Testament, references to tithing are sparse enough to raise serious questions as to whether tithing was ever practised extensively in the early churches, let alone being taken over spontaneously and without apostolic encouragement. But, before we examine these references to tithing in early Christian documents, we will delve into the complicated area of what the Old Testament teaches in relation to tithing.

---

[29] P. W. Thompson, *The Whole Tithe* (London: Marshall, Morgan & Scott, 1929), 101.
[30] Socrates Scholasticus: *The Ecclesiastical History*, Book 7, chapter 25.

Chapter 4

Tithing in the Old Testament

The Relevance of the Old Testament

Tithing may be mentioned infrequently in the New Testament, but there is substantially more material on the subject in the Old Testament. For advocates of tithing, who draw gratefully and heavily on this material, the Old Testament is a happier hunting ground than the New Testament – although, as we shall see, the prey is not easy to identify with the kind of precision that is often claimed.

However, we need to ask questions about the legitimacy of advocating tithing on the basis of Old Testament texts. It is unclear why anything taught about tithing in the Old Testament should be thought to apply to Christians today, who live under a new covenant and within a very different culture. It is even less clear why tithing, as one component of a complex and integrated socio-economic system, should alone be extracted from this context and applied to a different context, with little or no regard for the implications of detaching it from the other components of the system.

But for many centuries Old Testament texts have been mined to justify all kinds of practices for which it is difficult to find New Testament justification. Christocentric biblical interpretation, which recognises Jesus Christ as the pinnacle of God's revelation and takes seriously the newness of the new covenant, refusing to apply Old Testament norms without reference to Jesus, has been marginalised in mainstream Christianity since the fourth century. Only among radical renewal movements and dissident groups has this approach to biblical interpretation been popular – much to the dismay of establishment interpreters, who have frequently been appalled by the costly and socially disturbing implications of such an approach to the Bible.

Those who advocate tithing on the basis of Old Testament texts appear to be operating with the very familiar but deeply flawed principle that, just because a practice is biblical (in the sense that it can be found somewhere in the Bible and can make some claim to having been divinely approved at some point) it is therefore also Christian (in the sense of being appropriate for followers of Jesus). Practitioners of Christocentric biblical interpretation, most of whom have rejected tithing as inappropriate for Christians, have long objected to the Old Testament being used – they would say, abused – in this way. Tithing, like Christian participation in warfare, the swearing of oaths, infant baptism, priestly views of ministry, and a range of other 'biblical' practices, has often been justified on the basis of Old Testament passages. But it has been difficult to escape the suspicion that this justification is inadequate without a stronger New Testament witness.

This was the objection raised by the sixteenth-century Anabaptists, one of the better-known dissident groups. Their persistent claim that the New Testament taught the baptism of believers rather than the baptism of infants was rejected by both Catholics and Protestants, who insisted that infant baptism could be justified on the basis of Old Testament texts and by analogy with circumcision.

Balthasar Hubmaier, a leading Anabaptist theologian, in his *Dialogue with Zwingli's Baptism Book* of 1526, took the reformer Ulrich Zwingli to task for ignoring the difference between the Testaments. He wrote: 'For the sake of the last judgment, drop your circuitous argument on circumcision out of the Old Testament!'[1] Later in the same work he claimed: 'We have a clear word for baptizing believers and you have none for baptizing your children, except that you groundlessly drag in several shadows from the Old Testament.'[2] In his *On Infant Baptism Against Oecolampadius* of 1527, Hubmaier expressed the same concern about illegitimate appeals to

---

[1] H. Wayne Pipkin and John H. Yoder, *Balthasar Hubmaier* (Scottdale, Pa.: Herald Press, 1989), 180.

[2] Pipkin and Yoder, *Hubmaier*, 182.

the Old Testament made by another leading reformer. His exasper-
ation with this practice is apparent: 'Water baptism is a ceremony of
the New Testament. Therefore I demand from you a clear word
out of the New Testament with which you bring to us this infant
baptism . . . but you prove infant baptism from Exodus!'[3]

Advocates of tithing may be delighted to find renowned
reformers such as Zwingli and Oecolampadius endorsing their
position, but the discomfort in the writings of these theologians as
they face the accusation that they were misusing the Old Testament
is evident. This should at least alert those who base tithing on the
Old Testament to the fact that there is an important principle of
biblical interpretation at stake here.

Nevertheless, because of the acknowledged difficulty of finding
a New Testament basis for tithing, it is frequently argued that, since
the principle of tithing is firmly embedded in the Old Testament
and is not directly rescinded in the New, it should still be seen as
applying to Christians. Our response to this approach is that,
although there is no explicit New Testament abolition of tithing, it
simply does not fit with what Jesus and the New Testament writers
taught about sharing and giving. But, in order to deal more
thoroughly with the argument that Christians should tithe because
the Old Testament teaches tithing, we need in this chapter to
examine what the Old Testament actually teaches on this subject
and then assess the implications of trying to apply this Old
Testament teaching to the church.

Tithing in the Ancient Near East

Our starting point must be to set the Old Testament within its
wider cultural context. Tithing is mentioned early in the Old
Testament record and recurs in several periods of Israel's history. It
appears to be a principle that was deeply rooted in Israel's worship
life and social legislation and was applied more consistently and
more rigorously than similar principles in surrounding nations.

However, as already indicated, tithing was not unique to Israel.
There is evidence of tithing in many other Near Eastern and

---

[3] Pipkin and Yoder, *Hubmaier*, 288.

Mediterranean societies, with the earliest reference coming from Ur in about 2000 BCE.[4] The particulars varied from society to society, but property, produce, currency, work hours and the spoils of war might all be subject to a tithe. The requirement of a tithe might be imposed by a ruler on his own people or on a subject people. Often such tithing had religious connotations: the Arabians tithed to their god, Sabis; Carthaginians tithed to Melkarth, the god of Tyre.[5] Other societies in which there is evidence that tithing was practised include Ugarit in the fourteenth century BCE,[6] the Syrians,[7] the Lydians,[8] the Sumerians,[9] the Assyrians[10], the Babylonians[11] and the Phoenicians.[12] Sometimes tithing was used to raise public funds for a range of purposes: 'The tyrant Pisistratus about 600 BCE boasted to Solon: "Every citizen pays a tithe of his property, not to me but to a fund for defraying the cost of the public sacrifices or any other charges on the State or the expenditure on any war that may come upon us." '[13] An Old Testament reference to a form of tithing in a non-Israelite society (although a society influenced by the Israelites) occurs in Genesis 47:24, where the Egyptians gave two-tenths of the harvest to Pharaoh.

The limited information we have about tithing in these societies makes it difficult to be certain whether tithing in Israel was significantly different from tithing in other nations. But historians have demonstrated some common ground. Milgrom, for example, notes

---

[4] H. Jagersma, 'The Tithes in the Old Testament' in B. Albrektson et al., *Remembering All the Way* (Leiden: Brill, 1981), 116.

[5] According to Diodorus 20.14. See also Robert Hastings, *My Money and God* (Nashville: Broadman, 1961), 61.

[6] J. Milgrom, *Cult and Conscience: The Asham and the Priestly Doctrine of Repentance* (Leiden: Brill, 1976), 57. See also Augustine Pagolu, *The Religion of the Patriarchs* (Sheffield: Sheffield Academic Press, 1998), 175–176.

[7] See I Maccabees 10:31; 11:35.

[8] According to Herodotus 1.89.

[9] Pagolu, *Religion*, 173–175.

[10] Pagolu, *Religion*, 175.

[11] Milgrom, *Cult*, 55–62.

[12] Marvin Tate, 'Tithing: Legalism or Benchmark?', *Review and Expositor* 70(2) (1973), 153.

[13] Redmond Mullin, *The Wealth of Christians* (Exeter: Paternoster Press, 1983), 20.

some similarities between Old Testament tithing laws and regulations relating to the Babylonian temple tithe in the sixth century
BCE:[14] tithes of produce but not of animals were commutable;
temple officials were not exempt from the tithe; and tithes were
collected at source. However, other historians suggest that he may
be reading too much into the Babylonian material, which is rather
ambiguous in several places. Augustine Pagolu also demonstrates
areas of similarity between Israel and Sumerian, Assyrian, Ugaritic
and Babylonian practices.[15] It does seem, though, that tithing was
practised more systematically and over a longer period in Israel than
in other societies. Most of the instances of tithing in other societies
are from the twenty-first to the fourteenth centuries BCE and then
from the sixth to the fourth centuries BCE, with very little mention
of tithing in the intervening period.

Some have argued that tithing elsewhere was not theologically
motivated in the way that it clearly was in the Old Testament, that
such tithing was political, economic or humanitarian – a form of
tribute or taxation – rather than part of the religious cult. But it is
notoriously difficult to separate out religious and political or social
components in ancient sacral societies, where the modern compart-
mentalisation into religious and secular dimensions was unknown.
But it does seem that in Israel the theological significance of tithing
was more explicit and more developed. The Pentateuch contains
complex legislation about tithing, set in the context of covenant
language and obligations, by comparison with the much simpler
descriptions of tithing practices common in non-biblical texts.

The likelihood is that Israel adopted the familiar practice of
tithing from other nations, at first in a piecemeal fashion and then in
a more systematic way. But tithing became imbued with new
theological and ethical meaning as an important component in the
nation's worship life and social organisation. Nothing in the Old
Testament requires us to hold that tithing was originally introduced
into Israel as a result of divine revelation. But the significance of
tithing within the nation's developing theological and ethical
framework is clearly derived from principles and practices
associated with Israel's encounter with Yahweh at Sinai. This

[14] Milgrom, *Cult*, 58–60.
[15] Pagolu, *Religion*, 173–178.

connection between the tithe and the specific history of Israel is an important perspective to bear in mind as we consider Old Testament references to tithing and their possible contemporary application.

The terminology of tithing is used in various Old Testament books. *Tithe* as a noun occurs thirty-two times: in Genesis 14:20; Leviticus 27:30, 31, 32; Numbers 18:21, 24, 26 (thrice), 28; Deuteronomy 12:6,11,17; Deuteronomy 14:23,28; Deuteronomy 26:12 (twice); 2 Chronicles 31:5,6 (twice), 12; Nehemiah 10:38,39 (twice); Nehemiah 12:44; Nehemiah 13:5,12; Ezekiel 45:11,14 (the Ezekiel references are not to tithing but to tenth parts of a measure); Amos 4:4; and Malachi 3:8, 10. *Tithe* as a verb occurs nine times: in Genesis 28:22 (twice); Deuteronomy 14:22 (twice); Deuteronomy 26:12; 1 Samuel 8:15,17; and Nehemiah 10:38,39. We will consider each of these references within the different sections of the Old Testament.

Tithing in the Pentateuch

Genesis 14:17–20*: After Abram returned from defeating Kedorlaomer and the kings allied with him, the king of Sodom came out to meet him . . . Then Melchizedek king of Salem brought out bread and wine. He was priest of God Most High, and he blessed Abram . . . Then Abram gave him a tenth of everything.*

We have already encountered this incident in our study of New Testament references to tithing. The passage in Hebrews that retells this story and comments on the tithe collected by the Levites is, in fact, the only New Testament reference to the Old Testament practice of tithing. Much, therefore, is made of this story by advocates of tithing.[16] The status of Abram as spiritual father of Christians as well as progenitor of the people of Israel, combined with the designation of Melchizedek as a Christ-figure, are presented as compelling reasons for seeing in this incident a pattern for Christian giving – as Abram tithed to Melchizedek, so Christians should tithe to Christ.

---

[16] A typical example is R. T. Kendall, *Tithing* (London: Hodder & Stoughton, 1982), 39–50.

However, there are a number of difficulties inherent in this application. First, the status of Melchizedek is more doubtful than is often admitted. He is described as the 'priest of God Most High' and he distributes bread and wine, but it is far from clear that the author of Genesis regarded him as anything more than a powerful religious and political Canaanite leader to whom Abram wisely paid tribute in return for his support. This gesture can be seen as more than political expediency. Abram was a religious man. In recognition of God's help in this battle, he responded to the offer of support and blessing from a local high priest and tithed his booty to Melchizedek.

Whether the 'God Most High' whom Melchizedek represented was to be equated with the Lord whom Abram served was perhaps less of an issue for Abram at this time than it may be for later inter-preters. There is no doubt that the Psalmist[17] and the writer to the Hebrews accord to this shadowy figure a greater significance, but this may be best understood as a creative interpretation of the story, rooted in the fact that so little is known about this man. The fact that Abram paid to a local priest-king (whatever status is ascribed to him by later writers) a tribute consisting of a tenth of the plunder gained in a recent battle seems a dubious basis for using this story to persuade Christians to tithe their income.

A second difficulty is that Abram tithed to Melchizedek, not his regular income, but 'a tenth of everything'. If this means that Abram tithed all his possessions, we are dealing here with capital rather than income, which most advocates of tithing tend to exclude from consideration.[18] But this phrase probably refers to the spoils from a particular battle. This may just about qualify as a form of 'income', but it hardly indicates that Abram was in the habit of tithing his more normal income. Moreover, this is the only record of Abram tithing. There is no indication, either before or after this incident, that Abram tithed his herds or flocks or any of the other items that would be included within the Mosaic legislation on tithing.

Since tithing was a fairly common practice in Near Eastern soci-eties at this time, it is not impossible that Abram did tithe on other occasions. The fact that he gave a tenth of the battle spoils to

---

[17] Psalm 110:4.

[18] See, for example, comments on this phrase in Kendall, *Tithing*, 42–43.

Melchizedek may indicate familiarity with this practice. But there is no evidence for this in the biblical record. Nor would Abram's familiarity with and adoption in this instance of a common cultural practice be any reason for Christians to imitate his practice. Indeed, if Abram's tithing is any kind of model for Christians, it provides support only for occasional tithes of unusual sources of income. Perhaps a Christian who wins the lottery, a bingo jackpot or a battle with the Inland Revenue might consider tithing this!

Genesis 28:18–22: *Early the next morning Jacob took the stone he had placed under his head and set it up as a pillar and poured oil on top of it. He called that place Bethel, though the city used to be called Luz. Then Jacob made a vow, saying, 'If God will be with me and will watch over me on this journey I am taking and will give me food to eat and clothes to wear so that I return safely to my father's household, then the Lord will be my God and this stone that I have set up as a pillar will be God's house, and of all that you give me I will give you a tenth.'*

The only other indication that the patriarchs tithed occurs in this account of a pivotal incident in the life of the hitherto less than attractive Jacob. Following a dramatic encounter with God in a dream, in which God promised to bless, protect and restore Jacob, the startled man responded by making a simple shrine at Bethel and by vowing a tithe to God of all that God gave him in fulfilment of the promises in the dream. This promise of a tithe symbolised Jacob's commitment to God, with the implication that the tithe would be used to support 'God's house' at Bethel. It may also be seen as a form of bargaining, in which Jacob specialised[19] – God would only get his tithe if he honoured his promise to bless Jacob. Does this second reference to tithing in Genesis offer a better prospect for teaching tithing today on the basis that this was a biblical practice before the coming of the law?

There are difficulties with this reference also. First, there is no confirmation that Jacob ever fulfilled this promise to tithe what God gave him. He certainly returned to Bethel and built an altar there, prompted by a further divine visitation. In response to God's reassurance that he would inherit the promised blessings, he poured out oil and a drink offering on the altar. But there is no indication

---

[19] See Genesis 25:29–34; 29:18.

that Jacob, now a very wealthy man, tithed what God had given him.[20] If he did, the author of Genesis shows no interest in this. So if he is to be used as a model for tithing today, Jacob appears to be an example of the well-attested tendency for tithing to be talked about rather than practised.

Second, the ways in which Jacob gained and defended his wealth leave much to be desired. It seems that the promise to tithe was not accompanied by integrity in business dealings or by faith in the face of possible adversity. The belief that tithing represents a consecrated approach to financial matters receives little support from the story of Jacob.[21] Third, as with the previous reference to Abram tithing, there is nothing here to indicate that Jacob understood his promise to tithe as implying a regular and repeated practice. He promised to tithe if and when God blessed him, implicitly as a one-off response to this blessing, rather than tithing what he already had in the hope of future blessing or establishing a principle of annual tithing.

Systematic tithing is a feature of the Mosaic legislation but it cannot be traced back to the patriarchs. Not even voluntary tithing can be confidently ascribed to the patriarchs. The two incidents we have reviewed are presented as one-off instances of paying or vowing a tithe. Advocating regular tithing on the basis that this predates the law is illegitimate. Pagolu concludes in relation to references to tithing in Genesis: 'the text shows no concern that Abraham paid his tithe to a pagan king, or whether Jacob ever paid his promised tithes at all'.[22] Tithing appears to be almost incidental to the stories and no theological significance is accorded to this practice by the author.

Leviticus 27:30–33: *A tithe of everything from the land, whether grain from the soil or fruit from the trees, belongs to the Lord. If you redeem any of your tithe, you must add a fifth of the value to it. The entire tithe of the herd and flock – every tenth animal that passes under the shepherd's rod – will be holy to the Lord. You must not pick out the good from the bad or make any substitution. If you do make a substitution, both the animal and its substitute become holy and cannot be redeemed.*

---

[20] See Genesis 35:1–15.
[21] See Genesis 30:37–43; 31:43; 32:7–21; 32:1–3.
[22] Pagolu, *Religion*, 172.

When we come to the next reference to tithing in the Pentateuch in the final chapter of Leviticus, we find the subject of the tithe presented in a very different way. Tithing is now a legal requirement, set within the context of God's covenant with Israel, and specific instructions are given to ensure that reluctant tithers do not find ways to avoid what is, in effect, an agricultural tax. There is a clear theological basis for the tithe – that a tenth of everything the land produces is 'holy to the Lord'; and there is an implied rationale – that the land is God's and all that it produces. Giving back a tenth of the produce to God is a constant reminder that Israel owes the gift of its land to God and an acknowledgement that, though the farmers work hard to produce the harvests, it is God who makes things grow.

But the main concern in this passage is to identify and prescribe penalties for various kinds of sharp practice in relation to tithing. The history of tithing during the Christendom era, as we shall see in a later chapter, is one of constant disputes and ingenious attempts to avoid or mitigate the cost of tithing. It seems that such reluctance to tithe characterised tithing in Israel also, and that tithers were susceptible to the temptation to minimise the effect of tithing on their livelihood. It is evident also from this first reference to tithing in the Mosaic legislation that tithing was already well established in Israel at this point. At some point between the occasional tithing of the patriarchs and the framing of this legislation, tithing had become a regular feature of Israel's economy – but the Old Testament does not comment on this process. There is certainly no indication in this passage that tithing was a novelty and every reason to think that tithing was already familiar enough for tithers to have invented several moves to dilute its impact.

One stratagem was to 'redeem' part of the tithe by converting it into money. In other passages this practice is commended for pragmatic reasons when tithers lived a long way from the place to which the tithe had to be brought. But the temptation must have been strong to undervalue the tithe and so save money. Tithers are warned, therefore, that they must redeem the tithe at a fair price and are obliged to add one fifth of its value to ensure that they do not stray across the line here. A second ploy was to select weak or unhealthy animals to constitute the tithe. To counter this, the law insists that the tithe must be selected on a random basis – 'every

tenth animal' – and that the later substitution of a less valuable
animal for the original tithe will incur the penalty that both the
original animal and the substitute become part of the tithe.

Leviticus indicates that tithing was a well-established practice in
Israel at a fairly early date, although its origins within the legal
system are unclear. Pagolu writes: 'The pentateuchal tithe laws,
whatever their date, reflect only the time of standardization of
tithing in Israel, not the origin of the practice.'[23] There is evidence
also that tithing was as unpopular in Israel as in many other societies
in later centuries. Whether this legislation has any relevance to the
question of whether tithing is an appropriate model for Christian
giving will be considered after we have examined other references
to tithing in the Mosaic Law.

Numbers 18:21–32*: I give to the Levites all the tithes in Israel as their
inheritance in return for the work they do while serving at the Tent of
Meeting . . . They will receive no inheritance among the Israelites. Instead, I
give to the Levites as their inheritance the tithes that the Israelites present as
an offering to the Lord . . . The Lord said to Moses, 'Speak to the Levites
and say to them: "When you receive from the Israelites the tithe I give you as
your inheritance, you must present a tenth of that tithe as the Lord's offering
. . . In this way you also will present an offering to the Lord from all the tithes
you receive from the Israelites. From these tithes you must give the Lord's
portion to Aaron the priest. You must present as the Lord's portion the best
and holiest part of everything given to you . . . You and your households
may eat the rest of it anywhere, for it is your wages for your work at the Tent
of Meeting . . ."'*

The passage in Leviticus did not indicate who were the recipients of
the tithe. Here it is made clear that the Levites are to receive the
tithe as compensation for not having been allocated their own land
along with the other tribes, and in return for their service in the tent
of meeting. The tithe is the equivalent of their 'wages'. According

---

[23] Pagolu, *Religion*, 190. The dating of the various strands of the Pentateuch has been the subject of much debate, into which we have insufficient space to enter. We will concentrate in this study on the text itself and
its setting in the early period of Israel's history, recognising that many
scholars regard some of the Mosaic legislation as a projection back from a
much later period.

to this section of the law, 'all the tithes in Israel' are to be given to the Levites and their households. The Levites in turn are to tithe their tithe to the Aaronic priests – and it seems that they were no less susceptible than the original tithers to the temptation to keep the best portions for their own use, for they are instructed to pass on 'the best and holiest part of everything given to you'. Once again there are parallels between this situation and the disputes between bishops and parish priests in medieval times over the methods by which a portion of the priest's tithe was passed on to the bishop. Reluctance and cost-reduction seem to affect every part of the tithing chain.

A question that we cannot answer from the available evidence but which it is important to raise is whether this passage is simply giving further information about the tithing system described in Leviticus (specifying its recipients) or whether this passage marks a further development in the system. It is clear that tithes were already in existence, but are they now being adapted for a new context and a new purpose? This is the first of many such questions that will arise as we continue to explore the Mosaic provisions about tithing, questions which are impossible to answer with any degree of certainty and which point to the great difficulty of identifying or reconstructing the details of the Old Testament tithing system.

Deuteronomy 12:5–19: *But you are to seek the place the Lord your God will choose from among all your tribes to put his Name there for his dwelling. To that place you must go; there bring your burnt offerings and sacrifices, your tithes and special gifts, what you have vowed to give and your freewill offerings, and the firstborn of your herds and flocks. There, in the presence of the Lord your God, you and your families shall eat and shall rejoice in everything you have put your hand to, because the Lord your God has blessed you . . . there rejoice before the Lord your God, you, your sons and daughters, your male and female servants, and the Levites from your towns, who have no allotment or inheritance of their own . . . You must not eat in your own towns the tithe of your grain and new wine and oil, or the firstborn of your herds and flocks, or whatever you have vowed to give, or your freewill offerings or special gifts. Instead, you are to eat them in the presence of the Lord your God at the place the Lord your God will choose . . .*

It is in Deuteronomy that the bulk of the references to tithing in the Pentateuch are to be found. As in both Leviticus and Numbers, tithing is presented as an established practice and the legislation is

concerned to regulate certain aspects of the system. The primary
concern in this passage is that the tithe should be taken to the place
where the Lord would cause his name to dwell (i.e. Jerusalem),
rather than being administered locally. It seems that this stipulation
as to where the tithe was to be brought reflects a concern for unity
and purity at a time when strong centralising tendencies were
evident in Israel. It is likely that this was a change rather than merely
clarification of existing arrangements, a further development of a
system that had in the past been operating much more locally.

What is also made clear here in a way that was not spelled out in
the previous passages is that those who tithed also ate at least part of
their tithe. The passage in Numbers can legitimately be interpreted
as teaching that the tithe was to be given to the Levites and their
households for their exclusive use, whereas this passage includes the
Levites as beneficiaries but as guests at the feasts of the tithers'
households. Perhaps this was the case also in the context within
which the previous passage was written: when a system is familiar,
legislation does not need to rehearse every element of it. Or is this
passage a refinement or development of the tithing system? A
further possibility is that we are confronted here by two separate
tithes: one tithe that was given to the Levites as their wages (and
tithed on to the priests) and another that was consumed by tithers
and their households at the feasts. Does this mean that Israelites
were actually required to give two-tenths of their produce in tithes?

It is also worth noting that tithes are mentioned here alongside a
range of other offerings required of God's covenant nation: burnt
offerings and sacrifices, special gifts, what has been vowed, freewill
offerings and the firstborn of the herds and flocks. Tithing (whether
single or double) was not the only financial requirement on
Israelites at this time, but it is unclear – here and in other passages –
how tithing related to other offerings, especially the firstfruits and
firstlings. This raises again the perplexing question as to why tithing
(sometimes accompanied by freewill offerings) has been extracted
from a more complex system and advocated as the one economic
requirement that continues to apply to Christians.

Deuteronomy 14:22–27: *Be sure to set aside a tenth of all that your
fields produce each year. Eat the tithe of your grain, new wine and oil, and
the firstborn of your herds and flocks in the presence of the Lord your God at*

the place he will choose as a dwelling for his Name, so that you may learn to revere the Lord your God always. But if that place is too distant and you have been blessed by the Lord your God and cannot carry your tithe . . . then exchange your tithe for silver, and take the silver with you and go to the place the Lord your God will choose. Use the silver to buy whatever you like: cattle, sheep, wine or other fermented drink, or anything you wish. Then you and your household shall eat there in the presence of the Lord your God and rejoice. And do not neglect the Levites living in your towns, for they have no allotment or inheritance of their own.

This passage adds little to the information already given but it may represent a later gloss on the earlier requirement that the tithe was to be eaten in God's chosen place. It seems that this stipulation had been found to be excessively onerous for those living at a substantial distance from the central sanctuary. A practical solution is indicated that allowed tithers, if their home was far away from the sanctuary, to commute their tithe into money, which was easier to transport. They could then buy food for the feast when they arrived at the designated location. The final warning – that the Levites were not to be neglected – may indicate that some tithers were still looking for ways to avoid the full cost of tithing and were consuming the whole tithe within their own households.

The tone of this passage, however, seems rather lighter than the other passages. There is an emphasis on rejoicing, as there was in the previous passage, combined with the encouragement to 'learn to revere the Lord your God'. But there seems also to be more flexibility than is apparent in most legislative documents – 'Use the silver to buy whatever you like: cattle, sheep, wine or other fermented drink, or anything you wish.' This, coupled with the relaxation of rules about commuting the tithe (no mention is made here of adding a fifth to its value), may indicate an attempt to make tithing less taxing and more festive than previously.

Deuteronomy 14:28–29: *At the end of every three years, bring all the tithes of that year's produce and store it in your towns, so that the Levites (who have no allotment or inheritance of their own) and the aliens, the fatherless and the widows who live in your towns may come and eat and be satisfied, and so that the Lord your God may bless you in all the work of your hands.*

It is at this point that the difficulty of harmonising or tracing the relationship between the various laws about tithing becomes still more apparent. This passage seems to be differentiating between the normal tithe, which was taken to the central sanctuary and eaten there with the Levites, and a special tithe collected every three years that was to be administered locally (despite the strong resistance to such an idea in a previous passage). This tithe was to be stored in the towns and given not only to the local Levites but also to the sojourners, widows and orphans (presumably because none of these had land of their own and were likely to need community support).

Was this 'third-year tithe' an additional requirement, so that people were required to give an extra tithe every three years, or was the regular tithe redirected to local use in a way that is not indicated in any of the previous passages? If it were the former, this represents a very significant increase in the burden placed on tithers. It also again raises questions about the legitimacy of advocating tithing today as a simple 10% of income. If Israelites were giving an extra tithe every three years, why is this tithe not taken into account by most advocates?[24] If the various Old Testament passages are interpreted as referring to different tithes rather than developments in the system, it is possible that up to 23.33% of their income was designated for tithing (20% every year and an extra 10% every three years)! We will consider this issue again later in this chapter when we look at how tithing was understood in first-century Judaism.

Whether this is an additional tithe or a way of redirecting the normal tithe, it is unclear whether this procedure was an innovation at this point in the legislation or whether this had always been in view but had not been mentioned until now. It seems strange that the earlier passage should insist so strongly on tithes being brought to the designated place for consumption without mentioning that this only happened in two out of every three years. But, if this passage represents a development of the system, it becomes increasingly difficult to sustain an argument that Israel had a consistent

---

[24] Some advocates of tithing do, in fact, interpret the Old Testament in this way, but they generally continue to advocate the lower 10% figure – using the assumed additional giving of the Israelites as an added incentive.

tithing system that can function as a model for future generations. Tithing seems to have operated in different ways at different times, and it may have involved different percentages.

There is also a subtle but significant shift here in the underlying theology and social ethics of the tithe. Previous passages in Deuteronomy advocated tithing on the grounds that tithers have already been blessed by the Lord – tithing is an appropriate response of thanksgiving. But in this passage tithing is advocated 'so that the Lord your God may bless you in all the work of your hands'. Both theologies can be found in the arguments of contemporary advocates of tithing, although it seems that the 'tithe in order to be blessed' approach (which is evident in Jacob's promise to tithe) is more popular than the 'tithe because you have been blessed' approach (which seems to have been Abram's motive).

Tithing as a means of caring for the poor and marginalised members of the community also appears here explicitly for the first time in the tithing legislation. Giving the tithe to the Levites (or sharing the tithe with them, depending on which passage one reads) was linked with their need for support as members of the community without land of their own, but this support was advocated on the basis of their role in the worship life of Israel. Such tithing was cultic rather than humanitarian (although this distinction should not be pushed too far, as covenant legislation constantly relates responsibilities towards God with responsibilities towards others). But allocating some of the tithe every three years to sojourners, widows and orphans links tithing with a range of other Mosaic laws that are concerned to provide a safety net for the poor and to ensure that they are treated justly.

It is important that those who advocate tithing on the basis of Old Testament texts do not neglect this element. Tithing in the Mosaic law is not just an obligation towards God or a way of supporting the Levites and priests who minister in the tent of meeting. Nor is it only an investment with the hope that God will bless those who tithe. It is also a way in which resources are redistributed, albeit only periodically and partially, to ensure that those who are poor are not neglected. This component of tithing was built into the medieval tithing system, with a portion of the tithe being allocated to the poor rather than to the clergy. However, there is ample evidence that the poor frequently missed out on this provision and that the tithe was swallowed up in the costs of maintaining the clergy and church premises. Perhaps individuals and churches who practise tithing today need to check whether an appropriate portion of the tithe is being given to the poor rather than supporting the staff, premises and programmes of the church.

Given this background, it is perhaps not surprising that Jesus is scathing is his criticism of the Pharisees and teachers of the law who tithe their spices but whose treatment of poor widows demonstrates that they have neglected 'the weightier matters of the law'. The social ethics inherent in the tithing system cannot be neglected without incurring such condemnation, however scrupulously tithing is practised. Tithing that does not benefit widows – but is instead part of a system that impoverishes them still further – has no support in either Testament.

Deuteronomy 26:12–15: *When you have finished setting aside a tenth of all your produce in the third year, the year of the tithe, you shall give it to the Levite, the alien, the fatherless and the widow, so that they may eat in your towns and be satisfied. Then say to the Lord your God: 'I have removed from my house the sacred portion and have given it to the Levite, the alien, the fatherless and the widow, according to all you commanded.'*

This final reference to tithing in the Pentateuch adds little to what we have already studied. As in previous passages, tithing is again mentioned in connection with the offering of firstfruits.[25] It remains unclear how these two requirements are related, with some scholars suggesting that they are separate offerings and others that one is subsumed under the other. Popular advocates of tithing also vary on this issue, with some differentiating between them and others equating the tithe and the offering of firstfruits (the latter approach at least enables them to draw on more references in the Bible and patristic literature). Vischer insists: 'there is an essential difference between the presentation of the firstfruits and the tithe. The presentation of the firstfruits has more the character of a sacrifice about it . . . the tithe, however, has more the character of a tribute payment.'[26] This may be so but, as with so much about the Old

---

[25] See Deuteronomy 26:1–11.

[26] Lukas Vischer, *Tithing in the Early Church* (Philadelphia: Fortress Press, 1966), 2.

Testament tithing system, we do not have a clear picture of how these components fitted together.

There is also a new phrase in this passage. The third year, in which either the tithe is redirected to caring for the needy or an additional tithe is required for this purpose, is referred to as 'the year of the tithe'. There is also an emphasis on the liturgical aspect of tithing: those who tithe in this year are encouraged to testify before God that they have done what they were commanded to do. The tithe was never simply a tax.

Deuteronomy 16:13–17: *Celebrate the Feast of Tabernacles for seven days after you have gathered the produce of your threshing-floor and your winepress. Be joyful at your Feast – you, your sons and daughters, your male and female servants, and the Levites, the aliens, the fatherless and the widows who live in your towns. For seven days celebrate the Feast to the Lord your God at the place the Lord will choose. For the Lord your God will bless you in all your harvest and in all the works of your hands, and your joy will be complete. Three times a year all your men must appear before the Lord your God at the place where he will choose: at the Feast of Unleavened Bread, the Feast of Weeks and the Feast of Tabernacles. No one should appear before the Lord empty-handed: Each of you must bring a gift in proportion to the way the Lord your God has blessed you.*

Although this passage does not refer explicitly to tithing, the final statement about bringing 'a gift in proportion to the way the Lord your God has blessed you' can hardly mean anything else, given the familiar language of the preceding verses. What this summary of obligations adds to the passages we have already investigated is the emphasis on joy (which is the context for any offering mentioned in Deuteronomy) and the information that the tithe is to be used to supply resources for three feasts each year. It also seems to combine elements from other passages, suggesting that one tithe is in view throughout the Mosaic legislation, rather than two or even three. The tithe was to be used to supply resources for the feasts, but Levites and aliens, the fatherless and widows were all to be included in the celebrations. This further information may help to clear up one issue that is otherwise problematic in the passages we have studied – how an annual tithe could possibly be consumed in one feast or even one festival.

Whether this account reflects what really happened at any stage in Israel's history or whether this is a composite account of the tithing system is a moot point. This has been the problem we have encountered throughout our exploration of the Old Testament texts on tithing. It is unclear how they fit together. Do they apply to different stages in Israel's history? Were there different tithes for different purposes, which may have amounted in all to about one-third of a family's income? How do tithes relate to the additional requirements such as the giving of firstfruits and firstborn animals? As Clarence Lee concludes, 'the scriptural evidence is, to say the least, highly ambiguous and reveals that the practice of paying the tithe underwent so many modifications that it is almost impossible to determine what the "scriptural" practice really was'.[27] Menahem Herman, after surveying recent scholarship dealing with the tithe, comments: 'the nature of the tithe is perceived differently by each scholar. The tithe may be early or late, compulsory or voluntary, sacred or secular. Indeed, there is no consensus on approach or interpretation.'[28] S. L. Driver's terse comment sums up the state of the evidence: 'The data at our disposal do not enable us to write a history of the Hebrew tithe.'[29] Some theological coherence may be present throughout the Old Testament references to tithing, but any attempt to summarise the historical practice of tithing is likely to be artificial.

Tithing in the Historical Books

1 Samuel 8:11–17: *This is what the king who reigns over you will do . . . He will take a tenth of your grain and of your vintage and give it to his officials and attendants. Your male and female servants and the best of your cattle and donkeys he will take for his own use. He will take a tenth of your flocks, and you yourselves will become his slaves.*

---

[27] Writing in the foreword to Vischer, *Tithing*, ix–x.

[28] Menahem Herman, *Tithe as Gift: The Institution in the Pentateuch and in Light of Mauss's Prestation Theory* (San Francisco: Mellen Research University Press, 1991), 35–36.

[29] Writing in the International Critical Commentary on Deuteronomy, quoted in Hastings, *Money*, 62.

The plea of the Israelite elders to Samuel that he should 'appoint a king to lead us, such as all the other nations have'[30] prompted the elderly prophet to warn them that such an appointment carried costs as well as benefits. Among these costs was the probability that they would find themselves expected to pay the tithe that Near Eastern monarchs frequently demanded from their subjects as a royal prerogative. This form of tithing might be regarded as a secular charge, akin to modern taxation, and thus of no immediate relevance to our investigation. However, as with the tithing practices of other nations, it is likely that at least a portion of this tithe would have been used to support the royal sanctuaries. There is no indication in this passage as to whether such tithing would be an additional burden on those who were already tithing in the ways required under the Mosaic law or whether those tithes would be redirected, but Samuel indicates that the burden would be heavy. Even if the overall amount required did not increase, royal tithe collectors might be more efficient than Levitical collectors.

Tithing in the Pentateuch is generally presented as a joyful privilege – whatever those who were required to tithe may have actually felt about this obligation. But there is certainly no hint here that providing a tithe to support the royal entourage is anything but a tiresome burden – although Samuel, who disapproved of the request for a king, was no doubt painting the bleakest possible picture of the consequences.

2 Chronicles 31:4–12: *He [Hezekiah] ordered the people living in Jerusalem to give the portion due to the priests and Levites so that they could devote themselves to the Law of the Lord. As soon as the order went out, the Israelites generously gave the firstfruits of their grain, new wine, oil and honey and all that the fields produced. They brought a great amount, a tithe of everything. The people of Israel and Judah who lived in the towns of Judah also brought a tithe of their herds and flocks and a tithe of the holy things dedicated to the Lord their God, and they piled them in heaps . . . Hezekiah gave orders to prepare storerooms in the temple of the Lord, and this was done. Then they faithfully brought in the contributions, tithes and dedicated gifts.*

---

[30] 1 Samuel 8:5.

Whether or not the kings did indeed demand their tithe is unclear, as is any impact this may have had on the tithes to the Levites, but – for whatever reason – there was a serious problem with the tithing system by the time Hezekiah came to the throne. The priests and Levites were not receiving adequate support and so were unable to devote themselves to their ministry. As part of the religious reformation that took place during the reign of Hezekiah, a serious attempt was made to restore the tithing system. First in Jerusalem and then throughout the nation, people responded positively to the order that tithes, firstfruits, vowed gifts and other offerings should be collected. The fact that the king found it necessary to designate special storerooms in the temple for these gifts suggests that tithing had been obsolete for some considerable period and that there was not even a proper infrastructure for administering the system.

Two features of tithing that we have noted in previous passages are also apparent here. First, tithes were accompanied by various other forms of offerings and were not carefully differentiated from these. Second, the lack of tithing in preceding years (or decades?) is further testimony to the very limited popularity of tithing and the reluctance of people to sustain such a system. The generosity and whole-heartedness which accompanied the tithing recorded here, and which was no doubt associated with the spiritual renewal evident in this period of Israel's history, should not lead us to conclude that tithing was generally a matter for enthusiasm or celebration.

Nehemiah 10:36–39: *As it is also written in the Law, we will bring the firstborn of our sons and of our cattle, of our herds and of our flocks to the house of our God, to the priests ministering there. Moreover, we will bring to the storerooms of the house of our God, to the priests, the first of our ground meal, of our [grain] offerings, of the fruit of all our trees and of our new wine and oil. And we will bring a tithe of our crops to the Levites, for it is the Levites who collect the tithes in all the towns where we work. A priest descended from Aaron is to accompany the Levites when they receive the tithes, and the Levites are to bring a tenth of the tithes up to the house of our God, to the storerooms of the treasury . . . We will not neglect the house of our God.*

By the time of Nehemiah, when a further period of national reformation was under way, the tithing system had evidently again fallen into disuse. This is not surprising. During the period of the Exile, tithes might still have been paid to support the priests and Levites, but they could no longer have been used to provide food for the cultic festivals. Since the more popular use of the tithe was now redundant and the situation was chaotic enough for anyone who wished to evade the responsibility of tithing, it is understandable that the whole system appears to have collapsed, leaving the Levites to provide for themselves.

One of the many renewed commitments to the law made in the public ceremony recorded in this chapter involved the restoration of tithing, together with firstfruits and firstlings. The only new element in this passage is the information that the Levites, accompanied by an Aaronic priest, were to be involved in the actual collection of the tithes. While it is possible that this was a long-standing practice, which was being restored with the restoration of tithing itself, it may be that this represents an attempt to regularise the tithing system.[31] The initiative no longer rests with the tithers but with the recipients of the tithe – as would be the case in medieval times, when the priests and other tithe collectors became familiar and resented figures. The involvement of a priest might add solemnity to the collection process; it would also help to ensure that the priests received their designated share of the Levites' tithe.

Nehemiah 12:44: *At that time men were appointed to be in charge of the storerooms for the contributions, firstfruits and tithes. From the fields around the towns they were to bring into the storerooms the portions required by the Law for the priests and the Levites, for Judah was pleased with the ministering priests and Levites.*

It seems that this public commitment was put into effect and that tithing was, at least temporarily, reinstituted in this period. Not only were collectors dispatched to bring the tithes to Jerusalem, but administrators were appointed to manage the storerooms where the tithes were gathered. For a while, the priests and Levites were held in high regard and were properly supported by the tithes. But it is

---

[31] Some of the references in the Pentateuch, which we examined earlier in this chapter, may well date from this period and represent an attempt to clarify and regularise the tithing requirements.

not clear for how long the system operated. In the following chapter, Nehemiah returned to the city after a spell away from Jerusalem
to find that a man named Tobiah was occupying *a large room formerly
used to store the grain offerings and incense and temple articles, and also the
tithes of grain, new wine and oil prescribed for the Levites, singers and gate-
keepers, as well as the contributions for the priests.*[32] Although Nehemiah
promptly ejected Tobiah and ordered the rooms to be purified, this
passage provides further evidence that tithing, although embedded
in the Mosaic legislation, was practised less consistently, and
certainly less enthusiastically, than some advocates of tithing might
wish to suggest.

The references to tithing in Nehemiah do offer a further contribution to our attempt to understand how the tithing system
operated in the Old Testament. We noted above the apparent
discrepancies between the various references to tithing in the
Pentateuch, and we also indicated that these discrepancies can be
explained in various ways. They may be the result of historical
development, in that different forms of tithing were operative in
different periods of Israel's history. Alternatively, different aspects of
a more unified system may be presented in different passages
because their different authors or editors were interested in different
interpretations of the system – priestly or national, religious or
humanitarian.

The other possibility we considered is that there may have been
two or three different tithes: a first tithe to the Levites, from which a
portion was passed on to the priests; a second tithe that was set apart
and eaten by the tither's household at the feasts; and a third tithe
(every three years) for the poor. Or the third tithe may have
replaced the second tithe every three years. This attempt to
harmonise the tithing texts was the kind of interpretation favoured
by medieval theologians, who struggled with any indication of
inconsistencies in the Bible.[33] Nineteenth-century biblical scholars
mainly rejected this solution, preferring to live with the
discrepancies rather than trying to harmonise the texts. But several

---

[32] Nehemiah 13:5.
[33] Giles Constable, *Monastic Tithes* (Cambridge: CUP, 1964), 10–12.
Some medieval interpreters avoided the problem by using allegorical or
anagogical methods.

recent scholars have argued that this is the best way of making sense of the variations in the different passages, and this interpretation has certainly also found favour in many Jewish commentaries on the Old Testament. For example, the testimony given in Tobit 1:7–8 assumes that there are three different tithes: 'Of all my produce I would give a tenth to the sons of Levi who ministered at Jerusalem; a second tenth I would sell, and I would go and spend the proceeds each year at Jerusalem, the third tenth I would give to those to whom it was my duty.'

This Jewish testimony must obviously be given credence, despite the problems this interpretation of the Old Testament causes to those who want to advocate the model of a single tithe on the basis of Old Testament teaching and practice. But we must also pay attention to the evidence in another Jewish document – the book of Nehemiah. There is no indication of an awareness of more than one kind of tithe in the restoration of tithing recorded in this document. Gordon McConville writes: 'The idea of multiple tithes, having ancient Jewish tradition behind it, should not be lightly dismissed. But it fails because it is not the *most* ancient Jewish interpretation. That honour belongs to the book of Nehemiah, whose author knew all the relevant laws but only one tithe.'[34] The identification of three different tithes amounting to 23.33% of income appears to be a later development, although one which would have been well known to the Jews in the first century and which must be regarded as part of the background to anything Jesus said about tithing.

Tithing in the Prophets

References to tithing are not extensive in the prophetic literature of the Old Testament, whether because tithing was sufficiently well established and consistently practised in many periods of Israel's history or because the prophets were more interested in other aspects of the law. There are, in fact, only two instances where tithing is mentioned.

---

[34] J. Gordon McConville, *Law and Theology in Deuteronomy* (Sheffield: JSOT, 1984), 75.

Amos 4:4: *Go to Bethel and sin; go to Gilgal and sin yet more. Bring your sacrifices every morning, your tithes every three years.*

The concern in this prophecy is not that tithing is being neglected but that it is being practised in such a way as to incur guilt rather than release blessing. As so often in the writings of the prophets, Israel is condemned for failing to combine social justice with cultic acts of worship. Amos sees tithes being offered by those who are oppressing the poor – in effect, mocking one of the true purposes of tithing. Tithing is hollow if it is not accompanied by a concern for justice and righteousness, as Jesus was to tell the Pharisees and teachers of the law centuries later.[35] It is likely, Tate argues,[36] that what was intended to be a time of community and sharing at the feasts had become a time when the rich enjoyed themselves at the expense of the poor (a similar scenario to that condemned by Paul in 1 Corinthians 11). Once again we have a biblical reference to tithing that warns those who tithe to ensure that this practice is not disconnected from more important matters of justice and concern for the poor.

Malachi 3:8–12: *'Will a mere mortal rob God? Yet you rob me. But you ask, "How do we rob you?" In tithes and offerings. You are under a curse – the whole nation of you – because you are robbing me. Bring the whole tithe into the storehouse, that there may be food in my house. Test me in this,'* says the Lord Almighty, *'and see if I will not throw open the floodgates of heaven and pour out so much blessing that you will not have room enough for it. I will prevent pests from devouring your crops, and the vines in your fields will not cast their fruit,' says the Lord Almighty. 'Then all nations will call you blessed, for yours will be a delightful land,'* says the Lord Almighty.

No biblical text on tithing is quoted more frequently or more enthusiastically than this section of Malachi's prophecy. The prophecy is set in a period when tithing has been suspended or has fallen into neglect throughout the nation. Malachi's reference earlier in his message to instances of crippled and diseased animals being brought for sacrifice and his call to the nation to bring 'the whole tithe' into the storehouse may indicate that tithing was not

---

[35] Matthew 23:23.
[36] Tate, 'Tithing', 154.

defunct but was being practised partially and in ways that were contrary to the Mosaic legislation. Malachi insists that tithing should be resumed and practised properly. This clarion call is buttressed with warnings and promises, curses and blessings.

The power of this prophecy and its uncompromising language make it attractive to those who advocate tithing. However, there are problems with attempts to apply this text to Christians today. First, as we have already noted, it is very difficult to be sure what constituted 'the whole tithe' in the Old Testament – 10%, 20% or even more. At what point can someone be sure that they are no longer robbing God, that they are paying 'the whole tithe' and so are in line for the promised blessings?[37] Faithfully giving 10% of one's income may fall far short of what Malachi's prophecy requires. It might actually represent disobedience to the prophet's instructions and constitute only part of what is required.

More importantly, the language of this passage points again to an issue that has been evident as we examined the earlier Old Testament references to tithing, but on which we have not yet commented fully. The phrase 'so much blessing that you will not have room enough for it' is a clear echo of the covenant promises to Israel, promises that do not apply in the same way to any other people. Similarly, 'all nations will call you blessed' is an allusion to the promise to Abraham, the founder of the covenant nation.[38] Tithing operated in the context of a covenant nation with its own land, an agricultural society constituted as a theocratic state. The blessings and curses are also set in this context.

But many Christians today find themselves in a context with none of these features. Christians in Britain live in a society that is often described as post-industrial, at least two steps removed from an agricultural society. We belong to a new kind of covenant nation, the supranational community of the church that has no territory of its own. Blomberg notes a further difference: 'It is also important to remember the unique relationship between tithes and

---

[37] I have yet to discover any thoughtful response to this issue in the writings of those who advocate tithing. Kendall recognises that there is an issue but asserts that only 10% is required without giving any justification for this conclusion: see Kendall, *Tithing*, 70. Most simply ignore it.

[38] Genesis 12:1–3.

offerings and the temple cult. Without a similar centre for bloody sacrifices today, one cannot simply transfer all principles for giving to God's sanctuary in the Old Testament to church budgets in the New Testament age!'[39] And we live in a secular, pluralistic and non-theocratic state, which raises funds by way of a complex system of taxation. Many of us pay between 30% and 40% of our income through various forms of direct and indirect taxation. This system had no parallel in Israel – although the tithing system that Samuel threatened would result from the inauguration of the monarchy may have been the closest equivalent.

Tithing is an important, although somewhat obscure, component in the worship life and social legislation of the nation of Israel. Nothing more. It is biblical, but it is not Christian. It is not a fundamental principle that can or should be transferred from its Old Testament context into the experience of Christians and churches today. That this is so in no way implies that Christians in Britain (or elsewhere) should not be sharing their resources, supporting those who are set apart to provide spiritual leadership, giving to those in need or working for social justice and a more equitable distribution of resources. But the assumption that the principle of tithing can be extracted from a very different social, economic and religious context and imposed on Christians today, on the basis of verses such as these in Malachi, cannot be justified.

Tithing in Judaism

The evidence from the inter-testamental period and Judaism in the first and second centuries CE indicates that tithing remained an important, albeit never popular, aspect of Jewish religion. Indeed, by the time of Jesus, it was probably practised more consistently and rigorously than in most earlier periods of Israel's history. According to Herman, 'the tithe was recognized as the badge of personal piety for Jews . . . tithing came to be described as the mark of scrupulousness and trustworthiness in Jewish circles'.[40] Hastings

---

[39] Craig Blomberg, *Neither Poverty Nor Riches: A Biblical Theology of Material Possessions* (Leicester: Apollos, 1999), 80.
[40] Herman, *Tithe*, 2.

concludes: 'The acceptance of the tithing structure in Jesus' day was almost universal among devout Hebrews.'[41]

The Apocrypha mentions quite frequently the requirements of tithes, offerings and firstfruits.[42] Herman comments: 'The prominence of the tithe in talmudic texts is well attested . . . the tithe's significance for the rabbis is fully substantiated by the abundance of halakhic evidence in the Mishnah, Gemara and other writings.'[43] Three Mishnah tractates deal with the subject in considerable detail: *Maaserot*, *Maaser Sheni* and *Demai*. The third of these tractates, perhaps taking a lead from hints in the Pentateuch and certainly providing further evidence that tithing was not popular, deals with various forms of tithe evasion. The Mishnah (*Maaseroth* i.1) and Talmud (T.B. *Maaseroth* 1a) assert that: 'whatsoever is used for food and is kept watch over and grows from the soil is liable to tithes'.

The *Tractate Maaserot*, in the second century CE, reasserts the importance of tithing despite the catastrophic destruction of the temple, on the grounds that the underlying theological principle of God's ownership of the land and his covenant with Israel, on which tithing is based, is unchanged. The tractate repeats the familiar Old Testament injunctions but adds guidance on a range of practical issues, particularly about when tithes fall due and how food is to be treated when it is as yet untithed (for example, ripened grain which has not yet been harvested). It contains an amusing section about the difference between a meal and a snack, concluding that untithed food cannot be used for a meal but can be used for a snack, and that it is the intention not the amount that determines which it is. The tendency for tithing to become legalistic evidently was not confined to the first-century Pharisees![44]

In a succession of writings about tithing, the rabbis underlined the importance of the tithe and pronounced on various practical

---

[41] Hastings, *Money*, 62.

[42] See I Maccabees 3:49; 10:31; 11:35; 13:25–27; 32:10–15; Tobit 1:6–8; 5:13; Judith 11:3; Sirach 35:9; Jubilees 32:4–9. Some of these references suggest that the tithe is payable in this period to the priests rather than to the Levites.

[43] Herman, *Tithe*, 47–48.

[44] On this tractate, see Martin Jaffee, *Mishnah's Theology of Tithing: A Study of Tractate Maaserot* (Chico, Calif.: Scholars Press, 1981).

issues. They taught that the tithe was one of the three pillars on which the world rested (Midr. Gen. *Rabbah* i.6);[45] they insisted that the tithe due to the poor must go to the poor (Mish. *Peah* v.4f; viii.2f; *Aboth* v.9); they specified the sacred times when things were to be tithed; and the items liable to be tithed were extended to every conceivable possibility. This teaching is reflected in Jesus' conversation with the Pharisees and teachers of the law about their tithing of spices and garden herbs. As was the case with so much in first-century Judaism, Old Testament teaching on tithing had been overlaid with innumerable qualifications and extended through multiple refinements. If Jesus is to be understood as commending tithing, then it would certainly not have been clear to his disciples without further explanation that he was endorsing a bare 10% gift, as contemporary advocates of tithing so often assume, rather than the involved and highly technical system that tithing had become in his day.

Furthermore, it seems beyond dispute that the Old Testament was understood in first-century Judaism as requiring three separate tithes rather than a single tithe. This is the consistent teaching of the rabbis as well as the testimony found in Tobit. Josephus, too, mentions three tithes.[46] Redmond Mullin, surveying the literature of the period, concludes that, according to first-century Jewish teaching, 'there were three tithes: the first was for the Levite . . . the second was to be consumed in Jerusalem . . . (this tithe was in part a form of relief for the poor in the city); the third tithe was for the poor, and replaced the Levitical Tithe in the third and sixth years of each seven-year cycle'.[47]

We may agree with many biblical commentators that this is a misinterpretation of the Old Testament, but the fact remains that anyone – Jewish, Christian or Jewish Christian – mentioning tithing in the first century would undoubtedly have this more

---

[45] Although it has been argued that the reference here is to almsgiving rather than tithing, reflecting a development within Judaism in this period. See L. William Countryman, *The Rich Christian in the Church of the Early Empire: Contradictions and Accommodations* (New York: The Edwin Mellen Press, 1980), 105.
[46] Josephus, *Antiquities* 4.8.22.
[47] Mullin, *Wealth*, 26.

demanding requirement in mind. If the New Testament does advocate tithing in continuity with the Old Testament, as many claim, it certainly does not advocate a mere 10% of income. If for no other reason than this, advocates of tithing may be on safer ground if they base their advocacy on the Old Testament rather than on the New.

Conclusion

However, as we have seen in this chapter, while advocates of tithing may be on safer ground in the Old Testament, this ground may be no firmer than that provided by the few New Testament references to tithing. There is no basis whatsoever for transposing the tithe from its Old Testament context to the radically different context within which Christians today are called to work out what it means to follow Jesus in the sphere of financial discipleship.

Furthermore, as we have seen in our examination of the New Testament references to tithing, even in a culture where tithing was very familiar, there seems to have been a determined effort to encourage Christians to operate along different lines. Tithing is not even used as an illustration or as a starting point, so attempts to circumvent the problems we have identified by appealing to 'the spirit of the tithe' (rather than the letter of the law) do not appear to go to the heart of the problem.

Tithing was an entirely appropriate practice in Old Testament Israel when it functioned alongside other practices within the whole economic, social and religious system for which it was designed. But on what basis can we extract tithing as a bare percentage figure from the complex legal and fiscal system of ancient Israel? Can we with integrity rip out this one element and impose it unaltered in a very different social situation? Tithing was designed, as we will see in a later chapter, for a society where extremes of wealth and poverty were to be removed by the much more radical and comprehensive jubilee provisions and where there was no sacred/secular division such as there is in modern society. Separated from this context and these other practices, tithing is anomalous and anachronistic. It tends to become a component in a different kind of system that fails to engage radically enough with the challenges presented by Jesus and that allows inequality and injustice to go unchallenged. Tithing hinders the emergence of Christian communities that are 'good news to the poor' rather than institutions that have the reputation among non-members of being 'after our money'.

It was these kinds of communities which 'turned the world upside down' in the early centuries. So, in the next chapter, we will examine writings from this period to see if and how they used Old and New Testament tithing passages to guide their use of resources.

Chapter 5

Tithing in the Early Church

We return now to the question of how we should interpret the silence of the New Testament on the subject of Christians tithing. We have disputed the idea that this silence implies that tithing was accepted without question in the earliest churches, so that none of the New Testament authors felt they needed to teach on this subject. Our conclusion was that this silence is evidence, rather, that the early Christians were not interested in tithing and that this was neither advocated nor widely practised in this period.

In order to test these contrary claims, we will look in this chapter at evidence from the churches and Christian leaders in the period between the end of the New Testament and the development of the system that would become known as Christendom. This evidence has been assembled from an extensive, although probably not completely exhaustive, search for references to tithing in extant writings from that period.

We will be asking two main questions: How were references to tithing in either the Old Testament or the New Testament understood and applied by Christians in these years? And to what extent do the interpretations of these references to tithing indicate that Christians in this period were teaching or practising tithing? If we find that tithing was not widely taught or practised, we will need to consider a third question: What other principles for giving and sharing were operative in the early churches?

Tithing in the Pre-Constantine Church

Old Testament references to tithing quoted but not applied

Writers in this period quote from and comment on every section of the Old Testament, so they inevitably refer from time to time to the various passages about tithing. In most cases, however, they mention tithing without any suggestion that Christians should emulate this practice. This apparent lack of interest in the subject of tithing is not particularly surprising, for the context of most of the references to tithing suggests that the author's attention was on other matters. Tithing was incidental to his argument, mentioned only because it occurred in a passage he was interested in for other reasons.

The examples in this section should not, then, be given undue weight in our evaluation of the importance of tithing in this period. But they may, perhaps, offer a measure of confirmation if we find in other places evidence that patristic writers, even when they were writing about giving or other financial issues, showed a similar lack of interest in tithing as an appropriate model. Clearly, encountering a reference to tithing in Old Testament texts did not normally prompt these writers, even in passing, to apply this practice to their contemporaries. Even where tithing is commended as an aid to the Israelites' devotion, this commendation remains set within the Old Testament context and is not extrapolated to the early Christian communities.

The earliest reference I have found to tithing without any comment from the author is in the anonymous work usually dated to the first half of the second century known as *The Testaments of the Twelve Patriarchs*. In *The Testament of Levi* we read: 'And when we came to Bethel, my father Jacob saw in a vision concerning me, that I should be to them for a priest unto the Lord; and he rose up early in the morning, and paid tithes of all to the Lord through me.'[1]

Clement of Alexandria, writing early in the third century, refers twice to tithing in his longest work, the *Stromata*. The first reference reads: 'Wherefore the tithes both of the ephah and of the sacrifices were presented to God; and the paschal feast began with the tenth

---

[1] *Testament of Levi* ch. 9. Some scholars date this document much later.

day, being the transition from all trouble, and from all objects of sense.'[2] Clement then moves on without further comment. He returns to the subject in a later chapter, where he writes: 'Besides, the tithes of the fruits and of the flocks taught both piety towards the Deity, and not covetously to grasp everything, but to communicate gifts of kindness to one's neighbours.'[3] The spiritual and moral impact of the tithing system is noted, but Clement does not advocate the use of this in the churches.

Methodius, who was bishop of Olympus and Patara in Lycia, writing towards the end of the third century, also refers twice to tithing in *The Banquet of the Ten Virgins*. He writes:

> And the Lord spake unto Moses, saying, Speak unto the children of Israel, and say unto them, when either man or woman shall separate themselves . . . unto the Lord . . . one vows to offer gold and silver vessels for the sanctuary when he comes, another to offer the tithe of his fruits, another of his property, another the best of his flocks, another consecrates his being; and no one is able to vow a great vow to the Lord, but he who has offered himself entirely to God.[4]

Then, in a later chapter:

> Now the Jews prophesied our state, but we foretell the heavenly; since the Tabernacle was a symbol of the Church, and the Church of heaven. Therefore, these things being so, and the Tabernacle being taken for a type of the Church, as I said, it is fitting that the altars should signify some of the things in the Church. And we have already compared the brazen altar to the company and circuit of widows; for they are a living altar of God, to which they bring calves and tithes, and free-will offerings, as a sacrifice to the Lord.[5]

In both these passages the tithe is mentioned with other kinds of offerings as a form of sacrifice or consecration to God. In the latter passage the author compares aspects of worship under the old

---

[2] Clement, *Stromata* 2.11.
[3] Clement, *Stromata* 2.18.
[4] Methodius, *The Banquet of the Ten Virgins* 5.1.
[5] Methodius, *The Banquet of the Ten Virgins* 5.8.

covenant with their equivalents under the new covenant. There is an obvious opening here to affirm the importance of tithing (or some equivalent practice) in the churches, but Methodius does not develop this topic. The tithe appears to be of only decorative significance in this passage.

Tithing seems to have rather greater significance, however, in Origen's *Homilies on Numbers*, written during the first half of the third century. Origen asks:

> How can our righteousness exceed that of the scribes and Pharisees? For they did not dare to eat anything of the fruits of their fields until they had given the firstfruits to the priests and paid their tithes to the Levites. I, however, do not do any of this at all, but claim and use the fruits of the field for myself so that the priest does not know of them and the Levite does not see any part of them.[6]

Many later advocates of tithing would attempt to shame their readers into at least tithing by contrasting their paltry giving with the tithing practices of pious Jews, whose righteousness Christians should exceed. The line of thought here is similar enough for us to wonder whether Origen also was urging his readers to tithe. But the passage will not support this interpretation. Origen does not apply the Old Testament reference in this way; he uses tithing simply as an example of Israelite piety rather than commending it to his readers. Indeed, this passage provides explicit evidence that Origen himself did not tithe, so it is unlikely that he would have expected his readers to do this.

That Origen was not interested in advocating tithing is confirmed by a passage in his extensive *Commentary on the Gospel of John*, where he again mentions tithing and does suggest a contemporary application – but not one that encourages us to conclude that literal tithing was taught or practised in the churches of his day. He writes:

> Those of the tribes offer to God, through the Levites and priests, tithes and firstfruits; not everything which they possess do they regard as tithe or firstfruit. The Levites and priests, on the other hand, have no

---

[6] Origen, *Homilies on Numbers* 11.2.

possessions but tithes and firstfruits; yet they also in turn offer tithes to God through the high-priests, and, I believe, firstfruits too. The same is the case with those who approach Christian studies. Most of us devote most of our time to the things of this life, and dedicate to God only a few special acts, thus resembling those members of the tribes who had but few transactions with the priest, and discharged their religious duties with no great expense of time. But those who devote themselves to the divine word and have no other employment but the service of God may not unnaturally, allowing for the difference of occupation in the two cases, be called our Levites and priests'.[7]

Origen, like Methodius, here passes up a golden opportunity to urge Christians to tithe.

New Testament references to tithing quoted but not applied

Patristic writers similarly quote and comment on two of the passages in the New Testament which mention tithing. In most instances, they do not apply these texts in the ways that advocates of tithing apply them today, nor do they exhort their contemporaries to tithe.

Justin, in his *Dialogue with Trypho*, written in about 160, refers twice to Matthew 23:23. He writes:

> For He appeared distasteful to you when He cried among you, 'It is written, My house is the house of prayer; but ye have made it a den of thieves!' He overthrew also the tables of the money-changers in the temple, and exclaimed, 'Woe unto you, Scribes and Pharisees, hypocrites! because ye pay tithe of mint and rue, but do not observe the love of God and justice. Ye whited sepulchres! appearing beautiful outward, but are within full of dead men's bones.'[8]

Later, he returns to this theme: '. . . will they not deserve to hear what our Lord Jesus Christ said to them: "Whited sepulchres, which appear beautiful outward, and within are full of dead men's bones; which pay tithe of mint, and swallow a camel: ye blind guides!" '[9] In his dialogue with Trypho, a Jew, Justin quotes some of

---

[7] Origen, *Commentary on the Gospel of John*, Book 1.
[8] Justin, *Dialogue* 17.
[9] Justin, *Dialogue* 112.

the harshest words of Jesus to Jewish leaders, including his criticism of their tithing practice. Perhaps not surprisingly, he does not pause to suggest that Christians should copy this practice.

Elsewhere in this work he turns his attention to Hebrews 7:1–10: 'Melchizedek, the priest of the Most High, was uncircumcised; to whom also Abraham the first who received circumcision after the flesh, gave tithes, and he blessed him: after whose order God declared, by the mouth of David, that He would establish the everlasting priest.'[10] Later, he repeats this information: 'Melchizedek was described by Moses as the priest of the Most High, and he was a priest of those who were in uncircumcision, and blessed the circumcised Abraham who brought him tithes.'[11] But in neither place does he show any interest in the issue of tithing or even hint that the tithe paid by Abraham to Melchizedek is relevant to the way Christians share their resources.

Tertullian, writing early in the third century, also refers to the text in Matthew 23 in *Against Marcion*. He writes:

> In like manner, He upbraids them for tithing paltry herbs, but at the same time passing over hospitality and the love of God. The vocation and the love of what God, but Him by whose law of tithes they used to offer their rue and mint? For the whole point of the rebuke lay in this, that they cared about small matters in His service of course, to whom they failed to exhibit their weightier duties when He commanded them: 'Thou shalt love with all thine heart, and with all thy soul, and with all thy strength, the Lord thy God, who hath called thee out of Egypt.'[12]

Tertullian makes sure his readers do not miss the point of what Jesus said to the Pharisees, but he does not suggest that tithing might be relevant to them.

In a later chapter, he comments on the text in Hebrews:

> Now what had Hezekiah to do with Melchizedek, the priest of the most high God, and him uncircumcised too, who blessed the circum-

---

[10] Justin, *Dialogue* 19.

[11] Justin, *Dialogue* 33.

[12] Tertullian, *Against Marcion* 4.27.

cised Abraham, after receiving from him the offering of tithes? To Christ, however, 'the order of Melchizedek' will be very suitable; for Christ is the proper and legitimate High Priest of God'.[13]

Tertullian, like the author of Hebrews, is interested, not in the significance of tithing in this passage, but in the status and role of Melchizedek.

New Testament teaching on tithing explicitly superseded

The above examples indicate only that patristic writers were able to mention tithing in passing without suggesting this practice was applicable to their contemporaries. But we find a more negative attitude to tithing in the surviving writings of Irenaeus, who hailed from Asia Minor but was bishop of Lyons in Gaul during the second half of the second century.

His work *Against Heresies* contains the following passage:

> Instead of the law enjoining the giving of tithes, [He told us] to share all our possessions with the poor; and not to love our neighbours only, but even our enemies; and not merely to be liberal givers and bestowers, but even that we should present a gratuitous gift to those who take away our goods. For 'to him that taketh away thy coat,' He says, 'give to him thy cloak also; and from him that taketh away thy goods, ask them not again; and as ye would that men should do unto you, do ye unto them': so that we may not grieve as those who are unwilling to be defrauded, but may rejoice as those who have given willingly, and as rather conferring a favour upon our neighbours than yielding to necessity . . . Now all these [precepts], as I have already observed, were not the [injunctions] of one doing away with the law, but of one fulfilling, extending, and widening it among us.[14]

He employs a similar argument later in this book:

---

[13] Tertullian, *Against Marcion* 4.9.

[14] Irenaeus, *Against Heresies* 4.13.

They (the Jews) had indeed the tithes of their goods consecrated to Him, but those who have received liberty set aside all their possessions for the Lord's purposes, bestowing joyfully and freely not the less valuable portions of their property, since they have the hope of better things [hereafter]; as that poor widow acted who cast all her living into the treasury of God.[15]

Irenaeus appears to be arguing that, while tithing was appropriate for Jews under the law, a different approach to giving is appropriate for the followers of Jesus. He does not take the line adopted by some advocates of tithing that Christians should regard the tithe as the baseline for giving and then aim to move beyond this. Rather, working both from a theological point about the fulfilment and extension of the law and from quotations of Jesus' teaching in the Sermon on the Mount, he contrasts tithing with the very different way of giving that is applicable to Christians. Tithing, it seems, simply will not do as a model for the kind of community Jesus envisaged – not even as a starting point. Irenaeus' reference to the Sermon on the Mount would be repeated many times in later centuries by dissidents who rejected Christendom's endorsement of tithing and pointed back to the more radical teachings of Jesus about giving and sharing.

Irenaeus' comments about tithing are mirrored in a document emanating from Syria in about 225, known as the *Didascalia Apostolorum*. This was a church order regulating the life and worship of congregations in that period – an obvious context in which to prescribe tithing. At one point it seems that the document is advocating tithing, as readers are instructed:

Love the bishop as a father . . . your fruits and the works of your hands present to him, that you may be blessed; your firstfruits and your tithes and your vows and your part-offerings give to him; for he has need of them that he may be sustained, and that he may dispense also to those who are in want, to each as is just for him.[16]

---

[15] Irenaeus, *Against Heresies* 4.18.

[16] *Didascalia Apostolorum* 2.34. Text from R. Hugh Connolly, *Didascalia Apostolorum* (Oxford: Clarendon Press, 1929).

But in the following section it becomes clear that this language about tithes and other offerings is not being used or applied literally. The author insists that Christians have been freed by Christ from what he calls the 'second legislation' (the detailed legal prescriptions of the Pentateuch, which included tithing). The bishop is certainly to be supported, but Christians are to be guided instead by New Testament precepts:

> No more be bound with sin offerings, holocausts, etc., nor yet with tithes and firstfruits, and part-offerings, and gifts and oblations. For it was laid upon them to give all these things as of necessity, but you are not bound by these things. It behoves you to know the word of the Lord, who said: 'Except your righteousness abound more than that of the scribes and Pharisees, ye shall not enter into the kingdom of heaven.' Now thus shall your righteousness abound more than their tithes and firstfruits and part-offerings, when you shall do as it is written: 'Sell all thou hast, and give to the poor.' So do, therefore ... [17]

Both Irenaeus and the author of the *Didascalia Apostolorum* deal with tithing in the same context – a discussion of the relationship between the Testaments. Both insist that Christians are not bound by Old Testament laws or practices but should be guided by New Testament teaching. Irenaeus, writing from a Western perspective, and this church order that circulated mainly in the Eastern churches, appear to agree that tithing has been superseded. It is not an appropriate principle to guide the churches in the matter of sharing resources, whether to support church leaders or to relieve the needs of the poor.

We need also to consider the comments of other writers of this period who, while not mentioning tithing explicitly, describe the giving practices of the churches in language that seems to differentiate these quite clearly from the tithing system. Two examples from the second century are particularly instructive.

Justin, in his mid-second-century *Apology*, reports:

> We who valued above all things the acquisition of wealth and possessions, now bring what we have into a common stock (*koinonia*),

---

[17] *Didascalia Apostolorum* 2.35.

and communicate to every one in need . . . And they who are well-to-do, and willing, give what each thinks fit; and what is collected is deposited with the president, who succours the orphans and widows and those who, through sickness or any other cause, are in want, and those who are in bonds and the strangers sojourning among us, and in a word takes care of all who are in need.[18]

While the beneficiaries of such giving are comparable to those who received support through the Old Testament tithe in the third year, there is no mention here of support for church leaders, which has always been one of the primary purposes to which tithes are put. Two features of the practice Justin describes distinguish this from the tithing system: the emphasis on personal responsibility for deciding how much to give (which is unnecessary if a 10% rule were applicable); and the indication that giving is limited to those who were 'well-to-do'. It seems as if here the rich were mainly givers and the poor were mainly recipients, whereas under the tithing system no such distinction is made.

A similar description of how giving operated in some of the early churches is found in Tertullian's *Apology*, written in 197:

Though we have our treasure-chest it is not made up of purchase money, as of a religion that has its price. On the monthly collection day, if he likes, each puts in a small donation; but only if it be at his pleasure, and only if he be able: for there is no compulsion; all is voluntary. These gifts are . . . to support and bury poor people, to supply the wants of boys and girls destitute of means and parents, and of old persons confined now to the house; such too as have suffered shipwreck; and if there happen to be any in the mines, or banished to the islands, or shut up in the prisons, for nothing but their fidelity to the cause of God's church, they become the nurselings of their confession.[19]

Tertullian seems intent on hedging the giving around with qualifications, seemingly aware of the common accusation against organisations like the churches that they were really after the money

---

[18] Justin, *First Apology* 14, 67.
[19] Tertullian, *Apology* 39.5–7.

of their adherents and so put pressure on members to give. His terminology is reminiscent of Paul's in 2 Corinthians 9: giving is voluntary and depends on the wishes of the giver; there is no compulsion or set amount; what is given depends on a person's ability to give and personal choice; and a small donation is all that is required. Such gifts are to benefit those in need, not to guarantee rewards for the giver. Comparison with other patristic evidence, such as the passage from Origen quoted above, suggests this may be a somewhat idealised picture as Tertullian attempts to defend the churches against accusations, but the basic principles are very similar to those in the churches Justin describes – and to those in the New Testament. There is certainly no hint that tithing was advocated as an appropriate method of encouraging church members to give.

Old Testament references to tithing quoted and applied

There is, however, one seemingly more positive reference to tithing in a document from this period.[20] It does not attempt to advocate tithing on the basis of New Testament texts. In the writings of the pre-Constantine church leaders I have been unable to find any such line of argument. But it may suggest that the Old Testament practice was still of some relevance for Christians, if not directly applicable.

---

[20] It has been suggested that a positive reference is also to be found in the early church order known as the *Didache*. Mullin, for example, asserts that 'firstfruits and tithes were promoted by the *Didache* before AD 150' (Redmond Mullin, *The Wealth of Christians* [Exeter: Paternoster Press, 1983], 62.) However, although the author is clearly drawing on Old Testament parallels to encourage the support of Christian prophets and teachers, the text (*Didache* 13) refers to firstfruits, rather than tithes, and does so in the same manner as other early writings, with an emphasis on personal assessment of the amount that was appropriate. The phrase in question is rendered by Michael Holmes' revision of the translation by J. B. Lightfoot as 'take the "firstfruit" that seems right to you': see Michael Holmes (ed.): *The Apostolic Fathers* (Leicester: Apollos, 1989), 157. References to firstfruits in other patristic documents will not be considered here: although some of these references may conceivably be indicative of the adoption by early churches of tithing-like practices, there is no clear evidence of this.

Cyprian, who was bishop of Carthage in the middle of the third century, in a letter addressed to 'the Clergy and People Abiding at Furni', refers to the Mosaic legislation about the Levites being supported by tithes and argues that similar support should be given to the clergy in the contemporary churches. He writes:

> When the eleven tribes were dividing up and sharing out ownership of the land, the tribe of Levi, dedicated as it was to the temple, altar and sacred offices, received no allotment in that distribution – whereas the others turned to the cultivation of the land, they cultivated the favour of God exclusively and for their support and sustenance they received from the eleven tribes a tenth portion of the fruits of the soil. All this was done according to the arrangement and ordinance of God, so that those who were engaged in the works of God should not in any way be distracted nor should they be compelled to turn their thoughts or energies to worldly affairs. This is the arrangement and rule which applies to our clergy even today: those who are advanced in the Church of God by clerical appointment are not to be distracted in any way from their sacred duties; they are not to become entangled in the anxieties and worries of this world, but rather, receiving as they do in the gifts and donations of their brethren the tenth portion, as it were, of the fruits of the earth, they are not to withdraw from the altars and sacrifices but day and night are to be dedicated to heavenly and spiritual concerns.[21]

This is the only evidence we have so far found that might support a claim that tithing was taught and perhaps practised (since Cyprian appears to write descriptively rather than prescriptively) in some churches in this early period. However, the language used is quite indefinite and probably does not mean that the clergy were supported by literal tithes. Cyprian's main concern is to demonstrate the importance of church members supporting those appointed as church leaders adequately, so that they can be free to engage in ministry rather than being distracted by the need to support themselves financially. He compares church leaders with the Old Testament Levites, for whom similar provision was made. The emphasis is on adequate support, rather than the system that

---

[21] Cyprian, *Epistle* 1[65].1.2.

facilitated this, although Cyprian naturally mentions the tithe when he describes the Levitical support structure.

However, when he describes the parallel support system for contemporary church leaders, he portrays them as receiving 'as it were' tenths of the fruits of the earth. This rather vague phrase suggests that the reference to tithing is by way of comparison rather than an indication that Cyprian was instructing his readers to comply literally with this Old Testament principle. One scholar is more emphatic, arguing that the phrase in question, far from providing evidence that the churches in Cyprian's day practised tithing, 'must imply that a strict system of tithing did not operate at this time in this area'.[22] Cyprian seems to mean only that the clergy were supported by the gifts of church members in much the same way as the Levites had received tithes. If this is so, what we have here is a rare example in this period of a writer using tithing to illustrate the kind of giving required of Christians in order to support their leaders, but not a direct application of tithing to Christians.[23]

That this interpretation of Cyprian's letter is reasonable is confirmed by a passage in one of his major works, *On the Unity of the Church*, in which he contrasts the prayer life and unity of the early church in Jerusalem with the churches he served. He writes:

> Then they used to give for sale houses and estates; and that they might lay up for themselves treasures in heaven, presented to the apostles the price of them, to be distributed for the use of the poor. But now we do not even give the tenths from our patrimony; and while our Lord bids us sell, we rather buy and increase our store.[24]

---

[22] G. W. Clarke, *The Letters of St Cyprian of Carthage*. Ancient Christian Writers, 43 (New York: Newman Press, 1984), 156. The phrase in Latin is *tanquam decimas et fructibus accipientes*.

[23] There is also one brief reference in Cyprian's writings to a New Testament passage where tithing is mentioned. In his *On the Lord's Prayer* 6, Cyprian quotes Luke 18:12 but makes no comment on the reference to tithing there.

[24] Cyprian, *On the Unity of the Church* 26. See also the passage quoted later in this chapter from Cyprian's *On Good Works and Alms*.

This line of argument is familiar from other documents we have considered: tithing was a pre-Christian practice; Christians are called to more radical sharing of resources; we no longer even give tithes as the Jews did; so we should learn from the early Christians and (not start tithing but) obey what Jesus taught. Here the tithe is a provocation; in the letter it is an illustration.

Conclusion

Even if Cyprian's letter does indicate that tithing was taught and practised in some churches in this period, it represents a very meagre basis upon which to conclude that tithing was taught and practised widely in the first three centuries of the history of the church. There may have been individuals and whole congregations where tithing was practised, especially in the early decades under the continuing influence of Judaism. But there really are very few references to tithing in writings of this period.[25] None attempts to advocate tithing from the New Testament. Most writers demonstrate a complete lack of interest in the subject, even when they quote and comment on biblical passages which refer to tithing. Irenaeus, one of the very few who does comment on tithing, is convinced that tithing is inappropriate for Christians, as is the author of the *Didascalia Apostolorum*.

Admittedly, the conclusion that tithing was not a significant feature of church life in this period is again mainly an argument from silence. However, the almost complete silence on this subject of both the New Testament authors and Christian writers in the next 250 years is difficult to explain in any other way. This difficulty is enhanced by the fact that many Christian writers had plenty to say about financial matters.[26] They just chose not to refer much to

---

[25] There are occasional attempts to interpret the tithe allegorically, based on the significance of the number ten. See, for example, Origen, *Homilies on Genesis* 16.6; Clement, *Stromata* 2.11. These do not add anything significant to our investigation, save to confirm the apparent lack of interest in literal tithes.

[26] There are several helpful studies of this aspect of early church history. See, for example Justo Gonzalez, *Faith and Wealth* (San Francisco: Harper & Row, 1990); L. William Countryman, *The Rich Christian in the Church*

tithing. Not until the fourth century, when so much was changing in the church and in society under the influence of a new dynasty of Christian emperors, did some church leaders, hesitantly and unenthusiastically, begin to advocate tithing.

Tithing in the Post–Constantine Church

The division of this chapter into pre-Constantine and post-Constantine eras (rather than the more usual division of patristic writers into ante-Nicene, Nicene and post-Nicene periods) is deliberate. Although the ecumenical Council of Nicaea in 325 was theologically very important, it was the adoption of Christianity several years earlier by the Roman emperor Constantine I (who subsequently chaired the Council of Nicaea) that was of greater significance in the development of the church in Europe. The application of the tithing system to Christians throughout Europe in the decades after Constantine's conversion was one of the consequences of the social, economic and political changes that flowed from this event, rather than the result of any fresh theological or ethical insights generated by debates at the Council of Nicaea. While later councils did eventually discuss the question of the tithe, all that was by then left to them was to regularise a system that had been developing for a considerable time.

---

[26] (continued) *of the Early Empire: Contradictions and Accommodations* (New York: The Edwin Mellen Press, 1980); Martin Hengel, *Property and Riches in the Early Church* (London: SCM Press, 1974); Charles Avila, *Ownership: Early Christian Teaching* (Maryknoll, N.Y.: Orbis, 1983). Tithing is conspicuous by its absence in these surveys. Vischer refers to several of the passages we have examined in this chapter and suggests that tithing was taught and practised more widely than we have concluded, interpreting this as a patristic misunderstanding of the teaching of the New Testament: see Lukas Vischer, *Tithing in the Early Church* (Philadelphia: Fortress Press, 1966), 13–21. I am not convinced that his interpretation of these passages is justified.

The conversion of Constantine

By the beginning of the fourth century, the Roman Empire was in turmoil. After centuries of dominance, the empire was showing signs of age: the bureaucracy was creaking, moral standards were at an all-time low, the old forms of religion seemed empty and powerless, and barbarian tribes were attacking the frontiers. In spite of almost three hundred years of intermittent but sometimes vicious persecution, and despite still being officially an illegal society, the church was one of the few remaining stabilising and civilising influences. The sacrificial care Christians had offered to victims during a recent outbreak of plague had won them many admirers, even if their convictions and community life still seemed strange.

In 312, there were two claimants to the imperial throne. Maxentius held Rome and most of Italy, but Constantine held most of the Western empire and now marched on Rome. By October, he was camped north of the city preparing for what he intended to be the showdown with his rival, but he was worried because winter was coming on and he did not have the food or resources for a lengthy siege. Then, apparently, something unusual happened.[27] Constantine, a superstitious man from a family who honoured the sun, had a vision in which he saw the sign of the cross with the sun rising behind it, and saw or heard the words *in hoc signo vince* (in this sign conquer). In response, Constantine had the sign of the cross painted on his soldiers' equipment.

Shortly after this, and to everyone's surprise, Maxentius, instead of remaining safely within the well-defended city, decided to risk a pitched battle outside the city walls. Constantine's superior forces won a decisive victory, forcing their opponents back across the Milvian Bridge into the city. Constantine became emperor, convinced that the God of the Christians had given him victory. Within months he had issued the Edict of Milan, bringing to an end the threat of persecution and making Christianity for the first time in its history a legal religion.

---

[27] The main account is given in Lactantius, *On the Deaths of the Persecutors*, 44.5–6. Eusebius also describes this incident in his *Life of Constantine* 28–30.

Historians have argued for centuries about whether or not Constantine was genuinely converted, but what is certain is that he saw Christianity as a force that could unite and revive his crumbling empire. Constantine, therefore, invited representative church leaders to assist him in making the Roman Empire a Christian society. It is difficult to imagine the reactions that this turn of events must have caused in the churches. After nearly three centuries of persecution and survival, here was what most had to assume was a God-given opportunity to spread the gospel through the whole empire, to apply biblical principles in all areas of society, and to celebrate the victory of Christ. It seemed as if the millennium had arrived.

The following decades must have seemed like a time of revival. There was massive church growth as large numbers of people followed the emperor into this newly legal and socially acceptable religion. Wonderful new church buildings were erected with the help of state finance to accommodate these crowds and to provide fit meeting places for congregations that now included senators, aristocrats and members of the imperial household. Changes in the laws and customs of the empire were introduced in order to conform these more closely to Christian ideas, although in many areas some very creative compromises were reached. And church leaders found themselves increasingly taking on political and social roles, as members of the entourage of a man who saw himself in the role of a Christian emperor. By the end of the fourth century, the dramatic nature of the changes that had taken place over the past decades can be seen in two significant – and ominous – developments: Christianity had become the state religion, the only legal religion; and it was pagans who were now being persecuted by Christians rather than Christians by pagans.

The church under Christendom

The system known as Christendom was coming into being, an alliance between church and state that would dominate Europe for over a thousand years and which still impacts the way Christians think and act. The term Christendom (which, in its Latin form *christianitas*, was used from the seventh century) refers historically to the Christian civilisation which was dominant in medieval and early modern

Europe. This civilisation was the social, institutional, intellectual, cultural and spiritual consequence of the adoption of Christianity by Constantine, early in the fourth century, as the official imperial religion and the coercive measures taken by the emperor Theodosius at the end of that century to outlaw other religions.

Ideologically, however, the term denotes an understanding of Christianity that partially predated Constantine, was confirmed by his successors, and is the mindset that has dominated European church history. Assessments of the 'Christendom shift' that occurred during this period (roughly from the late second century to the fifth century) vary from enthusiastic endorsement, through grudging acceptance, to complete rejection. But there is general agreement that the changes were radical.

Familiar and fundamental features of Christendom include Christianity as the official religion of city, state or empire; the assumption that all citizens (except Jews) were Christian by birth; the development of a sacral society, where there was no effective distinction between sacred and secular, where religion and politics were intertwined; the definition of orthodoxy as the common belief, determined by socially powerful clerics supported by the state; the imposition of a supposedly Christian morality on the entire population; a political and religious division of the globe into Christendom and 'heathendom'; the defence of Christianity by legal sanctions to restrain immorality, heresy and schism, and by warfare to protect or extend Christendom; a hierarchical ecclesiastical system, based on a diocesan and parish arrangement, analogous to the state hierarchy and buttressed by state support; a generic distinction between clergy and laity, and the relegation of the laity to a largely passive role; obligatory church attendance, with penalties for non-compliance; and the practice of infant baptism as the symbol of incorporation into this Christian society (only first-generation adult converts were baptised as believers). The basis of the Christendom system was a symbiotic relationship between church and state. Its form might vary, with either partner dominant or with a balance of power existing between them. But the church was associated with the status quo and had vested interests in its maintenance.

Critics of Christendom claim that it is difficult to fit into the Christendom framework certain key elements of the Christianity of the New Testament and the first three centuries. Christendom thinking struggled with such New Testament ideas as believers' churches comprised only of committed disciples; a clear distinction between church and world; evangelism and mission (except through military conquest of or missions to heathen nations); believers' baptism as the means of incorporation into the body of Christ; the supranational vision of a new Christian nation; and faith as the exercise of free choice in a pluralistic environment. Other elements were redefined. 'Church' was defined territorially and the voluntary communities called churches in the New Testament were now called sects; a preoccupation with the immortality of the soul replaced the expectation of the kingdom of God, and the concept of the kingdom of God was reduced to a purely historical entity, coterminous with the state church; the church generally abandoned its prophetic role in society in favour of a chaplaincy role, sanctifying social occasions and state policies; and persecution was imposed by those claiming to be Christians rather than upon them.

Supporters of Christendom argue that this system enabled the lordship of Christ to be exercised over every aspect of society and demonstrated the triumph of the gospel. Critics contend that this apparent victory was achieved at the expense of compromising on important issues and that, in fact, Christianity was conquered and domesticated; rather than society being sanctified, the church had been secularised. A mediating view is that the church had no other realistic option in the fourth century but to accept imperial endorsement and that Christendom, despite its excesses, was a providential means of Christianising culture and advancing God's kingdom.

Tithing, for which biblical support was claimed, was the heart of the financial system which supported the church under Christendom. Tithing was at first voluntary but had become obligatory throughout Christian Europe by the end of the tenth century. It was administered by the clergy and enforced by the courts. It was a source of irritation, strife and poverty through the centuries. And it was a frequent factor in social and religious reform programmes. But tithing not only survived until the dying decades of Christendom but has in transmuted form outlasted Christendom. We will examine the history of tithing under Christendom in the next chapter. Here we will contrast the writings of post–Constantine church leaders with their pre–Constantine counterparts in order to discover how tithing was introduced into the church under Christendom.

Advocacy of tithing

With the possible exception of Cyprian (depending on how his words are interpreted), no pre–Constantine writer seems to have used Old Testament references to tithing to advocate that Christians should practise tithing. However, in the post–Constantine church, which was relying more and more on the Old Testament for guidance in a context where the New Testament and especially the teachings of Jesus seemed hard to apply (perhaps he had not anticipated a Christian empire?), this line of argument became increasingly common.

John Chrysostom, writing at the very end of the fourth century, probably in Antioch, argues:

> Woe to him, it is said, who doeth not alms; and if this was the case under the Old Covenant, much more is it under the New. If, where the getting of wealth was allowed, and the enjoyment of it, and the care of it, there was such provision made for the succouring of the poor, how much more in that Dispensation, where we are commanded to surrender all we have? For what did not they of old do? They gave tithes, and tithes again upon tithes for orphans, widows, and strangers; whereas some one was saying to me in astonishment at another, 'Why, such an one gives tithes.' What a load of disgrace does this expression imply, since what was not a matter of wonder with the Jews has come to be so in the case of the Christians? If there was danger then in omitting tithes, think how great it must be now.[28]

Chrysostom is, without doubt, advocating tithing to his contemporaries. But his comments reveal a number of things about the way in which tithing was understood in his generation. First, his reference to 'tithes again upon tithes' indicates that the traditional Jewish

---

[28] Chrysostom, *Homilies on Ephesians* 4, commenting on chapter 2:10. See also Chrysostom, *Homilies on Genesis* 35, 54.

interpretation of the Old Testament data as referring to three tithes rather than just one was still popular. It was this, rather than the single tithe, which he was using to measure the commitment of his contemporaries in the area of giving.[29] Second, although he records that tithing was being practised by some Christians at this time, it seems that this was unusual enough for others who became aware of this practice to express some astonishment. This reaction may indicate that tithing had recently been introduced and was still a novelty; or it may be a more general commentary on the increasing numbers of wealthy people in the churches and the much lower levels of giving that had been causing concern to church leaders for some time. Third, the emphasis here is on almsgiving rather than clerical support: the beneficiaries of this tithe are the poor, not the clergy.

But the central line of argument is clear. The Jews tithed (or maybe gave three tithes). Christians belong to a new dispensation and are under a new covenant where a higher level of surrender and care for the poor is expected. The failure of Christians even to tithe is disgraceful. This approach is taken also by Jerome, writing in the same period, in his commentary on Malachi.[30] Tithing is commended, not as a maximum or sufficient standard of giving, but as the minimum.

Another document which draws on Old Testament references to tithing in order to advocate tithing within the churches is the church order known as the *Apostolic Constitutions*, which can be dated to about 380 and probably originated in Syria. There are five passages in this church order that deal with the issue of tithing, the first of which is worth quoting at some length in order to follow the author's argument. The section is entitled *Of firstfruits and tithes, and after what manner the Bishop is himself to partake of them, or to distribute them to others.* Part of this reads:

> Let him use those tenths and firstfruits, which are given according to the command of God, as a man of God; as also let him dispense in a

---

[29] Indeed, throughout the patristic period, authors refer consistently to 'tithes' rather than 'the tithe'.

[30] See Giles Constable, *Monastic Tithes* (Cambridge: CUP, 1964), 13 (the reference is to J. P. Migne (ed.). *Patrologia Latina* (Paris, 1844–1864) 25, 1571.

right manner the free-will offerings which are brought in on account of the poor, to the orphans, the widows, the afflicted, and strangers in distress, as having that God for the examiner of his accounts who has committed the disposition to him . . . Here, therefore, the Levites also, who attended upon the tabernacle partook of those things that were offered to God by all the people – namely, gifts, offerings, firstfruits, tithes, sacrifices and oblations, without disturbance, they and their wives, and their sons and their daughters. Since their employment was the ministration to the tabernacle, therefore they had not any lot or inheritance in the land among the children of Israel, because the oblations of the people were the lot of Levi, and the inheritance of their tribe. You, therefore, O bishops, are to your people priests and Levites, ministering to the holy tabernacle, the holy Catholic Church; who stand at the altar of the Lord your God, and offer to Him reasonable and unbloody sacrifices through Jesus the great High Priest. You are to the laity prophets, rulers, governors, and kings; the mediators between God and His faithful people, who receive and declare His word, well acquainted with the Scriptures . . . For those who attend upon the Church ought to be maintained by the Church, as being priests, Levites, presidents, and ministers of God; as it is written in the book of Numbers concerning the priests: 'And the Lord said unto Aaron, Thou, and thy sons, and the house of thy family, shall bear the iniquities of the holy things of priesthood. Behold, I have given unto you the charge of the firstfruits, from all that are sanctified to me by the children of Israel; I have given them for a reward to thee, and to thy sons after thee, by an ordinance for ever.' Hear this, you of the laity also, the elect Church of God . . . Hear attentively now what was said formerly: oblations and tithes belong to Christ our High Priest, and to those who minister to Him. Tenths of salvation are the first letter of the name of Jesus . . . Those which were then firstfruits, and tithes, and offerings, and gifts, now are oblations, which are presented by holy bishops to the Lord God, through Jesus Christ, who has died for them. For these are your high priests, as the presbyters are your priests, and your present deacons instead of your Levites.[31]

In a later chapter there is a reminder of this requirement:

---

[31] *Apostolic Constitutions* 2.4.25.

You ought therefore, brethren, to bring your sacrifices and your oblations to the bishop, as to your high priest, either by yourselves or by the
deacons; and do you bring not those only, but also your firstfruits, and
your tithes, and your free-will offerings to him.[32]

And again:

Wherefore you ought to love the bishop as your father, and fear him as
your king, and honour him as your lord, bringing to him your fruits
and the works of your hands, for a blessing upon you, giving to him
your firstfruits, and your tithes, and your oblations, and your gifts, as to
the priest of God.[33]

Towards the end of the *Constitutions*, further details are given:

I the same make a constitution in regard to firstfruits and tithes. Let all
firstfruits be brought to the bishop, and to the presbyters, and to the
deacons, for their maintenance; but let all the tithe be for the
maintenance of the rest of the clergy, and of the virgins and widows,
and of those under the trial of poverty. For the firstfruits belong to the
priests, and to those deacons that minister to them.[34]

Finally, instructions are given about the distribution of such gifts
among church staff:

I the same make a constitution in regard to remainders. Those eulogies
which remain at the mysteries, let the deacons distribute them among
the clergy, according to the mind of the bishop or the presbyters: to a
bishop, four parts; to a presbyter, three parts; to a deacon, two parts;
and to the rest of the subdeacons, or readers, or singers, or deaconesses,
one part. For this is good and acceptable in the sight of God, that every
one be honoured according to his dignity; for the Church is the
school, not of confusion, but of good order.[35]

---

[32] *Apostolic Constitutions* 2.4.27.
[33] *Apostolic Constitutions* 2.4.34. This passage is adapted from the earlier
church order we considered above, the *Didascalia Apostolorum*, but has
been altered to emphasise the importance of tithing at the end of the
fourth century.
[34] *Apostolic Constitutions* 8.30.
[35] *Apostolic Constitutions* 8.31.

In this document the identification of church leaders with the priests and Levites of the Old Testament era is explicit and detailed. The bishop is the equivalent of the high priest of Israel and other orders are equated with the priests and Levites. Tithes are to be donated for the support of the clergy, and also to meet the needs of the afflicted, orphans, widows, strangers in distress and the poor – a similar list to that found in the Pentateuch in relation to the tithe of the third year. There seems little doubt that the author of this document regards tithing as a transferable system, as applicable to the church as to Old Testament Israel.

However, the issue we alluded to in connection with Cyprian's letter is even more problematic here – the transferability of tithing seems to depend on an argument that equates church leaders with Old Testament priests and Levites. For many advocates of tithing in recent years, this is not an equation they want to make. It is possible, of course, to argue that the equation of old and new covenant leadership structures is spiritual or metaphorical rather than literal. But, in that case, why should tithing be applied literally in the churches? And why should other features of the Levitical system not also be transferred?

A further complication is that throughout this document the tithe is accompanied by other kinds of gifts – offerings, freewill offerings, firstfruits, tithes, sacrifices and oblations – as we have noticed in some of the Old Testament passages. This again raises the question as to whether it is legitimate to advocate tithing without considering the other forms of giving which appear alongside the tithe. It is possible, therefore, that even in this document the use of the tithe is illustrative: what is important is that the clergy are properly supported, and the author finds the complex support system that sustained the Old Testament priests and Levites (which included the tithe) a useful source of encouragement when writing to Christians about the support of their church leaders.

Other writers in this period began to draw on New Testament references to tithing in order to advocate this system in the churches. As we have seen, there was apparently no precedent in earlier writings for such an application of these texts, and some of the advocates of tithing seem to have preferred to argue for tithing on the basis of Old Testament texts. Chrysostom, for example, in his *Homilies on Hebrews*, examines in some detail the passage about

Abraham tithing to Melchizedek and Levi tithing through Abraham, but he makes no attempt to use this to advocate tithing in the churches.[36] However, the changed circumstances of the fourth and fifth centuries seemed to require fresh approaches to this issue, and Chrysostom elsewhere argues, on the basis that Jesus did not abolish tithing in his conversations with the Pharisees, that tithing is not contrary to God's will.[37] This may not represent enthusiastic advocacy of tithing, but it does indicate a greater readiness to draw on New Testament references to tithing and apply them to Christians.

Jerome makes use of a New Testament passage which does not explicitly mention tithing. Commenting on Matthew 22:21, he writes:

> Give Caesar the things that belong to Caesar, namely, coins, taxes and money; and give God what belongs to God, namely, tithes, firstfruits, contributions, and sacrifices, just as Christ paid the tax for himself and Peter and gave God what belongs to God by fulfilling the will of the Father'.[38]

Although we may be right to interpret this as an example of the new advocacy of tithing in this period, there are indications that this line of argument was relatively new and uncertain. For Jerome has imported tithing into this passage and mentions this with other financial contributions, rather than advocating tithing alone as the measure to be used in the churches. His application also implies that 'fulfilling the will of the Father' is the equivalent of giving to God what belongs to God. The advocacy of tithing may be increasing during this period, but the use of the New Testament appears faltering, which may indicate that this was an unfamiliar way of interpreting it.

Augustine, writing early in the fifth century, also began to interpret the New Testament tithing texts in a new way. He reflects on the subject of tithing as he considers what is an appropriate amount for Christians to give away:

---

[36] Chrysostom, *Homilies on Hebrews* 12.
[37] Chrysostom, *Homilies on Matthew* 73.
[38] Jerome, *Commentary on Matthew* 2.22.

Let us give a certain portion of it. What portion? A tenth? The
Scribes and Pharisees gave tithes for whom Christ had not yet shed
His Blood . . . I cannot keep back what He who died for us said whilst
He was alive. 'Except your righteousness exceed the righteousness of
the Scribes and Pharisees, ye shall in no case enter into the kingdoms
of heaven' . . . The Scribes and Pharisees gave the tenth. How is it
with you? Ask yourselves. Consider what you do, and with what
means you do it; how much you give, how much you leave for
yourselves; what you spend on mercy, what you reserve for luxury.
So then, 'Let them distribute easily, let them share, let them lay up in
store for themselves a good foundation against the time to come, that
they may lay hold on eternal life.'[39]

In another sermon, commenting on Luke 11:39, Augustine notes
that the Pharisees 'tithed all they had, they took away a tenth of all
their produce, and gave it'. Drawing also on Matthew 23:23, he
continues:

It is no easy matter to find a Christian who doth as much. See what the
Jews did. Not wheat only, but wine, and oil; nor this only, but even the
most trifling things, cummin, rue, mint, and anise, in obedience to
God's precept, they tithed all; put aside, that is, a tenth part, and gave
alms of it.[40]

It is apparent from these comments that those to whom Augustine
was writing were no more enthusiastic about giving than those with
whom Chrysostom was concerned. So he advocates tithing as a
minimum standard. The line of argument here is very similar to that
of Chrysostom – that Christians for whom Jesus died should be
giving at least as much and as consistently as those under the old
covenant – but Augustine uses the Pharisees of the New Testament
rather than the Jews of the Old Testament as his example. He also
applies to this subject a text from the Sermon on the Mount that has
been used by many subsequent advocates of tithing – Matthew
5:20: 'For I tell you that unless your righteousness surpasses that of
the Pharisees and the teachers of the law, you will certainly not

---

[39] Augustine, *Sermons on Selected Lessons of the New Testament*, Sermon 35.
[40] Augustine, *Sermons on Selected Lessons of the New Testament*, Sermon 56.

enter the kingdom of heaven.' For Augustine, as for many advocates of tithing, this is interpreted as requiring Christians to regard tithing as the baseline for giving. Whether this is how Jesus would have applied what he said is at least doubtful given all that he said elsewhere in the Sermon on the Mount and throughout his ministry on the subject of giving.

Augustine seems to have become increasingly insistent in his advocacy of tithing. Even when he is commenting on an Old Testament passage which does not mention tithing, he returns to this theme. In his comments on Psalm 147, he urges his readers:

> Cut off then and prune off some fixed sum either from thy yearly profits or thy daily gains, else thou seemest as it were to give of thy capital, and thy hand must needs hesitate, when thou puttest it forth to that which thou hast not vowed. Cut off some part of thy income; a tenth if thou choosest, though that is but little.

Drawing on the reference in Luke 18:12 and apparently ignoring the context of this text, Augustine continues:

> For it is said that the Pharisees gave a tenth; 'I fast twice in the week, I give tithes of all that I possess.' And what saith the Lord? 'Except your righteousness exceed the righteousness of the Scribes and Pharisees, ye shall not enter into the kingdom of heaven.' He whose righteousness thou oughtest to exceed, giveth a tenth: thou givest not even a thousandth. How wilt thou surpass him whom thou matchest not?[41]

But even in Augustine's writings, tithing is not really presented as the norm that it would become in the hands of later advocates. He seems again in this passage to be using the New Testament references to tithing and to 'exceeding the righteousness of the Pharisees' as a way of establishing tithing as a guideline rather than a goal. And there is still a strong echo of the older emphasis on voluntarism. Tithing would in due course become a fixed and obligatory payment, but at this stage Augustine can still use less definite language – 'a tenth if thou choosest'. In the churches of early Christendom, where the radical sharing and giving of earlier years

---

[41] Augustine, *Psalm 147* para.13.

was a fading memory, but where the tithing system was not yet enforced, giving had become sporadic and minimal and Christian leaders felt obliged to try to shame church members into providing more realistically for their clergy by comparing their standards with those of the Pharisees.

Hesitancy about tithing

But the memory had not entirely faded. Augustine was well aware that the stance of Christian writers in earlier centuries was that Christ required his disciples to give up everything superfluous and to share their resources with the poor. His advocacy of tithing, therefore, has a somewhat reluctant tone. After a rather half-hearted attempt to teach this more radical way of living, he acknowledges that few Christians of his era will actually do this and suggests tithing as a minimum measure. Gonzalez comments:

> Augustine is apparently aware that in spite of all he says about giving up the superfluous, few will follow his advice. What, concretely, does he suggest that his flock do with their wealth? He tells them to set aside at least a tenth of all their possessions and income for the poor. After all, he declares, the Pharisees did as much, and the justice of Christians should be higher than that of Pharisees. Naturally, this must not be understood as contradicting all he has said about giving up everything superfluous, but rather as a concession to a flock that is not quite ready to take the drastic steps its pastor would rather recommend.[42]

Advocates of tithing may draw on Augustine's writings for support, but it is clear that he regarded tithing as a concession rather than an ideal and that he recognised he was not representing the historic stance of the churches on this subject.

Others were more wary of reliance on the model of tithing. John Cassian, writing from a monastic context in the first half of the fifth century, transcribes a number of testimonies from Christians who were committed to tithing. In *The First Conference of Abbot Nesteros*, he notes that 'the blessed John . . . had never used any of his crops

---

[42] Gonzales, *Faith*, 219. For comments on a similar reluctance in the sermons of Chrysostom, see Avila, *Ownership*, 146–148.

without having first offered to God their firstfruits and tithes'.[43] And in *The First Conference of Abbot Theonas*, he mentions a young man who 'had come in the eagerness of his pious devotion, bringing gifts of piety among other owners who were eager to offer tithes and firstfruits of their substance'.[44]

The same work contains the exhortation of Abbot John to Theonas and the others who had come with him:

> I am indeed delighted, my children, with the duteous liberality of your gifts; and your devout offering, the disposal of which is entrusted to me, I gratefully accept, because you are offering your firstfruits and tithes for the good and use of the needy, as a sacrifice to the Lord, of a sweet smelling savour, in the belief that by the offering of them, the abundance of your fruits and all your substance, from which you have taken away these for the Lord, will be richly blessed, and that you yourselves will according to the faith of His command be endowed even in this world with manifold richness in all good things.[45]

Finally, he reports that:

> The blessed Theonas was fired with an uncontrollable desire for the perfection of the gospel, and, committed, as it were, the seed of the word, which he had received in a fruitful heart, to the deep and broken furrows of his bosom, as he was greatly humiliated and con-science-stricken because the old man had said not only that he had failed to attain to the perfection of the gospel, but also that he had scarcely fulfilled the commands of the law; since though he was accus-tomed every year to pay the tithes of his fruits as alms, yet he mourned that he had never even heard of the law of the firstfruits; and even if he had in the same way fulfilled this, he humbly confessed that still he would in the old man's view have been very far from the perfection of the gospel.[46]

These testimonies indicate that tithing was being practised by at least some of the more pious and committed Christians in the fifth

---

[43] Cassian, *The First Conference of Abbot Nesteros* 7.
[44] Cassian, *The First Conference of Abbot Theonas* 1.
[45] Cassian, *The First Conference of Abbot Theonas* 2.
[46] Cassian, *The First Conference of Abbot Theonas* 8.

century, although they suggest that this was still far from wide-spread. Despite recording these testimonies, however, Cassian seems less than enthusiastic about the value of tithing. He writes:

> Wherefore we ought to know that we from whom the requirements of the law are no longer exacted, but in whose ears the word of the gospel daily sounds: 'If thou wilt be perfect, go and sell all that thou hast and give to the poor, and thou shalt have treasure in heaven, and come follow Me,' when we offer to God tithes of our substance, are still in a way ground down beneath the burden of the law, and not able to rise to those heights of the gospel, those who conform to which are recompensed not only by blessings in this present life, but also by future rewards . . . And so if even those who, faithfully offering tithes of their fruits, are obedient to the more ancient precepts of the Lord, cannot yet climb the heights of the gospel, you can see very clearly how far short of it those fall who do not even do this.[47]

Cassian returns to this theme in a later chapter:

> For one who is guilty as regards the precepts of the law will never be able to attain to the perfection of the gospel, even though he idly boasts that he is a Christian and freed by the Lord's grace: for we must not only regard as still under the law the man who refuses to fulfil what the law enjoins, but the man as well who is satisfied with the mere observance of what the law commands, and who never brings forth fruits worthy of his vocation and the grace of Christ, where it is not said: 'Thou shalt offer to the Lord thy God thy tithes and firstfruits'; but: 'Go and sell all that thou hast and give to the poor, and come follow Me'.[48]

He accepts, though without much enthusiasm, that tithing may be 'good for the weak brethren and could not do any harm to the perfect who were living under the grace of the gospel and by their voluntary devotion going beyond the law'.[49] But he contrasts the demands of the old and new covenants: 'The law says: "Thou shall not delay to offer thy tithes and firstfruits"; grace says: "If thou wilt

---

[47] Cassian, *The First Conference of Abbot Theonas* 5.
[48] Cassian, *The First Conference of Abbot Theonas* 7.
[49] Cassian, *The First Conference of Abbot Theonas* 30.

be perfect, go and sell all that thou hast and give to the poor." '[50]
And towards the end of this work, his evaluation of the benefits of
tithing becomes even more negative:

> Sin is alive . . . in one who is satisfied with merely paying his tithes and
> firstfruits . . . he who retains his goods of this world, or, bound by the
> rules of the old law, distributes the tithe of his produce, and his
> firstfruits, or a portion of his income, although he may to a consider-
> able degree quench the fire of his sins by this dew of almsgiving, yet,
> however generously he gives away his wealth, it is impossible for him
> altogether to rid himself of the dominion of sin, unless perhaps by the
> grace of the Saviour, together with his substance he gets rid of all love
> of possessing.[51]

The reluctance that can be detected in Augustine is stronger in these
extracts from Cassian, as he contrasts tithing with the teaching of
Jesus on giving. Tithing may be helpful for 'the weak brethren' and
is better than not even reaching this level of generosity. But it really
is not adequate for those seeking the graceful way of Christian
perfection. Those who tithe demonstrate that they 'are still in a way
ground down beneath the burden of the law, and not able to rise to
those heights of the gospel'. Furthermore, Cassian insists, tithing
does not deal effectively with the 'love of possessing'. Tithers can
still be very securely under 'the dominion of sin'.

Conclusion

In the churches of early Christendom and in the writings of church
leaders, tithing was becoming more familiar. Many writers continued to refer to the tithing passages in both Testaments without any
attempt to apply these to their contemporaries.[52] Some also, as we

---

[50] Cassian, *The First Conference of Abbot Theonas* 32.

[51] Cassian, *The First Conference of Abbot Theonas* 33.

[52] For example: Augustine, in his commentary on Psalms 61, 68 and 76,
in *Reply to Faustus the Manichaean* 16, in *On the Merits and Forgiveness of
Sins, and on the Baptism of Infants* 2.6,39,40, in *Treatise on Rebuke and Grace*
44; in *Of Holy Virginity*, and in Sermon 65.2; John Chrysostom, in his
Homilies on Hebrews 12, in his *Homilies on Matthew* 19,22,73, in his *Homilies
on John* 83, and in *Concerning Lowliness of Kind*; Gregory Nazianzen, in

have seen, were prepared to endorse tithing only as a concession rather than presenting it as an ideal. Enthusiastic advocacy of tithing as God's ideal in the area of giving was still some way in the future. But enough had been written about tithing for later advocates to claim at least some precedents from the early years of Christendom and from theologians like Augustine.

Alternatives to Tithing in the Early Church

We have listened to the early Christians. We have found that most pre-Christendom churches showed little interest in the tithe. For many decades even after the conversion of Constantine, tithing was advocated only reluctantly and sporadically. But we have not, with the exception of brief comments from Justin and Tertullian above, listened to these Christians describing alternatives to tithing. So here we will listen to some of them again as they explain how they and their contemporaries shared their resources, although we can do no more than sample the extensive literature on this subject. Our intention is not to affirm everything they did or to present this as some kind of church 'golden age', but rather to learn from the experiments and experiences of Christians who were closer in time to the New Testament era and were guided by practices that derived from this period, rather than by the Christendom assumptions that we can so easily adopt as normative. If most of them did not tithe, what did they do?

One of the earliest church orders, the *Didache*, written in Syria at the beginning of the second century, instructs Christians simply: 'Do not turn away the needy, but share everything with your brother, and do not say that it is your own.'[53] This approach to sharing resources, which echoes New Testament teaching, contains two emphases absent from the tithing paradigm: it prioritises the

---

[52] (continued) *Oration* 30; Sulpitius Severus, in *The Sacred History* 1.5,8; John Cassian, in *The Second Conference of Abbot Serenus*; Ephraim Syrus, in Hymn 3 of his *Fifteen Hymns for the Feast of the Epiphany*; Pope Anterus, in his Epistle; Jerome, in *Against the Pelagians* 3; and Theodoret, in *Dialogue* 2: *The Unconfounded*.

[53] *Didache* 4.8.

poor and it relativises the idea of private property. The focus is on receivers rather than givers, on capital rather than income, on 'everything' rather than a tenth. Was this an ideal, or did Christians actually live in this way?

Clement of Rome confirms that this kind of radical caring was operative in Rome early in the second century:

> We know many among ourselves who have given themselves up to bonds, in order that they might ransom others. Many, too, have surrendered themselves to slavery, that with the price which they received for themselves, they might provide food for others.[54]

The apologist Aristides, writing to the emperor Hadrian in about 125, describes the social practices of the Christian community:

> They walk in all humility and kindness, and falsehood is not found among them, and they love one another. They despise not the widow, and grieve not the orphan. He that hath distributeth liberally to him that hath not. If they see a stranger, they bring him under their roof, and rejoice over him, as it were their own brother: for they call themselves brethren, not after the flesh, but after the spirit and in God; but when one of their poor passes away from the world, and any of them see him, then he provides for his burial according to his ability; and if they hear that any of their number is imprisoned or oppressed for the name of their Messiah, all of them provide for his needs, and if it is possible that he may be delivered, they deliver him. And if there is among them a man that is poor and needy, and they have not an abundance of necessaries, they fast two or three days that they may supply the needy with their necessary food.[55]

From other writings, including those of Justin and Tertullian, we know that aid was given also to the elderly, exiles, victims of shipwrecks, those doing forced labour in the mines, and to cover burial expenses. Radical action was not uncommon – some, according to one report, even sold themselves into slavery to provide for the needs of others. A consistent picture emerges from these various

---

[54] Clement, *Epistle to the Corinthians* 55.
[55] Aristides, *Apology* 15.7f.

sources.[56] Some second-century Christians lived simply in order to release resources, and many gave generously into a common fund, managed by the deacons. The main task of these deacons was to search out poor people and make sure their needs were met. Giving was voluntary but substantial. Although individuals and families continued to own and manage their resources, these resources were available to those in need within the wider 'church family'. The concept of brotherhood in the church had economic implications, according to Tertullian: 'We are brothers because we live from the same inheritance. We who live united in spirit and soul have no hesitation in placing our goods at the common disposition.'[57]

Another feature of this period is that the Christians were not just concerned with eradicating poverty from their own churches. They gave generously to meet the needs of poor or persecuted members of other churches and those affected by disasters. Dionysius of Corinth, in about 170, testifies about the church in Rome:

> For this has been your custom from the beginning: to do good in divers ways to all the brethren, and to send supplies to many churches in every city: now relieving the poverty of the needy, now making provision, by the supplies which you have been sending from the beginning, for brethren in the mines.[58]

A letter from Dionysius of Alexandria to Stephen of Rome in 255 mentions financial assistance provided by the Roman church to Christians in Mesopotamia, Pontus and Bithynia.

The church in Rome was renowned for such generosity but other churches acted in similar ways. In 253, when a barbarian invasion had devastated Numidia, Cyprian collected from the relatively small church community in Carthage a spontaneous

---

[56] Some historians regard these claims as nothing more than attempts of apologists to impress a pagan audience: see, for example, Countryman, *Rich*, 77. But this seems untenable given the evidence from so many sources of such practices. The sources we are quoting may have presented the most striking examples and at times idealised the churches they were describing, but these ideals evidently resulted not infrequently in radical expressions of sharing and generosity.

[57] Tertullian, *Apology* 39.11.

[58] Dionysius of Corinth, *Ecclesiastical History*, 4.23.10.

contribution of 100,000 sesterces for Christians who had been made homeless. As well as helping meet material needs, such cross-cultural sharing of resources surely also enhanced the transnational self-understanding of the church. Countryman comments: 'Gifts from one church to another were . . . important in that they helped maintain ties of communion throughout the world.'[59]

More striking still was the readiness of Christians to provide for the needs of many people who were not church members at all. They surprised their contemporaries by caring for plague victims in Alexandria, Carthage and elsewhere. And such support was offered, not only in times of unusual need, but year after year. Eusebius reports that the well-established practice of caring for the poor was still operating in the year 250, when the church in Rome was giving regular support to 1500 people in need within the city. This commitment to providing aid beyond the boundaries of the church community was counter-cultural and had a powerful evangelistic impact in a society which was not used to such generosity. Indeed, many decades later, when this system of social support was evidently still functioning effectively, the emperor Julian the Apostate, frustrated by the failure of his efforts to encourage the empire to revert to paganism, blamed this kind of practice for the persistence of Christianity. He commented ruefully to Arsacius, a pagan high priest in Galatia, that 'the godless Galileans feed our poor in addition to their own'.[60]

This extensive poor relief was possible, not because the churches had many wealthy members or huge funds, but because giving to the poor was a high priority. After all, very little finance was needed to maintain their meeting places (which were generally private houses) or to pay their staff (some of whom were self-supporting). Even where church leaders did receive support, this was limited so as to ensure that the poor were not deprived of what they needed. Origen argues on the basis of Paul's teaching (in 1 Cor. 9:14) that church leaders deserve support, but he insists that they should only receive basic necessities – no more than the poor receive – so that the poor are not deprived of support. And Tertullian insists that one

---

[59] Countryman, *Rich*, 119.
[60] *Epistle* 84; p.430d, ed. Bidez.

of the qualifications for church leaders was that they must be 'friends of the poor'.

Neither the tithing system nor the expensive maintenance of staff and premises to which most tithed income is devoted today were significant features of church life in this period. Instead, despite a reputation for strange beliefs and bizarre rituals, many churches were recognised as communities that were 'good news to the poor'. It was not the tithing texts of either Testament to which church leaders looked back when they wanted to encourage their members to contribute financially to various needs, but to the model of sharing provided by the first church in Jerusalem.

Thus, Cyprian, writing in the first half of the third century, urged his at times reluctant church members to emulate the practices of the early church. In *On Good Works and Alms*, he writes:

> Let us consider, beloved brethren, what the congregation of believers did in the time of the apostles, when at the first beginnings the mind flourished with greater virtues, when the faith of believers burned with a warmth of faith as yet new. Then they sold houses and farms, and gladly and liberally presented to the apostles the proceeds to be dispensed to the poor; selling and alienating their earthly estate, they transferred their lands thither where they might receive the fruits of an eternal possession, and there prepared homes where they might begin an eternal habitation.[61]

By the third century, however, new attitudes to wealth and new approaches to giving and sharing were gaining ground in the churches. Radical generosity and a deep commitment to sharing resources within and beyond the Christian community were still evident, but the church was also struggling to come to terms with the influx of rich converts who were reticent about adopting such community practices.

In the early years the trickle of wealthy converts were urged to take seriously Jesus' teaching and to give away most of their possessions. The author of the *Shepherd of Hermas* is clear that rich people can only be fitted into the church once they had stripped themselves of their wealth and given it to poorer brothers and sisters: 'When

---

[61] Cyprian, *On Good Works and Alms* 25.

wealth, which today is their gladness, is trimmed from them, then will they become apt for God. For, just as a round stone cannot become square without being trimmed, so neither can the rich of this world become suitable for God unless their wealth be trimmed from them.'[62]

But as the flow of rich converts into the churches increased in the third century, such expectations were relaxed and church leaders began to teach that rich people need not give away their wealth. Alastair Kee writes with heavy irony about this period:

> The church welcomed into its midst the rich and property owning members of society. We can imagine how delighted were the Christians who could remember only a few years previously how such people had been on the side of the persecutors. Surely there would be no recriminations on that score? And surely no one would be so tasteless as to suggest that according to Jesus of Nazareth such people could not enter the kingdom of God? No doubt some bright young theologian would find a way of spiritualising these words: everyone is welcome if their 'hearts are right with God'.[63]

When Constantine professed conversion, the influx of rich and powerful converts became a flood. Ideas that had been voiced before in the churches now came into their own as church leaders struggled to come to terms with the end of persecution and the union of church and state. Theologians raided the Old Testament and various secular philosophies to develop a new system that would be acceptable in a much broader church. Among the main components of this system were:

- It was no longer a person's actual wealth that mattered but their attitude towards it: wealth could be retained provided one did not feel bound by it;
- Giving was no longer motivated primarily by concern for the poor but by a concern about one's own soul: the spiritual rewards available to givers were emphasised over the material needs of recipients;

---

[62] *Third Vision* 6.5–71. A later passage (in *Similitude* 9.30) moderates this comment a little but still requires that the wealth of the rich should be 'cut down'.

[63] Alastair Kee, *Constantine Versus Christ* (London: SCM, 1982), 161.

- Giving to others was presented as a good investment: what had previously meant living more simply was now seen as likely to result in God increasing one's wealth;
- The concept of *koinonia* was replaced by the concept of 'almsgiving',[64] and care for the poor was now regarded as an expression of 'charity' rather than justice;
- The maintenance of church buildings and providing appropriate financial support for church leaders took precedence: anything left over could still be given to the poor;
- Some church leaders began to advocate tithing.

This change in the way the church operated in relation to giving and sharing was neither total nor sudden. For many years before Constantine, theologians had been considering these issues and had suggested new ways of understanding the New Testament. At the beginning of the third century, for example, Clement of Alexandria wrote a lengthy treatise under the title *Quis Dives Salvetur?* ('Who is the rich man who may be saved?'), in which he spiritualises the incident of the rich young ruler and focuses attention, not on the needs of the poor to whom the rich man was to give his possessions, but on the state of the rich man's soul. Countryman concludes that this focus is apparent in many other writings from this period:

> The great emphasis on almsgiving in Early Christian writings un-
> doubtedly owed something to a genuine concern for the poorer breth-
> ren. But our authors made it quite explicit that they were also
> concerned about the souls of the rich and what almsgiving could con-
> tribute toward their salvation. In addition to these two motives . . . we
> can at least surmise a third – the institutional requirements of the
> churches.[65]

Nor was the more radical economic stance of the New Testament forgotten in the years after Constantine's conversion. Several influential writers (including Basil, Ambrose, Gregory of

---

[64] We will examine the concept of *koinonia* in chapter 9. Countryman suggests that the concept of almsgiving was imported into Christianity: 'The doctrine of redemptive almsgiving came to the church out of Judaism (where it was undergoing a parallel development during our period)': Countryman, *Rich*, 103.

[65] Countryman, *Rich*, 118–119.

Nazianzus, Hilary of Poitiers and John Chrysostom) called for generous giving, care of the poor, a rejection of the idea of private property and a refusal to accumulate unnecessary riches. Hilary of Poitiers wrote: 'Let no one regard anything as theirs, or as private . . . we must consider all things as being common to everybody, and not allow ourselves to be corrupted by the pride of luxury in the world.'[66] John Chrysostom was so clear on these issues that he incurred the wrath of rich churchgoers in Byzantium, who plotted his downfall. He has been described as 'a martyr of his preaching on behalf of the poor'.[67] And many church leaders gave away most or all of their possessions and devoted themselves to helping the poor.

There were also dissident movements, which regarded Christendom as the emergence of an unjust society. One of the earliest of these was the Donatist church of North Africa. This church flourished just as Christendom was developing and then suffered persecution from the new imperial church which could now impose its will on dissenters. Donatism, which cannot be understood in isolation from the social and economic conditions in North Africa, recovered the concern for justice that was rooted in the biblical tradition. Social justice was a key component in their programme and one of the reasons for the popularity of the movement. Zablon Nthamburi writes: 'the Donatists were prepared to challenge the established social and economic order in the name of social justice . . . the Donatist church was the first church in the ancient world that was prepared to challenge the social and economic order in the name of justice and religion.'[68] Joseph concludes: 'Justice to the poor became a theological category to the Donatists, and the attack on the State was in the name of a just social order.'[69]

Although earlier assertions that the movement was almost entirely made up of peasants have now been qualified, there is no doubt that

---

[66] Quoted in Gonzalez, *Faith*, 197.

[67] Gonzales, *Faith*, 201.

[68] Zablon Nthamburi, 'The Donatist Controversy as a Paradigm for Church and State', *Africa Theological Journal*, 13(3) (1988), 199–200.

[69] M. Joseph, 'Heresy of the Majority: Donatist Critique of the Church-State Relationship', *Bangalore Theological Forum*, 26(2) (1994),

resistance to the rich and oppressive overlords supported by Rome was an important factor in the development of the movement, alongside ecclesiastical issues. Although some Donatist churches were wealthy, there were also advocates of voluntary poverty within the movement, which was characterised by concern for the poor, the sharing of resources, and resistance to the identification of prosperity and spiritual blessing that was becoming accepted within the established churches as a result of the Christendom shift.

But as nominal Christianity in the newly Christianised empire spread, more and more church leaders bowed to what seemed inevitable and found a theology to fit the times. Lactantius presented, for the first time, a Christian argument in favour of private property.[70] Jerome distinguished between the 'commands' of Scripture which all must obey and the 'counsels' which were for those who were able to respond – much New Testament teaching on finance fell into the latter category. From now on monks could practise voluntary poverty and simple living, but others could adopt a more 'realistic' approach. And Augustine and others, as we have seen, began to advocate tithing as an expression of such realism.

For the tithing system was crucial for the continuing development of Christendom. The costs of maintaining the kind of church required in this society were enormous, and yet most members of this church showed little inclination to deal with their finances and share their resources in the radical ways that previous generations of Christians had. Of course, in these earlier generations, such shared resources were not used to support a huge ecclesiastical infrastructure. The church under Christendom not only cost much more; it also used its resources in quite different ways. Soon, as we will see in the next chapter, tithing would need to be imposed as a legal requirement. But in the meantime, some church leaders would struggle to persuade church members to tithe voluntarily, knowing that this system had no basis in New Testament teaching and little precedent in previous generations, but lacking confidence that a more radical approach would work in the new kind of church that was coming into being.

---

[70] Lactantius, *The Divine Institutes* 3.22–23.

Chapter 6

Tithing under Christendom

From Tithe to Tax

The cautious and somewhat reluctant advocacy of voluntary tithing in the late fourth and fifth centuries gradually evolved into the imposition of the tithe as a tax to support the staff, programmes and premises of the church. What had once been promoted as a moral and spiritual obligation was transmuted into a legal requirement. This – or something similar – was an inevitable consequence of the development of a state church and the proliferation of nominal Christianity.

For the church under Christendom was becoming a major land-owner and an institution with extensive jurisdiction over a wide range of social, political, cultural and economic issues. The maintenance of this church was expensive: not only its clergy and buildings but the burgeoning bureaucracy required to run such an organisation needed financial support. The church could not reasonably rely for this support on the voluntary contributions of those who were understandably less than enthusiastic about tithing their limited resources to support an institution to which many felt only a super-ficial allegiance. We do not know of latter-day Samuels in this era, warning of the cost of this emerging system, but the adoption of Old Testament models of ministry and government that characterised the early years of Christendom led inexorably to the same kind of taxation as Samuel had prophesied would result from Israel's insistence on having a king.[1]

---

[1] 1 Samuel 8:11–17.

By the end of the eighth century, this tax was in force in many areas of Western Europe, but the stages by which it developed are uncertain, as the history of the tithe between the fifth and eighth centuries is quite obscure. Many supporters of tithing in later centuries have argued (or more often simply assumed) that the tithe can be traced back in unbroken continuity to the early centuries of Christianity. But the evidence for this simply does not exist. In fact, some historians regard the imposition of the tithe in the eighth century in Western Europe as an innovation, unrelated to earlier sporadic instances of tithing in this area. It also seems clear that tithing had by this time died out even in the East, where it had been more strongly advocated in the early centuries than in the West. After the conquest of Constantinople in 1204, attempts to reintroduce tithing in the East were met with strong resistance.[2] The medieval tithe, it seems, was developed under Western Christendom and had little connection with earlier voluntary practices in either the East or the West.

We have already seen that there is hardly any mention of tithing during the first three centuries and that, in the fourth and fifth centuries, references to tithing are sporadic and largely unenthusiastic. These amount to little more than a few half-hearted attempts to advocate tithing as a method of giving that might be workable among often reluctant converts in the early years of Christendom. Furthermore, there are several indications in this period of resistance to the idea of fixed percentages or compulsory payments. The church in Rome, for example, designated certain days for public offerings known as the *collectio*, but it was made clear that such offerings were voluntary and that the amount was to be determined by those who gave. Both Pope Leo (440–461) and Pope Anthemius (467–471) condemned the growing trend in some Eastern churches towards fixed and compulsory contributions.[3]

Various sources from the sixth century indicate that interest in tithing developed in a piecemeal fashion. There are scattered references to tithing in the sermons and other writings of church leaders and in the deliberations of some provincial synods. It seems that

---

[2] Giles Constable, *Monastic Tithes* (Cambridge: CUP, 1964), 19.
[3] Catherine Boyd, *Tithes and Parishes in Medieval Italy* (Ithaca, N.Y: Cornell University Press, 1952), 29–30.

some individuals in this era tithed their income and that some church leaders and congregations taught this form of giving; but tithing was far from prevalent. There is some evidence of tithing in Gaul and Spain, and Eugippius notes that Severinus, a missionary who died in the final years of the fifth century, practised tithing and advocated this in Noricum (a territory covering much of modern Austria).[4]

Pomerius of Arles, writing at the end of the fifth century, and Caesarius of Arles, whose sermons date from the first half of the sixth century, both indicate that in southern Gaul the tithe was an established institution. The beneficiaries of the tithe were the clergy and the poor, although there were already ominous signs of a later and greatly resented development – the neglect of the poor by priests who used all they received on their own expenses. Pomerius, commenting on Ezekiel 34:3, writes: 'We take the milk and the wool from the sheep by accepting the daily gifts and tithes of the believers; and we free ourselves of the duty of feeding and caring for the flock by reversing the proper order and demanding that we ourselves should be taken care of.'[5]

Tithing is mentioned in several of Caesarius' sermons and is commended with the same combination of threats and promises, and the same reliance on Malachi 3, that we have noted in the writings of more recent advocates of tithing, although his emphasis on caring for the poor is significantly stronger. He writes:

> Our God, who has given us everything, requires of us only that we return a tenth part to him. He requires this of us not for His own benefit but without doubt for our own benefit . . . God promises eternal salvation to the man who gives tithes. Now since you can merit both earthly and eternal gifts for yourself by bringing tithes, why do you want to cheat yourself out of this double blessing through your own greed . . . God will leave nothing for the man who refuses to give the tithe except a tithe . . . Whoever does not give the tithe appropriates property that does not belong to him. If the poor die of hunger, he is guilty of their murder and will have to answer before God's

[4] Constable, *Monastic*, 20–21.
[5] Pomerius, *On the Contemplative Life* 1.21.3 (quoted in Lukas Vischer, *Tithing in the Early Church* [Philadelphia: Fortress Press, 1966], 29).

judgment seat as a murderer; he has taken that which God has set aside for the poor and keep it for himself.[6]

Caesarius also carefully distinguishes tithing from almsgiving. For example, he instructs his hearers: 'Above all, give tithes of your profits to the church for the clergy and the poor; from the nine-tenths which remain in your possession, give alms. By this means redeem your sins and prepare for yourself eternal rewards.'[7] Alms, which were believed greatly to benefit the soul of the donor, were given directly to the poor; tithes were to be paid to the church rather than directly to the poor and were used both to support the poor and to fund the clergy.[8]

Two synods in Gaul during the second half of the sixth century advocated a rigorous approach to tithing. The Synod of Tours in 567 urged Christians in the region to tithe their property and slaves to the church and instructed bishops to use what was given for the relief of the poor and the redemption of captives. The Second Council of Mâcon in 585 threatened those who failed to tithe with excommunication.[9] Although the jurisdiction of these synods was local, such pronouncements indicate that in some areas the potential of tithing was recognised as a means of funding the operation and programmes of the church – primarily poor relief and clergy support. There are also the first ominous signs of the transition from the tithe as a voluntary offering to the tithe as an ecclesiastical tax.[10] Certainly, pressure to tithe was increasing. The threat of excommunication was one incentive to tithe; another was the suggestion that certain calamities might be due to divine wrath incurred by the failure to tithe. Severinus had already blamed a ruined harvest in Noricum on this, and Hospitius told the people of Nice at the end of the sixth century that the Lombard invasions were punishment for their neglect of the tithe.[11]

---

[6] Caesarius, *Sermon* 277.1–3 (quoted in Vischer, *Tithing*, 19–20).
[7] Ceasarius, *Sermon* 14.3.
[8] Boyd, *Tithes*, 27; Constable, *Monastic*, 13, 21, 23.
[9] Constable, *Monastic*, 21–22.
[10] Boyd, *Tithes*, 28.
[11] Constable, *Monastic*, 21–22.

But tithing was certainly not practised uniformly during this period. There is evidence that some form of tithe was paid in Britain and Germany, as well as in Gaul, by the end of the seventh century,[12] but there is surprisingly little indication that the tithe was paid in Italy during this period (the region of Genoa may have been an exception), and the term is rarely used except in an allegorical sense. Indeed, the silence on the subject of tithing in most ecclesiastical documents from these centuries is remarkable. Tithing is not mentioned in the rules and deliberations of general church councils; there is no record of tithing or the failure to tithe in lists of ecclesiastical offences or causes of church discipline; the large number of deeds of donation and documents dealing with church property and finance make no reference to tithes. Nor is there any extant civil legislation dealing with the tithe.[13] Catherine Boyd summarises the significance of tithing in this period as consisting of 'a series of disconnected local experiments in the early Church' and concludes that 'the tithe existed as an idea for several centuries before it crystallized into an institution'.[14]

The imposition of tithing by legislation in the eighth and ninth centuries, then, appears to be an innovation rather than the extension of an ancient practice. Indeed, what evidence we have suggests that the compulsory church tax known for the next thousand years as the tithe resulted from the fusion of a common system of land leasing and yet another creative application of the Old Testament to the sacral society that was developing in Europe. Many aspects of Christendom emerged from just such a fusion of biblical and secular elements, combining Old Testament motifs and practices with Roman and pagan institutions and ideas. Familiar examples include the 'just war' theory, which has dominated Christian thinking on war for many centuries, and priestly concepts of church leadership, accompanied by hierarchical structures and clerical dress. Tithing emerged in the same period and under the same influences.

The leasing of land was a familiar feature of the European economy in the seventh and eighth centuries, for which a tenth of

---

[12] Constable, *Monastic*, 22–23.

[13] Edwin Hatch, *The Growth of Church Institutions* (London: Hodder & Stoughton, 1885), 102.

[14] Boyd, *Tithes*, 26.

the produce was the customary rent. The use of tenths, or tithes, to calculate payments to landlords seems as widespread as similar payments to political leaders or religious institutions in ancient cultures. This system had no theological or biblical justification, nor did it need any. Tithe as a rent-charge, though undoubtedly never popular with lessees, was a reasonable and straightforward payment. As the church increased its ownership of land across Europe, such tithes became an increasingly common feature of ecclesiastical finances: those who worked the land paid rent for it to the church as the landowner. But there was no inherent reason why the rent paid to the church should be regarded as in any different way from rent paid to other landowners.

During the eighth century, however, through a process that remains obscure, this rent-charge gradually became identified with the Old Testament tithe. Church leaders and the secular authorities began to urge an extension of this practice to the general populace rather than just those who leased church lands. Perhaps the most influential endorsement of tithing was to be found in the famous Anglo-Saxon work known as the *Penitential of Theodore*, which circulated widely in Europe during the first half of the eighth century.[15] At first, this extension was presented as a moral obligation rather than being legally enforced, and it is clear that few responded to the challenge to support the church in this way.

In 765, Pepin, the Frankish emperor and father of Charlemagne, invoked his imperial authority to put pressure on his subjects to tithe. He instructed the bishop of Mainz: 'You shall so provide and ordain on our authority that everyone, willy-nilly, must pay his tithe.'[16] Although some have interpreted this as the first empire-wide imposition of the tithe, it was probably a more limited measure; but it indicates growing imperial interest in the tithe. Some attempts were also made to compel newly conquered tribes to tithe, but wise church leaders advised against such impositions on the grounds that those in the heartland of Christendom rarely tithed, so it was unrealistic to expect newly converted people on the fringes to do so. Alcuin advised Archbishop Arn of Salzburg in relation to the Avars:

---

[15] Boyd, *Tithes*, 32–33; Constable, *Monastic*, 25–27.
[16] Constable, *Monastic*, 28.

Be a preacher of piety, not an exactor of tithes; for the new soul must
be suckled with the milk of apostolic goodness until it grows in health
and strength to take solid food. How can we impose on the necks of
the simple a yoke which neither we nor our brethren have been able to
bear?[17]

Such interventions, together with other documentary evidence,
indicate that, in the eighth century, tithing was still primarily a form
of rent for church lands rather than a general obligation, even
though connections were now being made with the Levitical tithe
and some were suggesting that tithing might be a more universal
requirement. Before long, however, the two forms of tithing would
become confused and conflated in a system that was neither
voluntary nor restricted to lessees of church lands. The system of
tithing which developed benefited from this dual origin: as an
extension of a rent-charge it constituted a legal requirement
enforceable by the state; and as an application of a biblical precedent
it could be advocated as a spiritual and moral duty.

By the end of the eighth century, there is clear documentary
evidence of a move in various places to standardise and enforce
tithing as a means of raising ecclesiastical revenues, but it seems that
this change took some time to apply. After the Frankish conquest of
Italy, Charlemagne codified tithing and made it obligatory
throughout his enlarged realm in capitularies of 779 and 794.[18] But
enforcement was less easy than codification, and further initiatives
were needed over the following decades, including pronouncements at the Council of Paris in 870.[19] That tithing was far from
universally applied in this period is apparent from a local council
only a few years earlier – the Council of Valence in 855. This
council, in line with the trend towards conflating the two kinds of
tithe and applying the tithe across society, not only urged lessees of

---

[17] Quoted in Richard Fletcher, *The Conversion of Europe: From Paganism to
Christianity, 371–1386 AD* (London: Harper Collins, 1997), 220–221.
See also Constable, *Monastic*, 33.

[18] Henri Daniel-Rops, *The Church in the Dark Ages* (London: J. M. Dent
& Sons, 1959), 416; Boyd, *Tithes*, 36–37.

[19] Henri Daniel-Rops, *Cathedral and Crusade* (London: J. M. Dent &
Sons, 1957), 245.

church lands to pay their tithes regularly but advocated that *all* Christians should offer to God a tithe of all they owned. But the council seems to suggest that such tithing remained a voluntary offering at this time.[20]

English monarchs were also beginning to recognise the potential of tithing – and were discovering how unpopular it was. There is no agreement as to when tithing was first introduced into England, but the *Penitential of Theodore*, mentioned above, suggests that tithing as a voluntary system may have been common in the seventh century. Two papal envoys and a representative from Charlemagne held two councils in England in 786, at which a canon concerning tithes was approved.[21] There is some indication that Offa of Mercia made tithes compulsory in 794,[22] and evidence that Alfred passed laws in Wessex in about 878 to enforce tithing and to punish those who withheld these payments.[23] A treaty between Edward of Wessex and Guthrum, king of Denmark, in 900 included penalties for non-payment of the tithe.[24] But tithing was not welcomed by English farmers and a succession of measures was required to enforce this payment. As late as 970, Edgar needed to reassert that the tithe was a legal requirement on all farmland.[25]

By the end of the tenth century, the distinction between the tithe as a rent-charge and the tithe as a moral obligation backed by Old Testament precedent had faded. Across Christendom the tithe was demanded by church leaders and enforced by the secular authorities. Legislators and theologians worked out the details of the system: who was required to tithe, what items were subject to the tithe, to whom tithes were to be paid, and how they were to be

---

[20] Hatch, *Growth*, 105.

[21] Constable, *Monastic*, 30.

[22] Alan Wharham, 'Tithes in Country Life', *History Today*, 22 (1972), 426. Wharham continues: 'tradition has it that he had, in the preceding year, treacherously murdered King Ethelbert of the East Angles, and, in order to expiate the crime and obtain absolution from the clergy, he granted them a tenth part of the produce of his kingdom for ever.'

[23] Doreen Wallace, *The Tithe War* (London: Victor Gollancz, 1934), 58–59.

[24] Eric Evans, *The Contentious Tithe* (London: Routledge & Kegan Paul, 1976), 17.

[25] Robert Morris, *The Tithe War* (Oxford: OUP, 1989), 1.

distributed. Over the following centuries the tithe would play a key role in the economic life of Europe and in the relationship between the churches and their parishioners.

The institution of the tithe has been designated as 'the most important tax in the economic evolution of the West'.[26] It was also, as we will see, probably the most unpopular. Whether this institution had any coherent link with the Levitical tithe, the financial practices of the early churches, or even the advocacy of voluntary tithing in the early Christendom years, seems very doubtful. But the combination of apparent biblical authority, sporadic experiments with voluntary tithing in some churches between the fourth and seventh centuries, and a longstanding and familiar land rental arrangement produced and undergirded a system of ecclesiastical taxation which adequately and efficiently financed Christendom for many centuries.

Collection, Administration and Distribution of the Tithe

Tithes, according to Kain and Prince, 'represented a tenth of the annual increase of the produce of the soil and were of three kinds: predial tithes, payable on the fruits of the earth . . . mixed or agistment tithes, payable on animal products . . . and personal tithes, payable on the clear gains of a man's labour and industry'.[27] Legally, then, not just agricultural produce but all forms of income were subject to the tithe: merchants, craftsmen and soldiers were also expected to pay tithes.[28] But there were many objections to tithing such personal income and it proved very difficult in early medieval society to enforce this measure. The Synod of Trosly in 909

---

[26] Boyd, *Tithes*, vii.

[27] Roger Kain & Hugh Prince, *The Tithe Surveys of England and Wales* (Cambridge: CUP, 1985), 7.

[28] This had been the assumption of earlier sermons on tithing, such as those of Cassian, Caesarius and Eligius: see Constable, *Monastic*, 17–18. Some historians have suggested that only agricultural produce was subject to the tithe, but it seems that they are reading back a later feature into an earlier period.

complained that 'many men . . . claim, at the risk of their own disaster, that they owe no tithes from military activity, trade, crafts, the shearing of wool, and other trades given to them by God'.[29] In practice, it seems, tithes were collected only sporadically from those engaged in such occupations.

The tithe, consequently, became increasingly associated with agricultural produce and summaries of what was required frequently refer only to such produce. Ladurie and Goy, for instance, do not include personal tithes when identifying the three main divisions of the tithe:

> Very roughly, and allowing for the inevitable regional variations, one can distinguish between: (1) the major tithes, which were levied on the basic components of agricultural production, wheat, barley, oats, rye and wine; (2) the lesser tithes or 'green tithes' on vegetables and fruit from gardens and orchards; (3) the tithes on livestock, commonly known as 'blood tithes'.[30]

Both the Old Testament tithe and the medieval tithe were designed for an economy which was primarily agrarian (indeed, it is doubtful whether the tithe would have been adopted with such enthusiasm if the economy of eighth-century Europe had been less obviously analogous to that of Old Testament Israel). The authorities may have been irritated that those not involved in farming often eluded the tithe, but these represented only a small percentage of the population in the early period. However, as the economy of Europe changed over the centuries, the anachronistic and unfair burden of tithing on farmers by comparison with other sections of the population led to frequent protests. But the tithe had by then been associated for so long with agriculture that attempts to extend it to other occupations were resisted as an innovation.

The tithe was normally payable in kind to the 'rector' of the parish in which the tithe-payer resided: this rector was often the parish priest, but tithes might also be paid to a bishop, prior,

---

[29] Constable, *Monastic*, 35.

[30] Emmanuel Ladurie & Joseph Goy, *Tithe and Agrarian History from the Fourteenth to the Nineteenth Centuries* (Cambridge: CUP, 1982), 14.

monastery, prioress or nunnery.[31] An absentee rector might appoint a 'vicar' to run his parish, for which he would receive a portion of the tithe. Tithes were payable by all those who worked on the land, nobles and peasants alike, with the exception of certain religious orders such as the Carthusians, Cistercians and Cluniacs. Tithes were gathered by tithe-payers into the 'tithe barns' close to the church and the rectory, ready for collection by the tithe-owner.[32] It was the responsibility of the tithe-owner to check and collect the tithe.

Although the institution of the tithe was firmly enshrined in the law, the mechanics of tithe assessment and collection varied from place to place and from time to time. The 'custom of the parish' was the general rule to which tithe-payers and tithe-owners appealed, but this was imprecise enough to lead to frequent disputes. When new crops, such as potatoes or maize, were introduced, which were not covered by parish custom, further disputes were inevitable as to whether and how these were subject to the tithe.

Over the centuries, the tithing system underwent several changes. First, many tithe-payers and tithe-owners preferred payment of a cash equivalent rather than a tithe in kind, and so arrangements were made for the 'commutation' or 'composition' of the tithe into money, based on acreage or rental value.[33] This became increasingly popular as the economy became more complex and cash replaced barter, but it was a source of further disputes over the value of crops in a changing economic context. Eventually, through the Tithe Commutation Act of 1836, a fixed

[31] On the monastic possession of tithes, see Constable, *Monastic*, 57ff. In this section, we will focus primarily on the development of the tithe in England. The story of the tithe in other European nations is not dissimilar. On the situation in Italy, see Boyd, *Tithes*; for France, see John McManners, 'Tithe in Eighteenth-Century France: A Focus for Rural Anticlericalism' in D. Beales & G. Best, *History, Society and the Churches* (Cambridge: CUP, 1985).
[32] These barns, which are a familiar and apparently quaint feature of the English countryside, are actually symbolic of centuries of rural oppression. They are found not only in England but across Europe and as far afield as Greenland: archaeologists have discovered remains of a 'substantial tithe-barn' near the cathedral in Gundar. See Fletcher, *Conversion*, 402.
[33] Wallace, *Tithe*, 20–21.

monetary amount would replace the uncertainties of the tithe in England.

Second, the tithe began to function as a form of property, which could be bought or sold. Many tithe-owners were not, in fact, representatives of the church but laymen who had acquired the right to collect tithes from a certain area. This practice, which further distanced the medieval tithe from any supposed biblical roots, began as early as the twelfth century in England; by the sixteenth century, roughly a third of all tithes were not owned by the church.[34] Further changes followed the dissolution of the monasteries, as first Henry VIII and then Edward VI allocated tithes previously held by the monasteries to a range of uses – the creation of new sees in Bristol, Chester, Oxford, Peterborough and Westminster; the endowment of schools and hospitals; and the disbursement of other tithes to various secular purposes.[35] This secularising and commercialising of the tithe irritated tithe-payers. Henri Daniel-Rops explains:

> the tithe, in fact, became an article of trade. This explains why the tithe, which was not in itself exorbitant (especially if we take account of the public services rendered by the Church), soon became unpopular. The common people were angered by this diversion of their pious offering from its lawful ends and by this misuse of the 'goods of the Crucified'.[36]

A third change was the attempt to bring other forms of income than agricultural produce within the scope of the tithe. As various forms of industry and mercantile activities proliferated, the church renewed its claim to a tithe of the profit or wages of those who worked in these occupations. But this attempt was only partially successful, especially after the Reformation, and farmers resented the fact that tithing fell primarily on them. It has been suggested that the tithing system was more extensive and more complex in England than in any other nation, and various additional burdens were associated with the tithe. Alan Wharham writes: 'Everyone

---

[34] Evans, *Contentious*, 8–12.

[35] A. G. B. Atkinson, *Tithe Rent-Charge* (London: SPCK, 1921), 3.

[36] Daniel-Rops, *Cathedral*, 247.

was tithed from cradle to grave: no one was exempt, whatever their religious beliefs . . . Mothers gave an "offering" to the Church after their babies were born, and after death a "mortuary" was payable from the estate of the deceased in recompense for any tithe accidentally overlooked during his lifetime.' He concludes wryly: 'but there is a strange dearth of information as to whether lawyers were expected to pay a tithe on their fees'.[37]

There were variations and developments also in the uses to which tithes were put. The traditional division of the tithe into four parts can be traced back to the custom of the early churches in relation to gifts they received in the centuries before tithing was adopted as the normal method of gathering gifts from church members. Perhaps the earliest rule is that promulgated by Pope Simplicius in 475 and repeated by Pope Gelasius in 494: one part to the bishop, one part to be divided among the other clergy, one part to church fabric, and one part to the maintenance of the poor and strangers.[38] Such fourfold arrangements can also be found in the writings of later church leaders.

When tithing became the accepted form of gathering such offerings, a similar fourfold division was often applied to the tithe, although the details of the division varied. In a letter to Boniface and Lull in 748, Pope Zachary instructs: 'provision shall be made for alms to the poor, the building of churches, the equipment of altars, and the decoration of every church, according to income'.[39] However, drawing on a ninth-century source, Hincmar, Janet Nelson offers an alternative interpretation of these four parts: 'the four shares of the priest's tithe went to: the upkeep of the church; the care of guests; the maintenance of the listed poor (*matricularii*); and the priest's own subsistence'.[40]

This quadripartite division, which was advocated by leading ninth-century theologians such as Walafrid Strabo, evolved in some areas into a tripartite division. This generally meant the bishop

---

[37] Wharham, 'Tithes', 432–433.

[38] Constable, *Monastic*, 44; Hatch, *Growth*, 110.

[39] Constable, *Monastic*, 27.

[40] Janet Nelson, 'Making Ends Meet: Wealth and Poverty in the Carolingian Church', in W. J. Shiels & Diana Wood (eds.): *Studies in Church History, 24: The Church and Wealth* (Oxford: Blackwell, 1987), 32.

losing his part, leaving one part to be allocated to the poor of the parish, a second part to the upkeep of the fabric of the church, and a third part to the support of the local clergyman. This was the arrangement agreed at the council of Aachen in 801, but there was evidently ongoing discussion about this issue for some time. At the Council of Paris in 829, the right of the bishop to a fourth part of the tithe was reasserted, but with the proviso that he should not claim this if he had sufficient income from his own church.[41] And at the Councils of Mainz in 847 and 852, the decree of Pope Gelasius was cited and the quadripartite division was stipulated. In England, however, the tripartite system continued to operate.[42]

Giles Constable summarises the widespread confusion over the distribution of the tithe: 'Throughout the Carolingian period, therefore, there was a wide variety of overlapping rules and opinions governing the distribution of tithes, and it is often impossible to say which practice prevailed in any particular region or period.'[43] It seems that regional synods reached divergent conclusions and that local negotiations were often required to settle this issue. Local circumstances might affect the distribution of the tithe in other ways too. At the Council of Aachen in 817, it was agreed that in richer churches two-thirds of the tithe should be allocated to the poor, with the remaining third to the clergy, whereas in poorer churches the poor and the clergy should receive equal support.[44]

Eventually, canonical rules were established to regularise this situation and standardise the tithing system. Even these, though, authorised two alternative divisions of the tithe, reflecting the divergent views in different regions: the 'Roman' quadripartite division between the bishop, clergy, fabric and the poor; and the 'Spanish' tripartite division between the bishop, clergy and fabric.[45] What is significant here is that it is the poor, not the bishop, who are left out of the tripartite division.

However, both the quadripartite and tripartite divisions gradually gave way to a system that left the tithe in the hands of the

---

[41] Hatch, *Growth*, 112–113.
[42] Constable, *Monastic*, 53–56.
[43] Constable, *Monastic*, 54.
[44] Hatch, *Growth*, 113.
[45] Constable, *Monastic*, 43–44.

clergy to distribute as they saw fit. At this point the tithe lost all claim to being a humanitarian instrument and was reduced simply to a church tax to support the clergy and the fabric of the churches. Although some local priests no doubt engaged in laudable charitable activities, the connection between the tithe and such care for parishioners had been broken. Eric Evans comments on the consequences of this development:

> By the sixteenth century . . . the old triple division of tithes, which ensured that a portion of tithe revenue went towards the upkeep of the poor and the fabric of the church as well as the maintenance of the clergyman, had fallen into disuse. Tithe, thus divested of mystical and charitable significance, became from the Reformation onwards fair game for vexation, evasion and dispute.[46]

Disputes and Complaints

The history of tithing under Christendom is a sorry tale of disputes and disagreements. Books and articles on the tithe sometimes indicate this in the titles they bear (e.g. *The Contentious Tithe, The Tithe War*). Many comment frequently on the unpopularity of the tithe, the disputes associated with it, and the unsavoury effects on all involved. The following sample of comments from various authors amply illustrates this.

> Payment of tithes in kind was a cause of endless disputes between farmers and tithe owners . . . Frequent disputes arose concerning the nature of titheable produce.[47]
> Tithe disputes are as old as the tithe system itself.[48]
> The subject of tithes has been the cause of much dissension and in some parts of the country has led to very unseemly strife.[49]

---

[46] Evans, *Contentious*, 17.
[47] Kain & Prince, *Tithe*, 16.
[48] Eric Evans, *Tithes and the Tithe Commutation Act 1836* (London: Bedford Square Press, 1978), 5.
[49] A. H. Cosway, *Guide to the Tithe Act, 1936* (London: Sir Isaac Pitman & Sons, 1937), v.

> Tithe was an irritating and harassing levy, as unpopular with many receivers as it was with most payers.[50]
>
> Tithe disputes were endemic in British society, and litigation was instituted by all manner of tithe owners.[51]
>
> Tithing was a cause of conflict from medieval times . . . right up to the 1930s.[52]
>
> Nothing put the clergy and laity at odds so much as money. Quarrels over tithe provide the background against which all the hostility between Londoners and their parish priests must be seen.[53]

That contributing a tenth of one's produce or income to the church was generally unpopular and that tithes were often paid grudgingly is hardly surprising, particularly given the poverty of most tithe-payers. Indeed, the absence of serious contention over the tithe in earlier centuries is perhaps more remarkable. This is explicable on a number of grounds. First, the tithe as a rent-charge (rather than as a voluntary contribution to the church) was recognised as a traditional measure that at least ensured that lessees were not subject to excessive or arbitrary rents. Second, tithing was encouraged by numerous sermons and tracts on the subject. Many of these advocated tithing as a vital religious duty and some made it clear that failure to tithe risked divine punishment. It is not just modern advocates of tithing who have employed threatening language to urge their readers to tithe. In the medieval period, such threats were taken very seriously.

Third, at many points in the history of Christendom, there was a genuine appreciation of the role of the church in society and a willingness to fund this institution. As Robert Morris writes: 'Many people complained about the hardship the tithe caused, but they were, on the whole, prepared to pay, as the Church was such an important part of their lives.'[54] Parish priests did engage in a wide

---

[50] Evans, *Tithes*, 8.

[51] Eric Evans, quoted in Kain & Prince, *Tithe*, 18.

[52] Redmond Mullin, *The Wealth of Christians* (Exeter: Paternoster Press, 1983), 150.

[53] Susan Brigden, 'Tithe Controversy in Reformation London', *Journal of Ecclesiastical History*, 32(3) (1981), 285.

[54] Morris, *Tithe*, 1.

range of social, charitable and educational activities, which were valued by their parishioners (the tithe perhaps equated here to a form of social security contribution).

> The clergy were alone responsible for services which today are provided by the State and for which the twentieth-century taxpayer has to find sums he might well wish reduced to a tithe rent-charge. Education, charitable institutions, hospices, parochial administration, and certain public works were among the numerous activities which fell to the clergy but which we now regard as the province of lay officials. Ecclesiastical revenues were by no means earmarked for the comfort and recreation of the clergy.[55]

But, even at its best, the tithing system was problematic. 'The tithe problem . . . derived from its unwieldiness, complexity and uncertainty. It was a valuable, though vexatious, property, and the system required a great deal of goodwill on both sides to function with even passable efficiency.'[56] But such goodwill was frequently missing, for there were several aspects of the tithing system which were deeply resented and which often resulted in disputes. We have already noted some of the causes of these disputes: the inexact rules that gave plenty of scope for different interpretations; changing economic conditions which introduced new elements and further fuelled arguments; the difficulty of finding fair ways of assessing the value of the tithe; the fact that an unfair burden seemed to fall on farmers; the increasing tendency for the tithe to be applied to clerical support at the expense of caring for the poor; and the realisation that the tithe operated in many cases as just another form of commerce. Between the twelfth and sixteenth centuries, it is disturbing to find tithing disputes increasing in frequency and intensity.

What is more disturbing still is the evidence that many disputes were caused less by the demands and deficiencies of the system itself than by the rapacity and insensitivity of the clergy to whom tithes were paid. Wharham claims: 'the evidence of the law reports and the text books indicates that, while some members of the clergy were favourably disposed towards their parishioners, many were

---

[55] Daniel-Rops, *Cathedral*, 248.
[56] Evans, *Tithes*, 36.

avaricious and ruthless men who had no hesitation in exacting the full amount to which they were legally entitled.'[57] Susan Brigden cites three particularly distasteful examples of clerical intransigence from early sixteenth-century London.[58]

The first involved Edward Pountesbury, rector of St Andrew Hubberd, who

> cited seven parishioners before the bishop's chancellor for not paying tithes, and they stood trial for over a month, to their great expense and inconvenience. The rector won his case, but it was another matter to extract payment from the defaulters, for the parish was united against him, even clubbing together to pay court costs. So incensed were the parishioners by what they saw as the malicious behaviour of their clergy that communally they brought a trespass case against the curate, William Peers, in the sheriff's court in 1531–2, and won.

The second started when Lewis More, rector of All Hallows, London Wall,

> brought a suit against a recalcitrant parishioner before Bishop Fitzjames's consistory court and won. In February 1521 More was himself cited before the commissary court charged with wrongly appropriating tithes. Later, More cited Robert Cockered before the ecclesiastical court for persistently refusing to pay his annual tithe of 22s. 9d. From the consistory court Cockered lodged an appeal to the Court of Arches, but sentence was given in More's favour; unsatisfied with this decision Cockered appealed to the Court of Audience and again lost. He then sought recourse to the rival jurisdiction of the temporal courts and obtained a writ of prohibition against More in the King's Bench, only to have More argue – successfully – that this was a case for the spiritual law.

The third concerned Robert Shoter, curate at St Botolph's, Aldgate, who

> came before the vicar-general for refusing communion at Easter 1523 to Edward Saunders and others who would not pay what they owed.

---

[57] Wharham, 'Tithes', 428.
[58] Brigden, 'Tithe', 289–290.

But Tudor Londoners expected certain moral standards of their clergy, and where their curate's personal behaviour scandalised them they would feel justified in withholding tithe. Shoter's certainly had. Some of his parishioners accused him of incontinence and refused their tithe, but Shoter still had the power to excommunicate them, and pronounced 'All you that did give evidence against Hertyswell (his concubine) to the Waremouth quest, you be accursed'. This curate was guilty of most of the failings that Londoners could complain of in their clergy: immorality, negligence and greed.

Reviewing these cases, Brigden concludes: 'Tithe litigation was the quickest way to poison relations within a parish.'[59] The fault was not all on the side of the clergy, as she acknowledges: 'In general, the clergy were right in believing that their parishioners allied to defraud them.'[60] There were many ways in which tithe-payers could defraud tithe-owners and reduce their liability. Some rural communities developed considerable experience in avoiding payment of the full tithe, as villagers conspired together to deceive and divert the parish priest. The arrival of a new and inexperienced incumbent was an opportunity to challenge old practices and establish new practices that were more beneficial to tithe-payers. Once established, these new practices could be appealed to as 'the custom of the parish'. Kain and Prince similarly recognise that: 'both tithe payers and tithe owners were guilty of pettiness and sharp practices', but they were in no doubt that 'the clergy [were] the worse offenders'.[61]

The impact of the unpopularity of tithing and of tithe disputes on the reputation of the church and the relationship between local priests and their parishioners was deeply damaging. As Evans comments: 'It was no doubt demeaning for a rector or vicar to appear in the guise of a tax collector. It was undoubtedly detrimental to a clergyman's social standing and pastoral relationships if he was involved in one of the all too frequent tithe disputes.'[62]

---

[59] Brigden, 'Tithe', 290.
[60] Brigden, 'Tithe', 287.
[61] Kain & Prince, *Tithe*, 18.
[62] Evans, *Tithes*, 8.

A further cause of resentment was the perception that the tithe seemed to fall most heavily on the poorer members of society. Complaints about this can be found in many periods. Christopher Hill gives two examples. In a book entitled *The Reformation of the Ecclesiastical Laws* (1571) the author complains: 'It is felt to be a great indignity that tithes are rendered each year to parochial ministers by the poor and labouring peasantry, whilst wealthy merchants and men abounding in learning and skill contribute practically nothing to the necessities of the ministry.' Almost a century later, Anthony Pearson, in *The Great Case of Tithes* (1657), concludes: 'The rich generally pay little, and the poor husbandman bears the burden.'[63]

Richer and more educated members of society seemed to be able to find ways of escaping liability. A. G. Little notes (echoing Wharham's comment above): 'Among the many classes mentioned in the provincial constitutions as liable to personal tithes the learned professions have no place nor have I so far found a single instance of a lawyer paying tithe on his fees.'[64] Even when the tithe was extended to those who did not work on the land, such people still seemed to be able to avoid the tithe. There were reasons for this, but not reasons that made such exemptions just or excusable. Brigden notes that, in the sixteenth century, 'no provision had been made for [tithing by those who paid] rent of over 40s. per annum, which meant that the rich escaped payment, an anomaly that angered poor Londoners as well as their clergy'.[65]

The richer the church grew, the more lands it owned, and the less it seemed to be in touch with the needs and conditions of the poor, the greater grew the disdain in which poor people held the clergy. It has sometimes been suggested that the poor have been alienated from the churches since the Industrial Revolution because the churches did not adjust effectively to the new urban context. The evidence from the history of tithing suggests that this alienation predates urbanisation and industrialisation and is rooted in the church's unwise and insensitive approach to the tithe through many earlier centuries.

---

[63] Christopher Hill, *Economic Problems of the Church* (Oxford: Clarendon Press, 1956), 77.
[64] A. G. Little, 'Personal Tithes', *English Historical Review*, 60 (1945), 82.
[65] Brigden, 'Tithe', 287.

Chapter 7

Tithing: Resistance and Dissent

Resistance to Tithing

Opposition to the tithe did not always stop at complaints, deception and litigation. There are instances of active and sometimes violent resistance to paying the tithe in many periods, although such incidents were relatively few in the earlier centuries and were normally provoked by assertive tithe-owners or proposed changes to the system. Daniel-Rops notes that in England: 'from about the year 1200 payment of tithes was stoutly resisted, complaints were made to the king, and organised strikes occurred . . . priests were beaten up when they came to collect tithes, and in 1226, at Dunkerque, some were actually murdered'.[1] Boyd, in her classic study of the history of the tithe in Italy, comments: 'One of the less-known conflicts between Church and State in the high Middle Ages was a struggle between the Italian episcopate and the communes over the tithe . . . In the thirteenth century . . . many communes launched an attack upon the tithe.'[2] There are occasional references in the fourteenth and fifteenth centuries to refusals to tithe and arguments against tithing, and tithing has been identified as one of the causes of the English peasants' revolt of 1325.[3] Hill cites the case of William Russell of Greyfriars, London, who 'taught that personal tithes

---

[1] Henri Daniel-Rops, *Cathedral and Crusade* (London: J. M. Dent & Sons, 1957), 247.

[2] Catherine Boyd, *Tithes and Parishes in Medieval Italy* (Ithaca, N.Y: Cornell University Press, 1952), 178.

[3] Redmond Mullin, *The Wealth of Christians* (Exeter: Paternoster Press, 1983), 150.

should not be compulsorily paid to the parish priest. Instead, an equivalent sum should be spent on the poor, *at the discretion of the payer*.[4]

By the sixteenth century, however, resistance to paying the tithe was becoming both widespread and persistent. There had been hopes that the Reformation that had begun in Germany and spread through much of Western Europe would remedy economic as well as ecclesiastical ills, but it soon became clear that the reformers had little interest in extending reform into these areas. At the same time, significant changes were taking place in the economic system as medieval practices associated with the feudal system began to evolve into early forms of capitalism, with the result that the tithe seemed anachronistic and an unfair burden on those who were already struggling to adjust to the new situation. Disappointment, coupled with these economic changes, resulted in outbreaks of resistance to the tithe in several places.

The most sustained resistance to the tithe in this period was orchestrated by leaders involved in the German Peasants' War of 1524–1526. This 'war' was, in fact, a series of loosely connected acts of resistance and skirmishes. Often the initial protest was peaceful and took the form of a strike or a protest march. Many of these activities were quite local and died down or were quelled before they could link up with similar activities elsewhere. Some, however, spread rapidly and took on regional significance, much to the dismay of the authorities. The organisation of the protests gradually developed from village assemblies to mobile peasant bands, some of which then allied themselves in regional *Landschaft* (territorial representative bodies), until eventually wider groupings emerged. The most important of these was the Christian Union of the Peasants of Upper Swabia, which had its own constitution and was an overtly political organisation. Once the protest became a military campaign, peasants operated a system of rotation, returning to their villages to continue farming while others replaced them in the peasant bands.

Various factors prompted the disturbances. The transition from a medieval to a capitalist economy involved the transfer of power

---

[4] Christopher Hill, *Economic Problems of the Church* (Oxford: Clarendon Press, 1956), 79 (italics his).

and wealth from the landed aristocracy to the emerging urban middle-class traders and businessmen, which resulted in economic pressure on landowners. The landowners responded by demanding from their peasant tenants both increased revenue and revenue in cash rather than in kind. In addition, inflation was becoming a problem and additional demands were placed on peasant tenants to offset the impact of this on landowners. The peasants protested against the attempt to move from fixed rents to rising rents, and against the demand for cash rather than payments in kind. Since the medieval church was a major landowner (about one-third of German lands were under ecclesiastical control) and senior clerics were almost all from the aristocracy, the church was perceived as implicated in the changing economic situation. There was also discontent that tithes frequently were used to finance activities or institutions far from the parish from which the income came.

Resistance to the tithe played a significant role in this peasants' movement. Laurence Buck, in his detailed study of tithe resistance in Nuremburg, reports that 'anti-tithe rebellions erupted throughout southern Germany in the summer months of 1524' and describes this issue as 'one of the most serious grievances of the German peasantry in the sixteenth century'.[5] His study conveys vividly the fear in the city of Nuremburg 'as the inhabitants of its territory began staging rallies and uniting in opposition to the payment of tithes'.[6] This opposition 'was characterised not only by refusal to pay the tithes but also by malicious destruction of them. Sometimes they were left exposed to the weather; in other instances they were actually burned.'[7]

Peasant leaders argued both for reform and abolition of the tithe. Some insisted that only the 'large tithe' of grain was payable and that this should be administered locally. This was the position of the peasants in Alsace and the Swabian-Franconian border region.[8] The

[5] Laurence Buck, 'Opposition to Tithes in the Peasants' Revolt: A Case Study of Nuremberg in 1524', *Sixteenth Century Journal*, 4(2) (1973), 11.

[6] Buck, 'Opposition', 12.

[7] Buck, 'Opposition', 21.

[8] Peter Blickle, *Communal Reformation: The Quest for Salvation in Sixteenth Century Germany* (London: Humanities Press, 1992), 42.

carefully worded Twelve Articles of the Upper Swabian peasants in
1525 proposed that

> the pastor 'who clearly preaches the Word of God' should be
> supported from the grain tithe, which 'from now on . . . our church
> wardens, appointed by the community, shall collect and receive'. It
> was the task of the wardens to use the tithe 'to provide our elected
> pastor with a decent and adequate living for himself with the consent
> of the whole community'. What was left from the tithe was to be
> distributed to the poor 'according to need and with the community's
> consent', all this 'as the Bible commands'.[9]

Other groups were more radical in their opposition to the tithe:

> The villages of the imperial cities of Memmingen and Solothurn
> rejected all legal claims to every kind of tithe, 'because', as the
> Memmingen peasants put it, 'the New Testament does not impose this
> duty on us'; they declared their willingness, however, to support the
> pastor. To the Salzburg peasants the tithe became the veritable work of
> the devil, because 'it has no foundation in Scripture'.[10]

Peter Blickle summarises the position on tithing that gradually came
to characterise the peasants' movement:

> What eventually prevailed were relatively uniform ideas regarding the
> obligation of paying the tithe and the use to which it should be put,
> ideas that were probably strongly influenced by the Twelve Articles,
> although we cannot be certain of that. The small tithe was in principle
> no longer paid. The large tithe was withdrawn (with or without
> compensation) from those who collected it (cathedral chapters,
> monasteries, hospitals, nobles) and redirected to new uses: to support
> the pastors, to help the village poor, and, if necessary, to pay for taxes.
> Control passed into the hands of the community, which collected the
> tithe and determined how much would be distributed to the pastor and
> the poor.[11]

---

[9] Blickle, *Communal*, 21.
[10] Blickle, *Communal*, 42.
[11] Blickle, *Communal*, 42.

There were also several instances of individual and organised resistance to the tithe in England during the sixteenth and seventeenth centuries. Brigden cites the example of John Rastell, who

> blamed the wealth of the Church for the impoverishment of the people and was imprisoned, terminally, in 1536 for arguing against the deleterious social effects of tithe: 'now not only the poor whose need ought to be relieved by the working of the curates be compelled to pay which they be not able, but the rich have thereby . . . a watergate to stop up the plenteousness of their hearts.'[12]

Margaret James also reports that

> in the sixteenth century the Privy Council imprisoned three Buckinghamshire men for the part they had played in the 'assembling of companies to withstand the payment of tithes', while in the early seventeenth century there appears to have been a general though possibly unconscious agreement all over England to keep back the small tithes of honey, eggs and such-like produce.[13]

From the middle of the seventeenth century, resistance to the tithe became a familiar feature on the agenda of several political and religious groups involved in the English Revolution. Indeed, though not all historians would agree with her assessment, James argues that

> at few points can [tithes] have played so important a part in determining the general history of a country as during the English Revolution, when, in the words of General Monk, they became an 'issue of blood', which divided parties, led directly to the overthrow of the 1653 Parliament, and contributed to the restoration of Charles II.[14]

Resistance to the tithe was combined with increasingly clear articulation of alternatives to this system of funding the established

---

[12] Susan Brigden, 'Tithe Controversy in Reformation London' *Journal of Ecclesiastical History*, 32(3) (1981), 293.

[13] Margaret James, 'The Political Importance of the Tithes Controversy in the English Revolution', *History*, 26 (1941), 3.

[14] James, 'Political', 1.

church. This was a new feature of the Reformation era. As Bridgen observes, prior to this,

> very few laymen denied the principle of paying tithe to their priest. Scripture, sermons and tracts proclaimed men's duty to render to God's ministers a tenth of the 'lively gift of God's grace' that was their earthly income. Refusal to pay was an act of ingratitude to God and would endanger the eternal salvation of the culprit. For those who found it difficult to envisage that handing money to the priest was tantamount to making an offering to God the Church emphasised the duty by making non-payment a sin punishable by greater excommunication.[15]

The long tradition of tithing and the deep-seated fears associated with the failure to tithe meant that, even in the sixteenth century, when opposition to tithing was widespread, in order to ease their consciences 'the majority of London citizens still made token provision for tithe in their wills'.[16] But the Reformation challenged many such notions and alternatives to the tithe were now thinkable.

One suggestion was that the tithe should be abolished and that the church should be supported by a fixed contribution from the state funded by additional taxation. This had the dual merit of recognising that the tithe was, in effect, simply another form of tax and of offering an opportunity to reform an unnecessarily complex and hopelessly outdated system. A more popular option was that tithes should simply be abolished and that ministers should be supported through voluntary donations from members of their congregation. This would mean that finance raised locally would be used locally, rather than being diverted to central church funds or applied to projects many miles away. It would also give parishioners an effective way of holding church leaders to account, since they could withhold contributions in situations where those leaders were not living consistent lives or fulfilling their pastoral responsibilities. A third option was that ministers should work for their own living. This was not as revolutionary a solution as it might appear, for many

---

[15] Brigden, 'Tithe', 288.
[16] Brigden, 'Tithe', 294.

parish priests in medieval times had been supported through a combination of tithes from parishioners and their own work on glebe land.

It is significant that opposition to the tithe was frequently based on biblical arguments, as the above extracts from various sixteenth-century documents demonstrate. Blickle concludes: 'It is quite clear that the fundamental attack on the tithe was launched from the basis of the "pure gospel" '.[17] Those who advocated reform of the tithing system or who resisted the tithe itself and proposed alternatives often did so on the basis that tithing – at least as it was currently practised – was contrary to the gospel or not supported by Scripture. Some accepted tithing as an Old Testament ordinance that was not explicitly rescinded in the New Testament and offered to continue paying the tithe if it were reformed in certain ways. Others rejected tithing itself as unbiblical.

In the more radical Articles of the Peasants of Memmingen (1525), this statement appears: 'Since we have been forced to pay the tithe, we think that we should not be obliged to give it any more, for the holy New Testament does not oblige us to give it. We will also provide for the pastor's bodily needs.'[18] Similarly, those involved in anti-tithe agitation in the Zurich area in the same year argued that the New Testament did not teach tithing as a divine requirement.[19] Such lines of argument against tithing were so common among the German peasants that their adversaries 'accused the peasants of hiding behind the name of the Gospel and claiming that Christian freedom meant freedom from secular responsibilities'.[20]

Nor should it be assumed that the clergy were united in their support of the tithe. Even though this system was the means by which they were supported, the evident injustice of the system and the deleterious effects tithing had on relations between priests and their parishioners prompted several clergymen to speak out against tithing. Some, including Luther, Melanchthon and Brenz,

---

[17] Blickle, *Communal*, 42.

[18] Tom Scott and Bob Scribner (eds), *The German Peasants' War* (New Jersey: Humanities Press, 1991), 79.

[19] Scott and Scribner, *German*, 111.

[20] Buck, 'Opposition', 16.

advocated continued payment of the tithe but insisted that this was a civil tax due to the secular authorities rather than a religious duty. Others, such as Karlstadt and Strauss, urged that the tithe should be administered locally rather than centrally. Some were more hostile to the tithe. Gabriel Biel and Konrad Summenhart at Tübingen, for example, declared that tithing was incompatible with the law of God.[21] Buck presents evidence that 'the Nuremberg peasants . . . were incited to revolt by clerical preaching against tithes'. He also refers to the work of J. E. Jorg, who 'notes several clerics through-out southern Germany who openly opposed the tithe system'.[22]

It is less certain that these clergy had thought through the impli-cations of their words or were expecting their hearers to act on them in the way that some did. It seems that, in the enthusiasm of the early years of the Reformation, some preachers spoke out against tithing because of their discovery that it lacked a New Testatent basis. Once they realised what would happen if the tithing system were to be abolished, however, they started to urge their parishioners to continue to tithe – not because this was biblical but because it was a long-established custom. But by then, it was often too late to prevent their parishioners resisting the tithe, and the preachers subsequently found themselves in the invidious position of being blamed by the authorities for instigating trouble and blamed by their parishioners for not supporting tithe resistance.

A report of tithe resistance in Zurich reflects this confusion:

> Many took the tithe into their own barns and were later punished for it. They laid all the blame for this on the preachers, since some of them were said to have proclaimed that the tithe was not demanded in the New Testament. Yet since they were ancient traditions, usages, and customs bequeathed to us, no Christian should refuse to pay them, but give the cloak as well as the coat. But this proposal vexed the peasants, who withdrew in great hatred of the preachers, where previously they would have given their right arm for the Gospel.[23]

---

[21] Tom Scott, 'The Reformation's Answer to the Tenth Portion or Tithing', *Catholic Historical Review*, 69(4) (1983), 610.
[22] Buck, 'Opposition', 15.
[23] Scott and Scribner, *German*, 113.

Tithing and Dissent

Resistance to the tithe might be based on political, economic or religious convictions, or prompted simply by disputes over tithe calculations in specific contexts. But it became increasingly clear – and worrying – to the ecclesiastical and secular authorities that opposition to the tithe was frequently associated with all kinds of other radical ideas and with groups who dissented from the established church. A pamphlet by Gerrard Winstanley, the leader of the radical group known as the Diggers, for instance, included 'the power of the tithing priests over the tenths of our labours' as one aspect of the oppression within seventeenth-century English society which the group opposed.[24] Evans concludes: 'Attacks on the tithe system formed part of [the radicals'] general pantechnicon of "Reform". Tithe was an integral part of Old Corruption and must be swept away.'[25]

It is, of course, not surprising that those who dissented from the established church should object to paying for this institution. But it is clear that many dissenting groups also objected to tithing for other reasons than that the tithe maintained the established church. This was sometimes because they had discovered in the New Testament more radical principles of dealing with their resources. There is, in fact, an alternative tradition – on financial discipleship and many other issues – running in parallel with Christendom, a tradition represented by various disparate movements. This tradition was generally regarded as heretical and dangerous and was marginalised by powerful opponents, who tried to eradicate from history all traces of its unsettling beliefs and practices. So we have less reliable information about this tradition than about the churches of the early centuries. But enough has survived to offer fascinating glimpses of communities that rejected Christendom and the tithing system which funded this and explored other ways of sharing their resources.

---

[24] Gerrard Winstanley, *A New Yeers Gift Sent to the Parliament and Armie* (London: Giles Calvert, 1650).
[25] Eric Evans, *The Contentious Tithe* (London: Routledge & Kegan Paul, 1976), 82.

This conjunction of dissent and opposition to the tithe was apparent as early as the fourteenth century, when the Lollards were causing concern in England. John Wyclif, whose writings inspired the Lollard movement, himself taught that tithes should not be paid to absentee incumbents, and that tithes should also be withheld from negligent and ignorant clergy.[26] Some of his more radical followers suggested that tithes should not be used to support the clergy at all but rather to support the poor. Others held that tithing was voluntary and that tithes should not be paid to unworthy priests. A few taught that tithing had no New Testament support and should not be practised. There is a report in the court records of one Thomas Compworth, a Lollard landowner in Kidlington, who refused to pay tithes to the local abbot. Mullin reports that 'the Lollards were blamed for asserting "that no man is bound to tithe in the manner now used by the church, but such tithes and offerings by the law of God should be given to the poor needy men".'[27]

Concern for the poor, then, seems to have been another component, alongside dissent from the established church, in the Lollards' opposition to the tithe. Wyclif had not only criticised the indiscriminate payment of tithes to unworthy clerics but had expressed concern about the wealth of the church, especially when it was surrounded by poverty. His influence on the Lollards ensured that they shared his critique of the wealth of the church and the corruption that resulted from this, and his concern for the poor. Their antagonism to images was in part prompted by their concern to see church resources used for the benefit of the poor; and they suspected that the ornate images tended to corrupt the clergy who were guardians of such treasures. They questioned also whether church buildings were really necessary and advocated simplicity in such buildings if they were used.

This perspective was shared by the Waldensians, continental dissenters who traced their origins to a businessman in Lyons by the name of Valdes who gave away his money and devoted himself to a life of voluntary poverty and itinerant preaching. Valdes was motivated less by criticism of the church than by a deep desire to imitate Jesus and to live a simple life. But he, too, took action to

---

[26] Brigden, 'Tithe', 291.
[27] Mullin, *Wealth*, 150.

relieve the hardship of the poor rather than simply choosing poverty as his way of life. His statement to the diocesan council in Lyons in 1180 makes this connection clear:

> We have renounced this world and have distributed to the poor every-thing we possess, according to the will of God, and we have decided that we ourselves should be poor in such a way as not to be careful for the morrow, and to accept from no one gold, silver or anything else, with the exception of raiment and daily food. We have set before our-selves the objective of fulfilling the Gospel counsels as precepts.[28]

It was not just what the movement taught, but the Waldensian way of life itself, with its emphasis on simplicity and on patterning their community life on New Testament principles, that was an implicit critique of the state church system. Jarold Zeman indicates how the tithe-collecting church was viewed from the perspective of this radical movement: 'The ideal of apostolic poverty was held up as a mirror to a Church which had become the wealthiest and the most oppressive collector of taxes and tariffs from birth to death.'[29] Although many of the Waldensians continued to pay tithes to avoid persecution, they were unhappy about this. There was opposition in many such movements to the tithing system – partly because they believed that it maintained a corrupt institution, and partly because they could not find clear New Testament support for this practice among Christians.

Jan Lochman, in his study of the Waldensian, Lollard and Hussite movements (which he characterises as 'the first reformation'), concludes:

> the entire first reformation repeatedly emphasizes in its understanding of the reform of church and life that the true church of Christ is apos-tolic in the sense that it understands itself as the 'church of the poor'. There is a double significance to this: the church, firstly, devotes itself to the poor, takes a stand for them . . . And then it lives as a poor

---

[28] Malcolm Lambert, *Medieval Heresy* (Oxford: Blackwell, 1992), 64 (footnote 11).
[29] Jarold Zeman, 'Restitution and Dissent in the Late Medieval Renewal Movements', *Journal of the American Academy of Religion*, 44 (1976), 9.

church: worldly domination jeopardizes and conflicts with the inner constitution of the church, destroys the credibility of its word and its mission. Therefore the first reformation challenges the established church as an institution: it reveals the church in its wealth and its power-interests to be a church in contradiction with itself.[30]

Within the medieval movements, different perspectives surfaced on issues of lifestyle and the sharing of resources. Some stressed the necessity of simple living in order to pursue spiritual development and to give integrity to other aspects of witness. Within the Waldensian movement, there were different views on whether this meant working for a living but refraining from accumulating wealth, or depending on charity for basic resources. In Wyclif's programme, and among some of the Hussites, voluntary poverty was replaced by enforced disendowment. Zeman writes:

> The Wycliffite and Utraquist leaders advocated 'coercive primitivism': the Church should be restored to poverty through confiscation of its property by secular authorities. The Waldensians and Bohemian Brethren represented 'voluntary primitivism' in the Franciscan tradition: individual Christians were called upon to choose poverty as one of the marks of Christian discipleship.[31]

Across Europe in the sixteenth century, the Anabaptist movement was causing concern to Catholics and reformers alike with their radical approach to ecclesiology and ethics. Many early Anabaptist leaders taught that tithing was not required of members of their congregations. Balthasar Hubmaier's views on tithing, expressed during his ministry in Waldshut, have been identified as a major factor in the opposition to the tithe of some of the groups involved in the Peasants' War.[32] Wilhelm Reublin, a first-generation Swiss Anabaptist leader, was personally involved in protests against the tithe and resisting its collection. Although this stance seems to have been a logical concomitant of the Anabaptists' dissatisfaction with the state churches, their rejection of warfare also played a part. They

---

[30] Jan Lochman, 'Not just one Reformation: the Waldensian and Hussite Heritage', *Reformed World*, 33 (1975), 222.
[31] Zeman, 'Restitution', 26.
[32] Scott, 'Reformation', 610.

regarded tithes and taxes as together supporting those who frequently advocated war, not only against the feared Turks but also against other 'Christian' states. This is particularly apparent in the writings of the Hutterites, a communitarian Anabaptist group, whose 'pacifist and anti-clerical consciences did not allow them to pay either taxes for war . . . or tithes'.[33]

There was considerable overlap between Anabaptist concerns and the programme adopted by peasant leaders for a more just distribution of resources within society. Like the peasants, they criticised the wealth and luxury apparent in the state churches and the lack of provision for the poor, regarding this as evidence that they were not true churches. Menno Simons wrote:

> Is it not sad and intolerable hypocrisy that these poor people boast of having the Word of God, of being the true, Christian church, never remembering that they have entirely lost their sign of true Christianity? For although many of them have plenty of everything, go about in silk and velvet, gold and silver, and in all manner of pomp and splendor; ornament their houses with all manner of costly furniture; have their coffers filled . . . yet they suffer many of their own poor, afflicted members (notwithstanding their fellow believers have received one baptism and partaken of the same bread with them) to ask alms; and poor, hungry, suffering, old, lame, blind, and sick people to beg their bread at their doors.[34]

Among Anabaptists there was a widespread commitment to simplicity of life and a strong emphasis on holding things in common. This is evident both in their writings and in the way they ordered their congregations. George Williams noted: 'Among the several New Testament ministries which the movement recognised, it was that of deacon or servant which was most characteristically given prominence by the Anabaptists.'[35] Other scholars agree that the role of deacon was as important as that of preacher, elder or overseer and that, until at least 1534, the only definite leadership office was that of

---

[33] Meic Pearse, *The Great Restoration* (Carlisle: Paternoster, 1998), 77.

[34] Menno Simons, *Complete Works 1496–1561* (Scottdale, Pa.: Herald Press, 1956), 559.

[35] George Williams, *The Radical Reformation* (Philadelphia: Westminster Press, 1962), 44.

the deacon who cared for the poor. This is a clear indication of the significance within Anabaptism of the church as a community of economic sharing. One of their earliest church orders in 1527 instructed:

> Of all the brothers and sisters of this congregation none shall have anything of his own, but rather, as the Christians in the time of the apostles held all in common, and especially stored up a common fund, from which aid can be given to the poor, according as each will have need, and as in the apostles' time permit no brother to be in need.[36]

Despite the phrase 'none shall have anything of his own' in this order, Anabaptist congregations generally practised mutual aid rather than full community of goods, following the pattern established by many earlier dissident groups (although Lollards occasionally expressed interest in the notion of community of goods). Most did not agree with the 'common purse' policy adopted by the Hutterites, who regarded as normative the example of the Jerusalem church and interpreted this as requiring the surrender of all possessions to the community. But the degree of economic sharing that was taking place and the various experiments with some form of community of goods frightened many in the turbulent sixteenth century.

Anabaptist opposition to the tithe was serious enough for many authorities to suspect any who protested about the tithe of being Anabaptists, whatever their actual religious views. 'Tithe abolition was said to be the first step leading down the slippery path to Münster.'[37] And the Anabaptist practice of community of goods was regarded as so dangerous that the 38th Article of the Church of England named the Anabaptists and explicitly outlawed this

---

[36] Quoted in Walter Klaassen, *Anabaptism in Outline* (Scottdale, Pa.: Herald Press, 1981), 120.

[37] James, 'Political', 6. Münster was a town in the north of Germany which some Anabaptists seized in 1535 and attempted to turn into the New Jerusalem before succumbing to an assault which turned into a massacre. Although rejected by almost all other Anabaptists as an aberration, Münster became the watchword for dangerous heresy in the sixteenth century and a stick with which to beat those accused of being Anabaptists and other dissidents in future years.

practice. This stance was not accepted by all, however, as is evident
in a seventeenth-century tract entitled *The Husbandman's Plea
against Tithes* (1647). The author argues that tithes were, in fact,
contrary to the 38th Article of the Church, and worse than the
community of goods condemned by that article, 'for if all things
should be common, then none should want if others had anything,
which were more agreeable to Christian doctrine than for these
tithe-mongers to take away other men's goods which they are not
able to spare'.[38]

Early English Baptists also struggled with the demand that they
should pay tithes to support the established church from which they
wished to dissociate themselves. The records of various church and
association meetings in the mid-seventeenth century reveal considerable discussion of this issue. The records of the 14th General
Meeting of the Abingdon Association on 27th March 1656, for
example, report arguments from some participants in favour of
paying the tithe because it was a civil law, not because it was a divine
right, although this position was rejected by the meeting.[39] Other
meetings reached similar decisions, although not without difficulty,
but in practice most Baptists chose to pay tithes, albeit grudgingly,
rather than disobey the civil law.

Association meetings also considered whether tithing might be
an appropriate way to support the ministers of their own Baptist
churches, but they rejected this on biblical and ethical grounds.
Tithing, several meetings concluded, was an Old Testament ordinance that was no longer appropriate under the new covenant. At
the Third General Meeting of the Midland Records on 24th
October 1655, for instance, it was argued that

> the paying of tithes as due by divine right, is such an establishing of the
> shadowish Levitical law, as in effect overthrows the priesthood of
> Christ, for the priesthood being changed, there is made of necessity the
> change also of the law, [Heb 7].12, which is clearly spoken of the law
> of tithing, among other parts of the shadowish law.[40]

---

[38] James, 'Political', 9.

[39] Barrington White, *Association Records of the Particular Baptists of England,
Wales and Ireland to 1660* (London: Baptist Historical Society, 1971),
153–157.

[40] White, *Association*, 48.

There was also concern about the ethical and pastoral implications of supporting ministers with tithes. A speaker at the same meeting of the Midland Records argued that 'enforced maintenance' is unchristian: 'Is not a preacher's taking an enforced maintenance an unlawful and shameful thing?'[41] Another participant reported: 'I next enquired whether you would have preached in a constant way as you have done . . . but for this maintenance and, consequently, whether you have not manifestly acted as one preaching for hire.'[42] It was also intimated that to use tithing as the state church did would be inconsistent with Baptist principles: 'all tithe paying now called for is an implicit holding of the pretended church state of the nation.'[43] And at least one speaker at this meeting argued that the tithing system was essentially unjust as well as inappropriate for the emerging Baptist churches: 'all those ordinances of men which now require the payment of tithes as things formerly due, rightfully belonging, at least by man's law, to the ministers, are indeed unjust and ought to be looked upon as such.'[44]

The Records of the 13th General Meeting of the Abingdon Association, on 11th January 1656, reached similar conclusions. The meeting decided:

> That such paying of tithes is an upholding . . . of that shadowish law of Moses which the saints are not now under. Neither may it be looked upon as remaining in force, unless we deny that Christ has come. The priesthood being changed there is made of necessity a change also of the law, Heb 7.12. And that this hath relation to the law of tithing plainly appears in v5.[45]

Not only was tithing devoid of New Testament support, but it was contrary to the spirit of the New Testament, which encouraged voluntary support of ministers:

---

[41] White, *Association*, 44.

[42] White, *Association*, 45.

[43] White, *Association*, 48.

[44] White, *Association*, 48.

[45] White, *Association*, 151.

The true ministers of Jesus Christ are to be supported, as touching their outward subsistence, not by tithes, nor by any enforced maintenance, but, as they shall be found worthy and as it shall be found needful and convenient and the saints shall be enabled thereunto, by the voluntary contribution of those that are instructed by them, Gal 6.6.[46]

It is interesting to note the use of Hebrews 7 to argue against tithing in these meetings, since this passage has been presented by some recent advocates of tithing as a New Testament basis for this practice. Early Baptists were concerned to avoid what they regarded as 'enforced maintenance'. They preferred to base their support of ministers on the voluntary principle they found in Galatians 6:6, as Roger Hayden notes in his examination of church records from Bristol in the same period. The meeting in Bristol endorsed 'our several voluntary and free subscriptions for the comfortable maintaining of a Pastor for this congregation'.[47]

But Baptists, though they disliked the tithing system, were wary of jeopardising the support and encouragement they were receiving from Oliver Cromwell at this time and the prospect of increased religious liberty. James reminds us that 'it was to Jessey, a Baptist minister, that Cromwell was said to have made his rash and unfulfilled promise to abolish tithes by 3 September 1654'.[48] Barrie White recognises the difficulty facing Baptists in this period:

On the one side those who were ministers had to decide whether to accept payment from the Cromwellian ecclesiastical establishment which would, inevitably, be very largely financed by tithes. On the other hand, Baptist church members had to decide whether they should withhold payment of tithes from the authorities because these would go to support a church settlement of which they disapproved ... on the whole, by the late 1650's, tithes were somewhat unwillingly paid by Baptist church members, while Baptist ministers were sharply discouraged from accepting any maintenance drawn from them.[49]

---

[46] White, *Association*, 151.
[47] Roger Hayden, *The Records of a Church in Christ in Bristol, 1640–1687* (Bristol: Bristol Record Society, 1974), 135.
[48] James, 'Political', 11.
[49] Barrington White, 'The English Particular Baptists and the Great Rebellion, 1640–1660', *Baptist History and Heritage*, 9(1) (1974), 20.

The most sustained opposition to the tithe was associated with the Society of Friends, or Quakers. George Fox, the Society's founder, often preached against tithing and lamented the fact that Cromwell 'had promised to the Lord that if he gave him victory over his enemies he would take away tithes or else let him be rolled into his grave with infamy' yet when 'he came to be chief, he confirmed the former laws'.[50] Many of his followers were willing to be imprisoned rather than paying tithes. It has been estimated that between 20,000 and 30,000 Quakers spent periods in prison for non-payment of the tithe,[51] although some historians regard this as an inflated figure. But there is no doubt that the threat of imprisonment and distraint of goods hung over the heads of Quakers throughout the seventeenth and eighteenth centuries. Not until 1835 was the threat of imprisonment for failing to tithe lifted. The Society of Friends kept careful records of the sufferings that resulted from the refusal to pay tithes. It also made repeated attempts to secure exemption from the requirement of the tithe and presented several petitions to Parliament calling for changes in the law.

Quakers objected, like most dissenting groups, to paying for the support of the state church, but it is clear from their sermons and writings that their objections to the tithe were more fundamental than this. They were as concerned as some Baptists about the issue of 'enforced maintenance', arguing on the basis of New Testament texts that tithing contravened Christ's command to his disciples: 'Freely you have received; freely give.' Payment of the tithe was treated as a 'crime' and carried the threat of expulsion from the Society (although there is no evidence this threat was carried out).

Meic Pearse, in his discussion of Quaker antagonism to tithing, refers with approval to the contention that

> the mid-seventeenth-century attack on tithes was not simply a religious protest, the refusal of those who had left the Church of England to support its ministry. Tithes were a form of real estate, and the rights to revenue from particular parishes could be inherited or sold. In practice, the recipients were often gentry, who might collect the money and pay a pittance to the vicar . . . Since tithes formed part

---

[50] Mullin, *Wealth*, 151.

[51] Doreen Wallace, *The Tithe War* (London: Victor Gollancz, 1934), 148.

of real estate, so the argument goes, the attack on them was actually an attack on the property system.[52]

Quakers rejected tithing as unjust, as well as declining to support a system from which they were dissenting.

By the early years of the eighteenth century, however, it seems that the enthusiasm of both Quakers and their prosecutors in relation to the tithing issue had waned. There are many instances of Quakers allowing tithes to be collected from their fields without protest. Sometimes the two sides reached a satisfactory compromise: the tithe-owner collected the tithe without waiting to be informed that it was ready for collection (which was the normal practice). This ensured that the tithe-owner received the tithe due but absolved the Quaker farmer from responsibility for paying it! Or a neighbour might collect the appropriate amount from a Quaker farm and deposit this with his own tithe on behalf of both farms. An attempt was made in 1736 to provide a quick and simple legal procedure in other cases where prosecutions were still needed to enforce tithes from reluctant Quakers, but the Quakers Tithe Bill did not receive sufficient support to become law.[53] The bill was limited in its scope but was seen by some as the thin end of a wedge that might eventually lead to the abolition of the tithe, and this prospect caused enough fear of the consequences to defeat the bill.[54] Prosecutions continued into the early years of the nineteenth century, but in most situations by then some form of accommodation had been found. Indeed, by this stage, opposition to the tithe was widespread and the protests of dissenters were swallowed up in the general dissatisfaction with a system that had long outlived its usefulness.

Tithing: Learning from History

We will chart the final demise of tithing as a legal requirement in the next chapter, but it is worth pausing here to reflect on some of the

---

[52] Pearse, *Great*, 273–274.
[53] See Stephen Taylor, 'Sir Robert Walpole, The Church of England, and the Quakers Tithe Bill of 1736', *Historical Journal*, 28(1) (1985), 51–77.
[54] Taylor, 'Walpole', 66.

lessons to be learned from the history of the tithe under Christendom. Those who advocate tithing today might protest that what
they are proposing is entirely voluntary and has little in common
with the legal requirement of tithing that we have been studying.
But it is this long period of history that constitutes the link between
tithing today and the biblical basis that advocates generally claim for
tithing. To leap over these intervening centuries and to ignore the
experiences with tithing of many generations seems illegitimate and
dangerous. Some of the concerns about tithing that are implicit in
this study may indeed relate to the specific ways in which this
principle was enshrined in legislation and applied; but there may be
other concerns which relate to the principle itself and which can be
seen clearly through the lens of the Christendom experience with
the tithe.

First, the claim that the tithe is a historic principle applicable to
the people of God in every generation needs to be tested against the
very complex history of the tithe. The same term may be used in
different eras, but it seems to refer to various concepts and practices:
the Levitical tithe, which was intended to support the Old
Testament priesthood and the poor within the community; the
triple tithe that pious Jews in the first century applied to their
income and which forms the background to the few New
Testament references to tithing; the voluntary payments to support
the church advocated by a few theologians in the early years of
Christendom; the rent-charge for church lands that constituted the
tithe in the sixth and seventh centuries; the conflation of this
rent-charge and the Levitical tithe that became the basis for tithing
as a tax to support the state church; and the attempt to revert to a
voluntary offering by advocates of tithing in the past century and a
half. Advocates of tithing may at least want to consider whether the
use of this term is appropriate; they might even want to look afresh
at the chequered history of this concept and ask whether it is time to
abandon the principle too.

Second, there is abundant evidence that the tithe has always been
deeply unpopular. The history of tithing is a history of contention,
evasion, strife and suspicion. Tithing rules are always surrounded by
provisions designed to prevent fraud, avoidance and sharp practice.
It is doubtful whether any other ecclesiastical strategy has done
more to undermine the church's standing and reputation in society

or hinder its witness and work. This is a powerful legacy, even though most Christians today may be unaware of it, and perhaps not a very good foundation upon which to build contemporary practice.

Third, tithing is presented by some contemporary advocates as an expression of radical commitment to Christ and a sign of spiritual renewal. This is rather surprising given the long history of sustained antagonism towards the tithe that we have discovered in many movements of spiritual renewal and in groups which taught radical discipleship. Nor will it suffice to dismiss such antagonism as no more than an expression of their dissent from the established church. In several radical groups, and in the writings of perceptive individuals, tithing is regarded as objectionable for other reasons: because it lacks a clear New Testament basis, because it imposes a fixed percentage rather than encouraging personal responsibility, or because it is unjust.

Furthermore, in most of these movements, more radical and yet more liberating approaches to the issue of sharing resources can be found – some tentative, some well developed. There are similarities in the principles and practices of such movements, and resonance also with the early churches. Only when tithing is set aside, it seems, do such approaches emerge. Today, as in earlier centuries, tithing distracts us from exploring other possibilities. Tithing is associated historically, not with radical renewal movements, but with establishment Christianity. As with many other aspects of Christendom, the tithe that funded this system seems to have been adopted from secular practice and covered with a veneer of biblical terminology. Despite claims that it is rooted in biblical precedent and teaching, tithing over many centuries has been rejected by many of those who have taken the Bible most seriously.

Fourth, tithing has not, throughout these centuries, enabled the church to be 'good news to the poor'. It is true that early experiments with tithing were mainly concerned with poor relief rather than the support of the clergy, and that, through much of this period, the clergy whom the tithe supported were engaged in a wide range of social and charitable activities. But a persistent complaint against the tithing system has been its failure to address issues of injustice within society. Tithing may have channelled some charitable giving towards the poor, but it did nothing to encourage a fairer distribution of economic resources. Indeed, tithing actually exacerbated the problem, in that poor people tended to suffer more than the rich under this system. Tithing seemed, in many places, to be a tax on the poor rather than a means of supporting them. The gradual erosion of the portion of the tithe that was intended for poor relief and the designation of an increasing proportion for the support of the clergy and church buildings did nothing to increase the popularity of the tithe. The tithing system seems to have been a major cause of the alienation of the poor from the church.

Advocates of tithing today may want to consider to what extent contemporary tithes equip churches to be 'good news to the poor'. Does tithing simply support church leaders and finance the construction and decoration of church buildings? Does the practice of tithing in any way sensitise those who tithe to the needs of the poor or to the injustices of the economic system upon which our society is based? Indeed, can such offerings be regarded as tithing at all if no part of them is allocated to the poor? Caesar of Arles, one of the early advocates of tithing, makes this link explicit in one of his sermons:

> Tithes are required as a due, and he who refuses to pay them has invaded other people's property. A man who does not pay his tithes will appear before the tribunal of the Eternal Judge charged with the murder of all the poor who have died of hunger in the place in which he lives, since he has kept back for his own use the substance which God has assigned to the poor.[55]

Tithing under Christendom (as in the Old Testament) at least made some attempt to redistribute resources to the poor, even if the system became in time little more than a tax on the poor. To what ends are contemporary tithes devoted? If the poor are not among the major beneficiaries of such gifts, perhaps these are not really tithes at all but simply an efficient way of funding church programmes and staff. If this is so, it may be that the present tithing system has not yet even reached the level of the Christendom

---

[55] Quoted in Edwin Hatch, *The Growth of Church Institutions* (London: Hodder & Stoughton, 1887), 117.

tithing system, with all its flaws, and that fundamental issues are being neglected. Perhaps we still need to reflect on John Rastell's evaluation of the effects of tithing that led to his imprisonment in 1536 for daring to challenge the system: 'now not only the poor whose need ought to be relieved by the working of the curates be compelled to pay which they be not able, but the rich have thereby . . . a watergate to stop up the plenteousness of their hearts.'

Chapter 8

Tithing: Demise and Recovery

The End of the Tithing Era

The Quakers were not the only ones protesting against tithing in
the late seventeenth and eighteenth centuries. Although the
Quakers Tithe Bill failed to become law, the debates associated with
this provided opportunities for many to voice their opposition to
the tithe. Speakers questioned the legitimacy of the tithe and many
insisted that it was simply a tax to support the clergy rather than a
divine institution. Recognising that opinions were shifting, some
tithe-owners accepted this redefinition and tried to defend the tithe
on this more limited basis. The most influential argument for
continued clerical support by the tithe was provided by the often
reprinted tract, *Original and Right of Tythes* by Prideaux.[1]

But by this time it was becoming obvious to all but the most
entrenched tithe-owners and church leaders that the tithe system
had outlived any usefulness it may once have had and that it had no
future. The way in which English society operated was now so
different from the agrarian economy for which the tithe was
originally designed (whether we have in mind Old Testament Israel
or early medieval Europe) that attempts to defend and maintain this
system attracted fewer and fewer supporters. The tithe was now
palpably unjust in its application only to those who worked the
land, patently anachronistic in an industrialising and urbanising
society and, in fact, hindering the development of a modern and
efficient agricultural economy.

---

[1] Stephen Taylor, 'Sir Robert Walpole, The Church of England, and the
Quakers Tithe Bill of 1736', *Historical Journal*, 28(1) (1985), 65.

Protests against the tithing system increased exponentially during the eighteenth century. Statements that in earlier days would have branded the speaker a heretic or dissident and might have resulted in imprisonment could now be heard on the lips of politicians, social commentators and even senior churchmen. The tithe was blamed for all manner of social and religious ills – often without foundation, as the Reverend Morgan Cove complained: 'Every shaft which ingenuity, wit or malice could devise hath been levelled against them [tithes] insomuch as there is hardly an imaginary or real grievance with which this country is so pathetically said to be oppressed which hath not been attributed to payment of tithes.'[2]

By now, though, even those representatives of the established church who benefited most from the tithing system had become painfully aware of its inadequacies and of the impact that this system was having on the church's reputation and on relationships between priests and their parishioners. Salim Rashid comments:

> Although it was the political economists who complained of tithes it is the clergymen who really suffered by such a system. Already in the 1750s perceptive clergymen, such as the Rev. Josiah Tucker, were asking that tithes be commuted into glebe. After noting that tithes were a tax on industry, hence injurious from a commercial point of view, Tucker goes on to show that they were also harmful from a religious one.[3]

The privately printed book by this clergyman to which Rashid refers, entitled *The Elements of Commerce and Taxes* (1755), contains the following scenario that Tucker asserts faced many clergy in his day:

> the poor man is reduced to this unhappy dilemma, either to sit down quietly, and see himself defrauded of half his income, while himself and his family are wanting it, – or to bear the character of an angry, litigious person, who, though the minister of peace, is always at war with his parishioners.

---

[2] Eric Evans, *Tithes and the Tithe Commutation Act 1836* (London: Bedford Square Press, 1978), 8.

[3] Salim Rashid, 'Anglican Clergymen and the Tithe Question', *Journal of Religious History*, 11(1) (1980), 70.

Many church leaders, like Tucker, realised that radical reform of the tithing system was vital – although abolition of the tithe was generally still regarded as too damaging a solution. Geoffrey Best observes in relation to church literature in this era: 'Many more books and pamphlets must have been written about tithes than about any other of the conventionally distinguished departments of church affairs.'[4]

Evans summarises the range of protests that the tithe problem attracted in this period:

> Discussion of it filled the pages of the agricultural and political magazines. In itself an inefficient and anachronistic impost, tithe symbolized far more. The agricultural improvers saw it as the major obstacle to increased cultivation and higher profits . . . many concerned for the welfare of the Church of England pointed to the huge number of disputes the system produced and argued that, while it lucratively lined the pockets of the lawyers, it set parson against parishioner and poisoned relations in a village community already subjected to great strain because of population pressures and growing poverty. The political economists attacked the irrationality of tithe, and some were prepared to suggest that it contributed to the massive problem of rural poverty by hindering projects for labour-intensive improvements. The radicals and political reformers saw in tithe the weakest link in the armour of the state church, through which an overall assault, aimed at disestablishment, could be mounted.[5]

The tithe also prompted the development of a rich and varied heritage of satire and humour, involving the use of poetry, drama, cartoons and symbolic protests.[6] Evans notes that 'the satirists and cartoonists of the period made much of the stereotype of the fat, bloated and gouty parson stripping poor farmers of their best beasts with singular avarice and lack of charity. The parson clutching his tithe pig symbolized clerical gluttony.'[7] Those who complain about the images of the clergy in the contemporary media might be

---

[4] Geoffrey Best, *Temporal Pillars* (Cambridge: CUP, 1964), 465.

[5] Eric Evans, *The Contentious Tithe* (London: Routledge & Kegan Paul, 1976), ix.

[6] Some examples of this genre can be found in Appendix 1.

[7] Evans, *Contentious*, 83.

grateful that they were not confronted by some of the images evoked by those who objected to tithing!

So entrenched was the tithe, however, that such protests were for a considerable time answered by attempts to relieve the most irritating and damaging effects of the system rather than dismantling the system itself. One of the main instances of this approach was the Tithe Commutation Act of 1836, referred to above, which 'sliced through [the tithe's] contradictions and complexities and made it possible for parties to effect a rational solution . . . For the first time after Commutation, the landowner knew clearly and in advance what he must pay, and the tithe owner what he might expect.'[8] Of course, tithes had quite often in the past been commuted into cash payments for the convenience of all concerned, but these had been purely local arrangements. Now there was a national system: a charge was calculated on the basis of an average of prices over the previous seven years. However, although this was an improvement on the older system, this Act merely converted the tithe into a local rate payment: it did not address the fundamental inequity and obsolete nature of the tithe. Furthermore, a fixed rate was disadvantageous to farmers in years when the harvest was poor or agricultural prices were low. It seems that the Act was passed primarily to assist tithe-owners rather than tithe-payers.[9]

The Tithe Commutation Act did not satisfy most tithe-payers. A further bill was introduced in the following year in an attempt to make the church responsible for its own maintenance, but this failed to gain sufficient support to become law. So the protests went on: tracts and pamphlets were produced, public meetings were held, politicians were lobbied, associations were formed and many campaigners used the language of battle.

Those who argued against the continuation of the tithing system did so on several grounds. First, they contended that this system was anachronistic and unjust. It was difficult to apply in an economy based largely on cash rather than exchange of goods. It imposed burdens on landowners that inhibited them from taking steps to develop the land and the use they made of it. It was a major contributory factor in the plight of agriculture in the late nineteenth and

---

[8] Evans, *Tithes*, 29.
[9] Doreen Wallace, *The Tithe War* (London: Victor Gollancz, 1934), 25.

early twentieth centuries. And it was unfair that tithes should be paid only by one sector of the population – and a declining sector at that in an industrialising society.

Second, they insisted that it was time to review the concept of a national church – especially when this institution was funded exclusively by landowners. Campaigners argued that only a minority of the population belonged to this church and yet Catholics, Jews, dissenters and agnostics were all expected to contribute towards its maintenance if they happened to be landowners. Two solutions were proposed, echoing earlier suggestions: either state churches should be funded by taxation like state schools – if there were sufficient national support for the institution to win consent for additional taxation; or else it should be left to church members to fund their own churches.[10] The former solution was acknowledged by most as unlikely to gain enough support to be feasible. The latter solution would certainly mean that the church would have to reduce its expenditure, for 'the faithful are not numerous enough to support such an extravagant organisation in the style to which it has been accustomed'.[11] But such an outcome was regarded by many critics as long overdue and an opportunity for the church to reform itself and live more simply.

A third line of argument, which is of particular interest to us, was that the tithe was not – and never had been – a Christian concept. This was the claim of Mr Kedward, the President of the National Tithepayers Association: 'Tithe and tithe rent charges had nothing to do with the Christian religion. They did not owe their origin to Christianity; the Founder of the Christian religion said nothing about them, and in the early centuries no tithes were payable: the Church was supported by the voluntary contributions of the people.'[12] A similar claim appears in the *Extraordinary Black Book* (1831): 'Christianity contains less authority for tithe than Judaism. Jesus Christ ordained no such burden; and in no part of his history is

---

[10] Wallace, *Tithe*, 9–11.

[11] Wallace, *Tithe*, 143.

[12] Wallace, *Tithe*, 146. Mr Kedward continued: '[Tithe] was bad for the Church and bad for the people. It had been an irritant in the national life for hundreds of years and would continue to be an irritant until Parliament . . . put an end to it': Wallace, *Tithe*, 147.

any compulsory provision for the maintenance of the clergy mentioned.'[13]

A further argument was used by others, namely that 'if tithes had any authenticity as compulsory payments, it had long since been ceded by the perversion of the original uses to which tithes were supposed to have been applied'.[14] This is a reference to the gradual diversion of tithe income from poor relief to the support of the clergy and church buildings. This aspect of the tithe system, which earlier critics had condemned, did seem particularly galling to tithe-payers. The tithe was never likely to be popular, but resistance to it might have been considerably more muted if the resources raised were distributed to those in need, rather than being retained by an institution widely regarded as already too wealthy.

What is interesting about these arguments is that they are identical to arguments that had been used for centuries by those who had dared to oppose the tithe. If they were more persuasive in the nineteenth century than they had been in the sixteenth, this was due to changes in the social context and the status of the established church, rather than to changes in the way the case against the tithe was argued. As with many other issues championed by radicals and dissidents throughout the Christendom era, so with the tithe: their arguments may have failed to convince their contemporaries, but in the long run they have been accepted by almost everyone.

Tithe disputes rumbled on during the final years of the nineteenth century and into the twentieth century, with fresh out-breaks of resistance to the tithe among Welsh non-conformists and Irish Catholics, both of whom objected to paying tithes to support an established church that was both English and Anglican. Historians have identified anti-tithe agitation as one of the factors that led eventually to the disestablishment of the church in Wales in the 1920s. To the majority of Welsh farmers, who were chapelgoers, there was no justice in the fact that the church claimed the tithe at all. They already contributed towards the upkeep of their chapels and towards the salaries of their ministers. Why should they be forced to pay money to a church they never attended? This,

---

[13] Quoted in Evans, *Contentious*, 82.
[14] Evans, *Contentious*, 83.

the standard argument of dissenters in previous centuries, was voiced again with renewed passion.

The most serious 'tithe war' took place in Clwyd, Wales between 1886 and 1891,[15] as non-conformist and impoverished farmers in several places refused to pay the required tithes. Although there were one or two incidents where intimidation and even a degree of violence were used, this 'war' mainly took the form of peaceful but vocal protests. One of the ringleaders was Thomas Gee, a Methodist minister and politician, who formed an anti-tithe league and wrote against the tithe in local Welsh-language publications. The protesters found many ways of making life difficult for the tithe-collectors: pelting them with rotten eggs or snowballs; sealing gates or covering them with tar or thorns; hiding cows or 'accidentally' releasing bulls; smearing their pigs with soft soap; or paying in very small change and jeering at the collectors as they counted this. There were many further examples of satirical humour: anti-tithe poetry was included in local papers; mock obituaries were tied to tithe cows; Gee even named his horse 'Degwm' (tithe in Welsh).

This rebellion had begun to run out of steam by 1891, partly due to some concessions made by the authorities, but discontent over the tithe was never far below the surface of Welsh rural society. When English tithe-payers in the 1920s and 1930s became increasingly vocal and active in their opposition to the tithe, more decisive action was finally taken. But it was not until a full century after the Tithe Commutation Act that the tithe was finally abolished by the Tithe Act of 1936.

Section 1 of the Tithe Act states:

> Subject to the provisions of this Act, all tithe rentcharge shall be extinguished on the second day of October, nineteen hundred and thirty six (in this Act referred to as 'the appointed day'), and accordingly as from that day the land out of which any tithe rentcharge issued immediately before that day shall be absolutely discharged and freed therefrom.

---

[15] A brief account of this is contained in *The Tithe War* (Hawarden, Deeside: Clwyd Record Office, 1978). Some of the satire and humour from this period is included in Appendix 1.

Remarkably, however, even this Act did not immediately and entirely relieve tithe-payers of their historic burden, for a further provision specified:

> In place of the tithe rent charge . . . an annuity is charged on the land out of which the tithe rentcharge was payable . . . This annuity is to continue for sixty years.

Not until 1996, then, were the final vestiges of tithing removed from English law. Despite its unpopularity, tithing survived far longer than many other vestiges of Christendom, and it is only at the beginning of the twenty-first century that it has finally been laid to rest. As Evans comments wryly: 'One can only wonder at the tenacity and resourcefulness of those who kept the ailing patient alive for so long.'[16]

The Renewed Popularity of Tithing

More remarkable than the resilience and longevity of tithing as a legal requirement, though, is the surprising popularity of tithing today in many church circles. No sooner had the Tithe Act of 1936 finally abolished the system of compulsory tithes to support the established church than voluntary tithing began to be taught and advocated in British free churches as a biblical principle and as evidence of serious discipleship. Dissenters and free church leaders in earlier generations had protested vigorously against the tithe (not only because they did not wish to support the established church but also because they regarded other biblical principles and practices as more appropriate). Now their descendants, apparently oblivious to their history and heritage, ensured that the tithe would rise phoenix-like from the ashes of the Tithe Act and enjoy renewed life and influence in churches where it had never before been practised.

Although the roots of this renewed interest in tithing are not easy to detect, it seems that advocacy of voluntary tithing began to develop in North America (which lacked the long history of tithing that European nations shared) in the final decades of the nineteenth

[16] Evans, *Contentious*, 168.

century. During the previous fifty years, there had been an increasing emphasis on 'stewardship', prompted in part by the expanding
missionary movement and the need to find ways of providing
adequate financial support for missionaries. In his book, *The Story of
Stewardship in the United States of America*, George Salstrand traces the
development of what he calls 'the great stewardship awakening' and
the plethora of sermons, books and tracts which urged a revival of
giving to support missionaries and ministers.[17]

But it was not until the 1870s that tithing began to be promoted
as the primary means by which finances might be collected from
devoted Christians and channelled towards these objectives.
Salstrand credits 'the rediscovery of the tithe' to Thomas Kane, a
Chicago businessman, who published millions of pamphlets on the
tithe and founded the 'Layman Foundation' to continue his
endeavours.[18] Several congregations – including Episcopalian,
Methodist and Presbyterian churches – began to teach and advocate
tithing, resulting in huge increases in their financial resources. News
of this spread and many other congregations adopted the tithe as the
measure of giving they expected from their members.
Organisations such as 'The Tenth Legion' and 'The Twentieth
Century Tithers' Association of America' were established and, in
1906, Henry Lansdell's *The Sacred Tenth* was published – an
important and much-quoted two-volume work that offered a
scholarly basis for the practice of tithing.[19]

The reputation and influence of some of those who were
involved in the stewardship movement in North America, and the
demonstrable results of substantially increased offerings in churches
which advocated tithing, ensured that tithing began to be taught
and promoted in other nations, including Britain. Many books and
tracts on tithing appeared during the middle years of the twentieth
century, many sermons were preached on this subject and, with
hardly a question being raised about the biblical basis, history,
legitimacy, ethics or pastoral consequences of this practice, the prin-

---

[17] George Salstrand, *The Story of Stewardship in the United States of America*
(Grand Rapids: Baker, 1956).
[18] Salstrand, *Story*, 41–46.
[19] Henry Lansdell, *The Sacred Tenth; or, Studies in Tithe-Giving Ancient and
Modern* (1906; reprinted, Grand Rapids: Baker, 1954).

ciple of tithing has attained normative status in many congregations and in some denominations. The Southern Baptists and various Pentecostal denominations are perhaps the most thoroughly committed to tithing and their denominational leaders have been prepared to commend this officially. They have also advocated tithing in many other nations through their extensive missionary activities, with the result that tithing is also regarded as the normative biblical approach to giving in many of the younger churches and denominations across the world.

Enthusiasm for tithing has perhaps been less marked among Catholics and in the Church of England, where it may be assumed that memories of past problems with the tithe are clearer than in other churches. But many Anglicans recognise that the tithe is a useful means of encouraging more responsible giving to an institution that struggles to persuade its members to contribute as generously as in many of the free churches. Some Catholic parishes have welcomed visits from 'tithing teams', whose mandate is to persuade members of the congregation that tithing is a biblical practice that they should adopt in order better to support their church.[20] Tithing is also taught in many individual congregations from Methodist, United Reformed, Episcopalian, Lutheran, Presbyterian, Baptist, Brethren, Seventh Day Adventist and several other traditions.[21]

The popularity of tithing in Britain has been enhanced in recent decades by its promotion within some of the fastest-growing churches and movements in British Christianity. One of the more influential developments during the past twenty-five years has been what was known in its earlier years as the House Church Movement and is now more often designated as 'the New Churches'. Although this movement, which appears to have peaked in the 1990s, has not been theologically innovative, its teaching and practices in the areas of authority, the use of homes,

---

[20] Eileen Flynn, 'Beware the Tithing Team', *Theology Today*, 40 (1983/84), 195 (reprinted from *America*, 6 November 1982, 262).

[21] Before advocates of tithing celebrate such widespread support too enthusiastically, it is worth noting that tithing is taught also by a range of other organisations, including the Mormons, the Worldwide Church of God and some that are much further from orthodox Christianity.

corporate worship, relationships, discipleship, spiritual gifts and eschatology have had a remarkable impact on Christians in other traditions. The way this movement has operated has frequently caused pain and division, and some of its principles and practices have received sustained criticism, but the movement has undoubtedly also made some very positive contributions. Evident even in the writings of its fiercer critics are frequent, albeit sometimes begrudging, comments of appreciation for its approach to a range of issues.

These comments sometimes relate to the way the movement deals with the issue of finance. One of the distinctive marks of the House Churches over the past quarter of a century has been the teaching and practice of tithing. As we have already indicated, and as House Church teachers would acknowledge, tithing is certainly not unique to these churches. One of the historical roots of the movement is Pentecostalism, within which tithing has been widely and enthusiastically advocated. Stanley Horton writes about the Pentecostal movement: 'Tithe giving has always been emphasized and plays an important part in the teaching and preaching of the churches. There is hardly a pastor who has not preached a sermon based on Malachi 3:8–10 . . . interpreting the "storehouse" to mean the local church in our time.'[22] Tithing was also taught and practised in the Brethren circles from which several early House Church leaders came.

House Church leaders do not present tithing as a recent innovation, but as a biblical practice that needs to be included in the contemporary restoration of New Testament Christianity to which the movement is dedicated. Thus Ron Trudinger, in his influential book on the principles of restoration, *Built to Last*, presents tithing not only as a component in the contemporary restoration of the church but as an element in previous periods of restoration from biblical times.[23]

It is within the House Churches that tithing has been taught most persistently and accepted most enthusiastically in Britain. Introduced to new members in commitment courses, encouraged

---

[22] Stanley Horton, 'Tithe Giving', *Dictionary of Pentecostal and Charismatic Movements* (Grand Rapids: Zondervan, 1988), 846.

[23] Ron Trudinger, *Built to Last* (Eastbourne: Kingsway, 1982), 143–147.

both in public and in private, regarded as a sign of commitment to Christ and his church, tithing is practised by a substantial number of House Church members. Furthermore, church members are often encouraged to give 'tithes and offerings' rather than just tithes. Differentiating between tithes and offerings may be a rather artificial interpretation of Old Testament texts, but the result is a useful practical distinction between the minimum contribution expected from all church members (the tithe) and additional gifts designated for special purposes. Money raised through the tithe is generally used to support the local ministers (by whatever title these may be known), with offerings being collected to fund projects, programmes and new buildings.[24] On the basis of the phrase in Malachi 3:10 about bringing 'the whole tithe into the storehouse', church members are taught to give their tithe to the local church for distribution and to use their offerings to support other causes or people.[25]

Critics express concern about the pressure to tithe which leaders within the House Churches are supposed to exert; and some raise questions about the level of salaries paid to these leaders and other uses to which the tithes are put. They also note that teaching about tithing is sometimes (although certainly not always) accompanied by advocacy of what is known as the 'prosperity gospel'.[26] But many critics are honest enough to recognise that churches where tithing is not only taught but practised are relieved of the financial worries and limitations with which so many others struggle year after year. Members of such churches who tithe seem also to demonstrate in various other ways a deep commitment to Christ and to their local church. Tithing does seem to have very significant practical and spiritual benefits. Not surprisingly, then, even those who criticise the way the House Churches practise tithing often acknowledge these positive features and covet them for their own churches.

Roughly contemporaneous with the emergence of the House Church movement has been the development in England of many networks of Caribbean churches; and more recently there has been a proliferation of African churches, which are being planted in large

---

[24] Andrew Walker, *Restoring the Kingdom* (Guildford: Eagle, 1998), 167.
[25] Trudinger, *Built*, 145–146.
[26] See, for example, William Davies, *Rocking the Boat* (Basingstoke: Marshall Pickering, 1986), 72–80.

numbers and are growing rapidly, especially but not exclusively in London. Many of these Caribbean and African churches are linked with Pentecostal denominations or are at least as deeply indebted to Pentecostalism as the House Churches. In most of these churches, too, tithing is taught and practised as the biblical standard and method of giving – although, as in many of the House Churches, both tithes and offerings are expected from the faithful.

Why have these new churches so enthusiastically embraced tithing, a practice which for many centuries was associated with the establishment form of Christianity that these churches so often dismiss as defective or even illegitimate? There seem to have been a number of influences. Certainly the teachings of both evangelical and Pentecostal American church leaders, by whom tithing was presented as the biblical norm, have been persuasive,[27] as have the writings of some prosperity teachers. But the adoption of tithing in these movements may owe as much to their criticism of the undisciplined patterns of giving evident in the older churches and their own need to find effective ways of funding their new churches. Fundamentally, however, it is the literalistic approach to biblical interpretation apparent in these movements, together with their lack of interest in church history, that has allowed them to appropriate the tithe with little or no appreciation of the complex contextual issues that surround it.

Tithing may be associated particularly with these newer and more independent evangelical and charismatic groups, but it is also a familiar concept within churches on the evangelical wings of most of the older denominations and has the support of several well-known evangelical leaders. North American influence is certainly apparent here too. In 1982, a book by R. T. Kendall, the American minister of Westminster Chapel, London, simply entitled *Tithing*, powerfully advocated the practice.[28] On the back cover of the book are commendations and endorsements of tithing from three other respected evangelical leaders – Sir Fred Catherwood, John Stott and

---

[27] Walker, *Restoring*, 166.

[28] (London: Hodder & Stoughton, 1982). This small but influential paperback is clearly and persuasively written and avoids many of the excesses often associated with the advocacy of tithing. But the case it presents for tithing is deeply flawed in most of the areas about which we

Billy Graham. The appearance in 1992 of a revised version of Kendall's book, now called *The Gift of Giving*, is a recent indication of continued interest in this subject among evangelical Christians.

That tithing remains normative (at least in theory) among many evangelicals is apparent also from a recent unpublished paper by David Hilborn of the Evangelical Alliance. Responding to a question which had been raised as to whether the Alliance should tithe gifts it received from its members,[29] Hilborn surveys biblical references to tithing and concludes that tithing is a biblical mandate. Before proceeding to deal with the specific question under review, he concludes that 'most evangelicals would accept the principles and key functions of tithing listed above'.[30] Mann, an Anglican, also recognises – and offers an explanation for – this evangelical enthusiasm for tithing: 'It does seem that giving is higher . . . where the Church has a stronger identity and a clearer boundary with the world . . . This particularly applies to Churches with an evangelical tradition, where teaching of the tithe combines effectively with a conservative view of biblical authority.'[31]

---

[28] (continued) have expressed concern in this study: though full of biblical references and detailed exegesis, there is almost no attention to hermeneutical issues; no justification is provided for using the tithe as the controlling paradigm; no attention is given to the history of tithing and the problems encountered over the centuries; testimonies are included without critical reflection; many unwarranted assumptions are made and many points are asserted rather than established by careful argument; there is no engagement with wider questions of justice and lifestyle; and those who challenge the practice of tithing are dismissed as unwilling to obey God.

[29] The background to this question is the practice in some churches of tithing the tithed income they receive from members. As the Levites tithed their tithe to the priests, so these churches give away to other causes a tenth of what they are given. This practice seems commendable until one realises that it often means that (a) the local church spends 90% of its income on itself; (b) only 1% of a tither's giving is really given away, since the other 9% is spent on the church that serves the tither.

[30] David Hilborn, 'Should EA Tithe?' (private paper, 1998), 5.

[31] Adrian Mann, *No Small Change* (Norwich: The Canterbury Press, 1992), 158–159.

The main difference between these evangelical churches and the newer independent churches is that tithing often remains a theoretical standard in the former, whereas in the latter it is more likely to be practised. A recent report into giving among evangelical Christians in Britain concludes:

> While conducting this survey we noted that 'tithing' – giving 10% of one's income, traditionally the benchmark for giving to the church – is not widely practised among evangelicals. Survey data indicates that the average amount of money given today by evangelicals is 5% of their monthly income to church and 2% to Christian charities.[32]

Evangelicals reading this report might argue that this is no time to jettison tithing. Rather than questioning the legitimacy of tithing, as this study does, perhaps attention needs to be given to teaching this principle more effectively and encouraging more consistent practice?

Nor do the experiences of churches in traditions where tithing is not advocated offer much incentive to abandon this system. Advocates of tithing are dismissive of the feeble attempts to raise funds in many churches – 'fund-raising campaigns, wheedling money from reluctant members, fêtes, bazaars, lotteries, garden parties and all the rest'.[33] In those churches where tithing is not taught, the only alternative appears to be haphazard, sporadic and severely limited financial support, both for the local church and for the denomination to which the church belongs. Decisions about their level of giving are left to individual church members, who are informed about needs and opportunities but are not encouraged to respond within a framework such as the tithing system offers.

---

[32] 'Who Gives to What and Why? . . . Getting to Know Evangelical Donors' (a survey carried out by Redina Kolaneci under the auspices of the Whitefield Institute, 1998), 13. That Christians in North America do not practise tithing consistently is indicated by research noted by Blomberg that 'the amounts of money theoretically needed to eradicate world poverty could be amassed simply if all American Christians would tithe': Craig Blomberg, *Neither Poverty Nor Riches: A Biblical Theology of Material Possessions* (Leicester: Apollos, 1999), 252.
[33] Trudinger, *Built*, 145.

The results of this approach are less than encouraging. Mann, writing as the director of the Anglican Stewardship Association, concludes:

> The figures are difficult to analyse, but the most optimistic view of giving by [Anglican] Church members . . . is that it is around 2% of income for Church attenders . . . It is generally accepted, too, that in almost every parish current levels of giving are maintained by a small proportion of active members. The giving of the majority of Church members must still be reckoned to be inordinately low.[34]

Keith Tondeur, the director of *Credit Action*, a Christian money education charity, suggests that there is an even lower level of giving across all the churches: 'If every committed Christian in this country tithed giving would increase nearly ninefold.'[35] Chronic financial shortages result from this situation, not only precluding new initiatives but, in some cases, threatening the viability of existing causes.

Those with responsibility for finance in such contexts are often torn between wanting to suggest a set percentage (tithing or a lower proportion) and the assumption that giving is a private matter with which the church should not interfere. Mann reflects on this dilemma:

> In 1982 the general Synod . . . called for a standard of giving of 5% of net disposable income. Obviously, if this standard was accepted, the finances of the Church would be transformed. There would be a lot more money in the common purse, but this has not been the case . . . The espousal of such a standard of giving is very problematic, because regular and systematic giving is in the end a matter of personal, ethical decision. For the institutional Church to claim that decision for itself is hard to justify.[36]

Those who speak or write from an influential but less official perspective also grapple with the dilemma of how to advocate

---

[34] Mann, *No*, 137.
[35] Keith Tondeur, *Your Money and Your Life* (London: SPCK, 1996), 102.
[36] Mann, *No*, 141.

responsible giving without being unduly prescriptive; but they are more likely to opt for tithing as the way forward. Thus, in his practical manual on financial matters, Tondeur explores the issue of tithing and insists (despite centuries of historical evidence to the contrary) that 'tithing has always been a voluntary act for God's people'; but he argues that 'you cannot sit under the teaching of a local church and not support it financially'. His conclusion is categorical: 'Everyone who is working should tithe.'[37] Similarly, Michael Bond, a former provincial treasurer of the United Reformed Church, encourages his readers to 'think about what God wants of them' but feels free to advocate tithing with enthusiasm as a secure basis for the support of his denomination in the twenty-first century.[38]

But denominational statements on stewardship tend not to advocate tithing in this way. Some mention the tithe as one model that church members might consider. Such lukewarm advocacy may represent the worst option. The tithe may be objectionable for the reasons we have identified in this study, but at least those churches that teach this wholeheartedly are generally well financed and their members know what is expected of them. Those that neither endorse tithing enthusiastically nor offer a compelling alternative should not be surprised if their members regard giving as an optional extra.

If the alternative to tithing is undisciplined giving and under-resourced churches, we are unlikely to find much enthusiasm for exploring these alternatives – either within those churches where tithing is operating well, or within other churches where tithing is taught but not practised, or where some form of proportional giving like tithing is seen as the answer to financial problems. The renewed popularity of tithing despite its legacy and so soon after its demise as a legal requirement may be due, as much as anything else, to the apparent lack of viable alternatives. It is, therefore, to an exploration of such alternatives that we now turn.

---

[37] Tondeur, *Money*, 90–92.
[38] Michael Bond, *Dying to Give* (Nottingham: United Reformed Church, East Midlands Province, 1988), 72.

Chapter 9

Alternatives to Tithing

Our aim in this chapter is to be indicative rather than exhaustive, to provoke further exploration rather than attempting to reach final conclusions. Rejecting tithing is not intended as the precursor to imposing a different system, but as an invitation to look afresh at the issues involved in sharing resources, to study and pray, to be creative, to engage in discussion with others, to learn from Christian churches and communities in other times and places. We have already noted some alternative principles and practices in the early churches and in movements that dissociated themselves from Christendom and the tithing system which funded this arrangement. Here we will consider two biblical models – one from the Old Testament and one from the New.[1] Might these principles, rather than tithing, prompt new ways of thinking and acting as we struggle to discover what it means to be communities of justice and generosity at the start of the third millennium?

That Jesus did not encourage his disciples to tithe and that the early churches did not, on the whole, adopt this traditional Jewish practice seems clear, both from the New Testament record and from the documentary evidence we have of church life in the following centuries. But it would be very surprising if Jesus had not

---

[1] Both models have received considerable attention from scholars and have been the subjects of popular treatments of stewardship issues. What follows makes no claim to originality. But they are conspicuous by their absence in books or articles advocating tithing. There are also other principles and practices that we might have examined: sufficiency (*autarkeia*), contentment, simplicity, hospitality, table fellowship, and 'good news to the poor'.

drawn on Old Testament principles, particularly those emphasised within the prophetic tradition, in his teaching about possessions, giving and sharing. It would be equally surprising if the financial practices of the early churches were not informed by their reflection on both the Old Testament and Jesus' often creative and radical interpretation of this.

If we are searching for principles and models in the New Testament which might guide our contemporary practice in relation to our finances, then, we will want to be alert to echoes of Old Testament teaching as we listen to Jesus and his disciples. We will expect to find new approaches that are consonant with the changed context, but we will anticipate discovering elements of continuity as well as discontinuity. Our conviction that the principle of tithing was not regarded by New Testament writers as a suitable practice under the new covenant does not prevent us from recognising the appropriation by Jesus and the early churches of other Old Testament principles.

The basis upon which we are challenging the advocacy of tithing as a Christian practice is not that it is an Old Testament concept or a provision of the Mosaic Law, but that it is not endorsed in the New Testament. We have already intimated that tithing does not fit easily into the teaching of Jesus and his disciples because of the new approaches to giving and sharing they taught. But this does not mean that all that the Old Testament teaches and models in relation to economic matters is now obsolete. Indeed, as we will see, these new approaches may not draw on the tithing passages, but they were greatly influenced by other Old Testament paradigms.

Jubilee

The most fundamental of these paradigms – in terms both of its significance in the Old Testament and its appropriation in the New Testament – is the remarkable institution of the Year of Jubilee, to which Leviticus 25 (and a section of Leviticus 27) introduces us:

> *Consecrate the fiftieth year and proclaim liberty throughout the land to all its inhabitants. It shall be a jubilee for you; all of you are to return to your family property and to your own clans. The fiftieth year shall be a jubilee for you; do*

not sow and do not reap what grows of itself or harvest the untended vines. For it is a jubilee and is to be holy for you; eat only what is taken directly from the fields. In this year of Jubilee all of you are to return to your own property . . . You are to buy from your own people on the basis of the number of years since the Jubilee. And they are to sell to you on the basis of the number of years left for harvesting crops . . . what is really being sold to you is the number of crops . . . What was sold will remain in the possession of the buyer until the Year of Jubilee. It will be returned in the Jubilee, and they can then go back to their property . . . If any of your people become poor and sell themselves to you, do not make them work as slaves. They are to be treated as hired workers or temporary residents among you; they are to work for you until the Year of Jubilee. Then they and their children are to be released . . . (Lev. 25:10–41)

Once every fifty years the trumpets were to be sounded throughout the land on the Day of Atonement and liberty, or release, was to be proclaimed. The Year of Jubilee was to be a holy year, a year of celebration, and a year the Lord told his people was 'for you'. It was a year when radical action was to be taken, a year of winners and losers, a year of costly and revolutionary behaviour.

This chapter has attracted plenty of scholarly attention, and in recent years there have been several more popular treatments of the jubilee provisions described here. We do not need to engage with all of these since we are not suggesting that the jubilee described here is applicable to Christians. Just as the tithe cannot be extracted from its social, economic and religious context, and from the many other components of the Mosaic legislation to which it relates, without doing violence to the meaning of this institution, so with the Year of Jubilee. This chapter is part of a complex set of regulations that can properly be understood only as an interconnecting whole.

What we are suggesting is that the legislation that formed the basis of the Year of Jubilee expressed certain values, hopes and ideals. These continued to inspire Israel over the centuries and formed part of the prophetic vision and challenge that acted both as a critique of the present and a call to a transformed future.[2] Further, we are arguing that Jesus, standing within this prophetic tradition,

---

[2] Many scholars regard the jubilee legislation as dating from the period of the exile, interpreting it as a manifesto for social reform couched in ancient language, or as a utopian ideal. Others argue for the historicity of

used the imagery of jubilee in his teaching in order to impart to his disciples some of the fundamental values of the new community they would lead. The disciples, in turn, drew on jubilee language and ideas as they began to work out in their own context what Christian discipleship meant in the area of economics.

To substantiate these claims, we need to make sure we understand the main elements of jubilee and then explore the ways in which these were taken up by the prophets, by Jesus and in the early churches. Jubilee was about release and restoration: all debts were to be cancelled, all slaves were to be released, capital wealth was to be redistributed by land being restored to its original family ownership, and the land was to enjoy rest.[3]

Leviticus notes a number of exceptions and qualifications to these requirements, but nothing that undermines the basic principles we have identified or the radical nature of this institution. This was to be the foundation stone upon which so much else was built, the pivot about which the rest of the Mosaic economic legislation revolved, the central reference point in Israel's environmental, economic, social and religious system. Old Testament scholar, Christopher Wright describes the Year of Jubilee as the 'central core of Old Testament economics'.[4]

Jubilee deeply impacted concepts of property and ownership. On the one hand, the idea of ownership was strengthened in that owners had an immutable title to their ancestral property; on the other hand, purchasers of property could never attain such ownership – land was not really sold under this system, but loaned to a buyer and returned to its original owner in the fiftieth year. Personal and social relationships were also governed by the principles of the jubilee. Robert Gnuse comments: 'The jubilee laws reflect a

---

[2] (continued) the legislation – or at least that a historical practice lay behind texts that may have been written much later. A helpful discussion of the issues involved in this debate is contained in Robert Gnuse, *You Shall Not Steal* (Maryknoll, N.Y.: Orbis, 1985), 36–45. Although we will adopt the latter perspective, our primary interest here is the motif of jubilee and its significance within the prophetic tradition and in the New Testament era.
[3] The more frequent Sabbath years involved three of these four elements, but not the most radical one – the redistribution of capital wealth.
[4] Christopher Wright, *Living As the People of God* (Leicester: IVP, 1983), 83.

courageous vision for society . . . [Jubilee] gave hope to the impoverished by offering a promise of return to their land and a place of equality in the community. It became an aid to prevent the breakdown of the family as a social element.'[5]

The Year of Jubilee had a didactic and liturgical purpose. It was intended to remind the Israelites that they owned nothing in an absolute sense. Everything they had was held in trust from the Lord, whom they were to fear and obey. They were to release slaves because they had been released from slavery in Egypt. They were to forgive debts because their God forgave them. It was also part of the justice tradition that runs through the Pentateuch and is interwoven with the cultic tradition. Jubilee was designed to prevent the development of gross inequalities of wealth and poverty in Israel, to redistribute possessions and opportunities regularly, to give those who had done badly a chance to start again. Paul Hertig writes: 'Jubilee . . . can be summarized as . . . a redistribution of resources, and a flattening of pyramids . . . Jubilee is a profound spiritual and social event.'[6] Jubilee was gracious, redemptive and creative.

What is the relationship between the jubilee and the tithe? Both are rooted in the history and culture of Old Testament Israel. They are linked together within the overall economic system of the Pentateuch that includes Sabbath years, gleaning rules and various other kinds of offerings. Both have liturgical and humanitarian dimensions, although it seems that the liturgical element is stronger with the tithe and the humanitarian element is more pronounced with the jubilee.

But there are some significant differences. Tithing, as we have seen, was practised in other nations than Israel, even if its theological significance was more developed in the Old Testament. Jubilee, however, appears to be unique to Israel. Although there are some instances in other ancient societies of edicts to release slaves, cancel debts or return land seized by creditors, these are occasional and extraordinary measures rather than a basis for the kind of regular redistribution of resources envisaged by the author

---

[5] Gnuse, *You*, 36.

[6] Paul Hertig, 'The Jubilee Mission of Jesus in the Gospel of Luke: Reversals of Fortune', *Missiology*, 26(2) (April 1998), 171.

of Leviticus.[7] If we are searching for the distinctive mark of the covenant people of God in the sphere of economics, jubilee appears a much stronger candidate than tithing.

Tithing, as a percentage measure, applied equally to everyone, but jubilee would have markedly different implications for those who were rich and those who were poor. The tithe was concerned with income, whereas jubilee dealt with capital. By comparison with the social upheaval envisaged by the jubilee provisions, the tithe involved a fairly minor redistribution of resources in favour of the Levites and the poor. Tithing, unlike the jubilee, could not prevent the development of a widening gap between rich and poor.

Absent from most books on tithing is any reference to jubilee. There is an appendix on the subject in Thompson's book, prefaced by the assertion that the jubilee can be ignored for the purpose of his study![8] Most other authors appear to have no interest at all in this topic. The question we asked previously confronts us with renewed force: on what basis is the tithe chosen as the controlling paradigm for interpreting and applying Old Testament – let alone New Testament – texts on the subject of possessions? The jubilee provisions are so much more wide-ranging and far-reaching than the tithe: surely the tithing passages should be interpreted in light of the jubilee?

One thing that the tithe and jubilee have in common is that neither was practised consistently by the Israelites. Tithing was certainly practised by some people some of the time and there were periods when this was implemented enthusiastically. After the exile and at least into the New Testament era, as we have seen, even augmented tithing was generally accepted. But there is no clear evidence that the jubilee system was ever fully implemented. The relationship between the Year of Jubilee and the Sabbath year is unclear. Three of the four main components of the jubilee provisions were required every seven years. It has been suggested that the jubilee provisions

---

[7] For a helpful summary of the evidence, see Gnuse, *You*, 37, 41. For a more detailed examination of similar practices in other societies, see Raymond Westbrook, *Property and the Family in Biblical Law*, JSOT 113 (Sheffield: Sheffield Academic Press, 1991), 44–50.

[8] P. W. Thompson, *The Whole Tithe* (London: Marshall, Morgan & Scott, 1929), 237.

were a post-exilic attempt to replace earlier economic legislation,[9] but it seems very unlikely that such a radical approach would have been used as a remedial measure. It may be, then, that we should rather understand the Sabbath year as forming part of the jubilee system. If this is so, then three of the jubilee requirements may have been operative in some periods of Israel's history, since the release of debts and slaves did occasionally take place and there is some evidence that the land was allowed to lie fallow.[10] But it seems that the central requirement – the radical redistribution of land, the major resource in an agricultural economy – did not take place. Certainly the prophets frequently denounce the many social injustices relating to the accumulation of land.

It does not require a fertile imagination to understand why the nation managed to forget to blow the trumpet in the fiftieth year. Unlike the tithe, jubilee was 'good news to the poor' but 'bad news to the rich'. Those who had done well over the past five decades, whose families had flourished, whose wealth had grown and who had accumulated property and servants, would find the approach of this year of economic redistribution profoundly threatening. Why should they be required to give so much of this up in favour of those for whom the past fifty years had been very different – a downward spiral of crop failures, indebtedness, loss of property and even slavery? There was a certain cost to tithing, but it did not threaten a person's economic status in the way that the jubilee provisions did. Tithing provided some charitable support for widows, orphans and other needy members of the community, but jubilee offered such people a new beginning and new hope.

So the jubilee legislation was not implemented. Nor has it appealed to the advocates of tithing, many of whom seem not to be attracted to the limitation it implies on the concepts of 'ownership' and 'private property', the questions it raises about capital resources as well as income, the threat it poses to the social and economic status quo, or the unavoidable communitarian ethic that it embraces, which is so much less evident with the tithe.

---

[9] Gnuse, *You*, 37.

[10] The release of debts and slaves is mentioned, for example, in Nehemiah 5. There is intriguing evidence of grain shortages every seven years during the first century, which may indicate that a significant number of Jews were observing the Sabbath year legislation.

But, largely thanks to the prophets, the ideal of the jubilee was
not entirely lost. It may not have been implemented in Israel, but it
remained in the nation's sacred literature as a reminder and stimulus. The foundational passage in Leviticus was not excised and
echoes of the jubilee legislation could be heard from time to time in
the prophetic literature. The central jubilee concepts of release and
restoration are used sometimes by the prophets to describe the new
age of salvation that would follow the great Day of the Lord.[11]
Although this was not now regarded as something that could be
achieved in this age, jubilee formed part of Israel's hopes for the
coming age, the Kingdom of God, the new heaven and new earth.

One of the classic passages is Isaiah 61:1–11, with its proclama-
tion of good news for the poor, liberty for the captives, hope for the
hopeless, release for those in bondage, social and spiritual
restoration, and even a renewed creation. The terminology of this
passage resonates deeply with the jubilee provisions, as many
commentators have recognised. Walter Pilgrim writes: 'What has
especially caught the eye of numerous commentators is the precise
language that is used to portray the coming liberation. It is the
language of Jubilee Year.'[12] Hertig concurs:

> This phrase [the year of the Lord's favour] and the phrase 'sent me to
> proclaim release to the captives' are rooted in the jubilee language of
> Leviticus 25:10, 41. Furthermore, the word 'release' . . . meaning
> 'freedom' or 'liberty' is a technical expression referring to the release of
> Hebrew slaves and of property every 50 years in the year of Jubilee.[13]

---

[11] See, for example, Isaiah 27:13; Isaiah 60; Ezekiel 39; Ezekiel 46; Joel
2:32; Amos 9:11–15; Zephaniah 3:20. If the jubilee legislation in Leviticus is dated later than we have suggested, this would indicate strongly that
the idea of jubilee was being promulgated later in Israel's history.

[12] Walter Pilgrim, *Good News to the Poor* (Minneapolis: Augsburg
Publishing, 1981), 69.

[13] Hertig, 'Jubilee', 171. Some scholars do not regard this passage as
referring to the Jubilee: see, for example, Roland De Vaux, *Ancient Israel:
Its Life and Institutions* (New York: McGraw Hill, 1965), 176. But the
linguistic links and overall tenor of the passage make it likely that the
prophet had this institution in mind, even if he was not explicitly
announcing a Year of Jubilee.

Some scholars reject the conclusion that 'the year of the Lord's favour' announced in this passage was intended by the prophet to mean the long-delayed Year of Jubilee and suggest that he was prophesying a less specific period of renewal and restoration. But it seems that in first-century synagogues, those who listened to Isaiah 61 would have understood this passage as referring both to the jubilee vision and to the coming of the Messiah.[14]

No wonder, then, that Jesus created a stir in Nazareth when he read part of this passage (Lk. 4:18–21) and announced that the time had come for these hopes to be realised! His hearers knew this familiar passage well, understood its messianic significance and were familiar with its jubilee themes. The fact that Jesus abruptly stopped reading after the phrase 'year of the Lord's favour' would have increased the air of excitement and disbelief in the synagogue. Was this what he was saying? Could it really be jubilee time? Was he claiming to be the Messiah? What about the 'day of vengeance', the next phrase that Jesus had not read out? Surely vengeance on their enemies was necessary for them to enjoy the promised blessings of the new age? How could Israel have one without the other?

Commentators have argued over whether Jesus intended to proclaim the Year of Jubilee (or whether Luke intended to portray Jesus as doing this), and if so what he meant by this. Some scholars have even attempted to demonstrate, on the basis of careful calculation, that the year in which Jesus read this passage in Nazareth was actually a fiftieth year![15] There seems to be a growing consensus that the language of jubilee does indeed underlie this passage and that Jesus (or Luke) was using this in order to interpret his ministry in terms of the jubilee paradigm. Clearly Jesus was not implying that the provisions of Leviticus should be implemented literally. This was not feasible in Roman-occupied Palestine without some manifestation of the 'day of vengeance', which seemed not yet to be on

---

[14] See John Howard Yoder, *The Politics of Jesus* (Carlisle: Paternoster, 1994²), 29; Pilgrim, *Good*, 71.

[15] David Seccombe refers to the calculations of August Strobel and seems inclined to accept his view. See David Seccombe, *Possessions and the Poor in Luke-Acts* (Linz: Studien Zum Neuen Testament Und Seiner Umwelt, 1982), 54–55. Several more popular books also mention Strobel's argument. But this kind of claim seems impossible to substantiate.

his agenda. But he may have been telling his hearers that the spirit and values of jubilee would be evident in his ministry and in the community that was already beginning to form around him.

In a previous chapter we rejected the attempt by some advocates of tithing to base their teaching on the 'spirit of the tithe' rather than its literal meaning in the Old Testament. We seem now to be adopting just such an approach to the jubilee. Why is this legitimate in relation to jubilee when it was not in relation to the tithe? There are two reasons. First, there is no evidence that Jesus showed any interest at all in the tithe, whether interpreted literally or symbolically, whereas the language and values of jubilee are evident not only in Luke 4 but, as we will see, throughout his ministry and teaching. Second, the first-century Jewish community understood tithing texts and jubilee texts in quite different ways. Tithing was applied literally and had even been extended to cover details not mentioned by the Mosaic legislation. By contrast,

> in . . . later Jewish literature the Jubilee vision of Isaiah 61 is not interpreted literally as a kind of legal prescription, but as a symbol or vision of the new age . . . this is also the way it would have been interpreted by Jesus and by the early church, including Luke . . . it is not the Mosaic Jubilee which is announced by Jesus but the coming of the kingdom, which is then described in the language of the messianic and Jubilee vision of good news to the poor and release for the captives.[16]

His ministry and teaching over the next three years made it clear that Jesus had the jubilee very much in mind. John Howard Yoder, in his influential study *The Politics of Jesus*, provides a helpful summary of various ways in which the Gospel writers portray Jesus drawing on jubilee concepts.[17] Among these are:

- the echo in Luke 12:29–31 of the concern expressed in Leviticus 25:20–21 about what those who let the land rest would eat if they did not sow or reap;

---

[16] Pilgrim, *Good*, 71.

[17] Yoder, *Politics*, 60–75 (adapted freely, with permission, from a pioneering study of this theme in André Trocmé, *Jesus and the Nonviolent Revolution* [Scottdale, Pa.: Herald Press, 1973]).

- parables dealing with the concept of debt and the hope of being released from debt (Mt. 18:23–35; Lk. 16:1–12);
- the use of debt language in the Lord's Prayer (Mt. 6:9–13), where the word used for 'release' (a better translation than 'forgive') is the term used in the Septuagint for jubilee;
- Jesus' instructions to his followers to 'sell your possessions and give to the poor' (Lk. 12:33) and to the rich young ruler to 'sell everything you have and give to the poor' (Lk. 18:22), which reflect the redistribution of capital envisaged by jubilee.[18]

As with so much in the Old Testament, Jesus reinterpreted and expanded the concept of jubilee. Noting that the restoration of sight for the blind went beyond anything mentioned in Leviticus, Virgil Vogt comments: 'Jesus proclaimed a more profound and comprehensive Jubilee, one in which all sins (i.e. all debts) could be cancelled, all bondages – psychological and spiritual, as well as economic – could be broken and all captives could go free.'[19] Not only was it no longer feasible in first-century Palestine to blow the trumpet and declare a Year of Jubilee; this was not adequate under the new covenant. Why wait fifty years before practising the kind of social justice that the jubilee provisions suggested? Why not find creative ways now of dealing with debt, of sharing resources and of bringing 'good news to the poor'? Why not build the kind of community, energised by the spirituality of jubilee and captivated by jubilee values, which would frequently redistribute resources and remove inequalities, develop a sustainable rhythm of work and rest, and release people from debt and other forms of slavery?

---

[18] Other scholars, building on or challenging Yoder's interpretation, have explored the use of jubilee concepts in the Gospels and have offered further insights and additional examples of jubilee concepts and language in the New Testament. See especially three works mentioned by Yoder in the revised version of his book: Robert Sloan, *The Favorable Year of the Lord* (Austin, Tex.: Schola Press, 1977); Sharon Ringe, *Jesus, Liberation and the Biblical Jubilee* (Philadelphia: Fortress Press, 1985); and Donald Blosser, 'Jesus and the Jubilee: The Year of Jubilee and its Significance in the Gospel of Luke' (PhD thesis, University of St Andrews, 1979).
[19] Virgil Vogt, *Treasure in Heaven* (Ann Arbor: Servant Books, 1982), 75.

And it seems that the early church caught the jubilee vision. When the Spirit came at Pentecost, one of the first things that happened was that the Christians in Jerusalem began to practise jubilee. There is not a hint that tithing was practised, but a radical redistribution of capital resources took place as houses, fields and goods were sold and the proceeds were made available to those in need. Luke's claim that 'there were no needy persons among them'[20] echoes the promise to Israel that if they were obedient to God's covenant legislation (which included the jubilee) 'there will be no poor among you'.[21] The impact on slavery and debt can already be seen in a number of places in the New Testament[22] and even more clearly in the writings and experience of Christians during the next two centuries.

These early Christians did not, of course, attempt to apply the detailed provisions of Leviticus. The original Year of Jubilee was designed for Israel as a nation in its own land. It could not be applied literally by the church, a new kind of 'nation' without land of its own. But the spirit of jubilee – the kingdom hope of justice and equality that the prophets had looked forward to – this they could begin to work out in their own community, as a testimony to a society disfigured by economic injustice and plagued by poverty, and as a sign that a new age was dawning, to which the church was a signpost.

What happened at Pentecost and in the days and weeks that followed was only a beginning. But, having listened to Jesus' teaching on finance, having received the Holy Spirit's power to live radically new lives, 'wasn't it appropriate', asks Alan Kreider, 'that they on the fiftieth day (Pentecost) should do what God had called his people to do in the fiftieth year – make Jubilee?'[23] Many experiments, setbacks, joys and struggles would follow over the coming years, as Christians continued to grapple with the disturbing teaching of Jesus and how this applied to practical issues of financial discipleship. But it was this initial outburst of joyful jubilee action (rather than the familiar but much less exciting model of the tithe)

---

[20] Acts 4:34.

[21] Deuteronomy 15:4.

[22] See, for example, Philemon; Romans 13:7–8.

[23] Alan Kreider, *Journey Towards Holiness* (London: Marshalls, 1986), 164.

which inspired and challenged subsequent generations. It is this jubilee model which has continued to offer an alternative paradigm whenever Christians have looked for fresh ways to live justly together and to be 'good news to the poor'.

Unlike tithing, with its miserable history and moribund heritage of fixed percentages and obligatory payments, jubilee has been a less familiar concept but one which is now used quite widely, within and beyond the churches, and which conveys images of liberation, joyful celebration and social justice. Unlike tithing, which is now used almost entirely within churches or religious groups to support their own activities, jubilee invites creative, daring and imaginative approaches to entrenched problems and issues of justice within the global economy. The recent Jubilee 2000 campaign, for example, has attracted widespread support for its attempt to persuade wealthy nations to release poorer nations from crippling debt.[24] What might be the impact of churches all over the country becoming known as 'jubilee centres' rather than institutions that are 'after our money'?

Koinonia

Although jubilee is not a term that occurs in the New Testament, we have suggested that the spirit of jubilee pervades the ministry of Jesus and the practice of the early churches. But for those who are eager to identify a New Testament term that might indicate an alternative model to tithing, we need look no further than the familiar term *koinonia*.

Koinonia has in recent years joined a select group of Greek words that readers of popular Christian books may encounter without

---

[24] A leaflet produced in November 1998 by Christian Aid and CAFOD for Churches Together in England, 'New Start for the World's Poor', included a practical section entitled 'What can you do locally? Ten Steps to Jubilee'. The same leaflet suggested, with references to both Leviticus 25 and Luke 4, that the millennium should be seen as a jubilee and celebrated by action to reduce debt and global injustice. Other examples of organisations using jubilee language are Jubilee Housing, run by the Church of the Savior in Washington D.C. and the Jubilee Centre in Cambridge which campaigns on debt issues.

translation. It is normally used to describe a quality of fellowship or depth of personal relating within a community that is regarded as highly desirable. But it has a broad semantic range and can legitimately be translated as fellowship, community, communion, intimacy, joint participation, intercourse or association.[25] Its root meaning is 'commonness', and it is used in the New Testament in connection both with God's communion with humanity and with human relationships. These two dimensions come together in the communion meal: 'Is not the cup of thanksgiving for which we give thanks a participation (*koinonia*) in the blood of Christ? And is not the bread that we break a participation (*koinonia*) in the body of Christ?' (1 Cor. 10:16). Renewed interest in this concept has provided churches with a necessary and helpful response to the prevailing individualism within Western society and has encouraged the development of mutual commitment and strong friendships in the church.

But *koinonia* was also an economic term, which referred to business partnerships in the Roman world, to joint benefactions (donations made by more than one donor) and to financial collections. Twice in the New Testament the term is used to describe a financial contribution.[26] In the early churches the *koinonia* was the common fund out of which the deacons administered care for the poor, or the box into which gifts were placed as people arrived at church meetings. So, without wanting to devalue the important aspects of fellowship and mutual commitment to which the term can also refer, it is important to recognise that *koinonia* is concerned with the sharing of resources, with responsibility for the needs of others within the community, with the just distribution of wealth, and with very practical action to relieve needs.

This understanding of *koinonia* invites us to see the church as a kind of business association, with each member acting as a partner in the enterprise. This partnership is a voluntary association but carries with it certain responsibilities. All the partners renounce sole right to their possessions. In return, each partner can rely on practical assistance from the other partners. One of the primary goals of the

---

[25] Craig Blomberg, *Neither Poverty Nor Riches: A Biblical Theology of Material Possessions* (Leicester: Apollos, 1999), 161.
[26] Romans 15:26; 2 Corinthians 8:4.

association is to abolish extremes of wealth and poverty among the partners and to work towards increasing equality. The division in churches which practise such *koinonia* will be between givers and receivers, not between rich and poor, with a constant flow of resources making it likely that givers will sometimes also become receivers and receivers in turn become givers.

Surely this is the basis for Jesus' promise to Peter (Mt. 19:29) that his disciples, as they gave away their possessions in response to the jubilee vision, would have at their disposal hundreds of houses, fields and families? This is simply another way of describing how the early churches practised jubilee. *Koinonia* is identified by Luke as one of the defining marks of the church that was formed on the Day of Pentecost: 'They devoted themselves to the apostles' teaching and to the fellowship (*koinonia*), to the breaking of bread and to prayer' (Acts 2:42). Just in case we are tempted to interpret this term in less tangible ways, Luke adds: 'All the believers were together and had everything in common (*koina*). Selling their possessions and goods, they gave to everyone who had need' (Acts 2:44–45).

The phrase 'everything in common' has sometimes been inter-preted as meaning that personal ownership of property was abolished in the Jerusalem church. Many groups have, on the basis of this passage, advocated the practice of 'community of goods' and the formation of 'common-purse' communities. But neither jubilee nor *koinonia* implies this, nor does the language used by Luke support such an interpretation.[27] Jubilee radically relativised personal ownership but did not abolish it. What Luke describes here is an ongoing and voluntary process of redistribution from those who had much to those who had little. He tells the story of Barnabas, who sold a particular field (rather than all his possessions) and brought the proceeds to the church leaders for distribution.[28] Ananias and Sapphira are not condemned for their failure to divest

---

[27] The imperfect tense of the verbs indicates a continuing process rather than a single event. This does not, of course, preclude the adoption of 'common-purse' policies, but advocates of these will need to look else-where than Acts 2–4 for a biblical foundation. A more appropriate prece-dent is provided by the common purse from which Jesus and his disciples were supported.

[28] Acts 4:36–37.

themselves of personal property, which Peter explicitly recognises was theirs to do with as they wished, but for their dishonesty.[29] Furthermore, the size of the community in Jerusalem was such that just seven men could not possibly have coped with a common-purse community, however 'full of the Spirit and wisdom' they were. But they could administer a communal fund and a programme of food distribution.[30]

Koinonia clearly left individuals free to retain or give away their property, but it called for a new understanding of economic responsibility for one another. As needs arose, resources were shared. Vogt helpfully summarises the situation: 'individuals still possessed things, yet they had all things in common. Their attitudes towards economic things were so changed that individual ownership did not define individual use. Everything that everyone owned was available for common use. It didn't matter who possessed it.'[31] It was not that everything was held in common ownership so that no one had their own possessions, but that 'no one claimed that any of their possessions was their own' (Acts 4:32).

Koinonia is also one of the principles behind Paul's detailed instructions on giving to the church at Corinth. That he does not advocate the kind of system practised in the Jerusalem church is an indication that *koinonia* can be worked out in diverse ways. It seems that the story of the sharing in the Jerusalem church was inspirational rather than normative, even in the first century. Two whole chapters of Paul's second letter (2 Cor. 8–9) and a number of other passages[32] are devoted to the subject of the collection he is gathering in order to make a contribution (*koinonia*) to the impoverished Christians in Jerusalem.[33] The attention he gave to this subject, by comparison with many other ethical, pastoral and doctrinal issues, is remarkable and indicates the importance he attached to this kind of mutual support among Christians. Economic *koinonia* is a firm basis for other dimensions of community life.

---

[29] Acts 5:1–11.

[30] Acts 6:1–7.

[31] Vogt, *Treasure*, 80.

[32] See Romans 15:25–27; 1 Corinthians 16:1–4; Galatians 2:10; Acts 20:24; 24:17.

[33] For a detailed but accessible study of Paul's collection, see Dieter Georgi, *Remembering the Poor* (Nashville: Abingdon, 1965).

Advocates of tithing have tended to deal with this body of teaching by imposing on it the paradigm of the tithe. Although Paul nowhere mentions this concept, they argue that he certainly assumed it and that his readers would have interpreted what he wrote as implying that they should tithe. We have already indicated that the evident lack of interest in the tithe, not only in the New Testament but also in the following two and a half centuries, makes such an interpretation highly unlikely. Furthermore, Paul's teaching is clearly based on quite different principles. He employs a range of arguments, supported by several Old Testament quotations,[34] but he does not refer to the tithing passages or suggest that setting aside a fixed percentage is an appropriate response to the challenge he is bringing.

The collection for the church in Jerusalem has also been used as evidence by those who reject as reckless and ill-conceived the form of *koinonia* in Acts 2–4. Obviously, they argue, the church in Jerusalem soon got into financial difficulties by adopting jubilee-like practices and needed to be baled out by gifts from other churches that had handled their finances more responsibly. But this conclusion, though ostensibly plausible, is not supported by the New Testament itself, which records instead that Judea was badly affected by a severe famine and that Christians in other churches, alerted to this prophetically, decided to send help to their sister church (Acts 11:28–29). Whether or not the Jerusalem expression of *koinonia* should be regarded as a model for others or as an experiment that might inspire similar creativity and mutual commitment, the New Testament contains no criticism of their practice.[35]

But if we refrain from reading into Paul's teaching either tithing or criticism of the Jerusalem model, what principles can we discover that might help us understand how the early churches shared their resources?

First, there is a consistent emphasis on voluntarism rather than compulsion. Though Paul feels and writes passionately about the collection, he does not use the 'ought' language so often associated with tithing, nor does he suggest his readers should contribute a

---

[34] See above in chapter 3.

[35] Indeed, there are indications that other early churches operated in similar ways. See Vogt, *Treasure*, 81–82.

fixed percentage. Willard Swartley points out that the term 'grace' occurs ten times in these two chapters.[36] Paul expects his readers to be motivated by thanksgiving rather than duty. The only phrase that might be understood as implying tithing is 'in keeping with your income', which occurs at the end of Paul's first letter to Corinth (1 Cor. 16:2). But this might just as well imply that wealthier members should give larger percentages of their income. Otherwise, these passages are full of phrases like 'as much as they were able' (2 Cor. 8:3), 'entirely on their own' (2 Cor. 8:3), 'I am not commanding you' (2 Cor. 8:8), 'according to what one has' (2 Cor. 8:12), 'what you have decided in your heart to give' (2 Cor. 9:7), 'not reluctantly or under compulsion' (2 Cor. 9:7). If Paul was an advocate of tithing and so expected his readers to tithe, this is a very oblique way of saying so!

Second, Paul testifies to an enthusiasm about giving which is markedly absent from the history of tithing and which seems to resonate more with the celebratory feel of the jubilee tradition. He refers to the givers' 'overflowing joy' (2 Cor. 8:2), their sense of 'the privilege of sharing (*koinonia*)' (2 Cor. 8:4), their 'eager willingness' (2 Cor. 8:11), their 'eagerness to help' (2 Cor. 9:2), and their 'enthusiasm' (2 Cor. 9:2). He concludes with the well-known phrase that 'God loves a cheerful giver' (2 Cor. 9:7). Those who tithe – and those who advocate tithing – may experience such excitement and joy as they contribute in this way, as testimonies in various books on tithing show. But paying a fixed percentage does not lend itself naturally to the kind of spontaneity evident in these chapters.

Third, the giving Paul describes and urges here is wholehearted, generous and even sacrificial: 'their extreme poverty welled up in rich generosity' (2 Cor. 8:2), they gave 'beyond their ability' (2 Cor. 8:3), Paul is anticipating 'a generous gift' (2 Cor. 9:5) and he is not afraid to encourage them to 'sow generously' (2 Cor. 9:6). *Koinonia*, like jubilee, is not a soft option for those who are reluctant to tithe, but a far more demanding approach to financial discipleship. Rather than being restricted by the fixed percentage of the tithe or seeing

---

[36] Willard Swartley & Donald Kraybill, *Building Communities of Compassion* (Scottdale, Pa.: Herald, 1998), 25. His chapter entitled 'Mutual Aid Based in Jesus and Early Christianity' provides a useful theological introduction to the concept of *koinonia*.

this as a maximum (which, contrary to the claims of those who advocate tithing, is actually what usually happens), those who are motivated by the 'privilege of *koinonia*' (2 Cor. 8:4) are encouraged to regard neither a tenth of their income nor even 'their ability' to give (2 Cor. 8:3) as caps on their generosity.

Fourth, though Paul does not refer to any of the Old Testament passages associated with jubilee, he does advocate the principle of 'equality' (2 Cor. 8:13) and presents a vision of *koinonia* in practice that looks remarkably like what would happen if some form of jubilee were practised regularly. He writes: 'Our desire is not that others might be relieved while you are hard pressed, but that there might be equality. At the present time your plenty will supply what they need, so that in turn their plenty will supply what you need. Then there will be equality' (2 Cor. 8:13–14). Those families who had more than enough at the start of one Year of Jubilee, and so were required to release their slaves and debtors and return property they had acquired to its original owners might in the next Year of Jubilee (if Israel had implemented the legislation) be in need and receive such treatment from others. Similarly, in the churches of the New Testament era, the interchange of resources might flow now in one direction and now in another, with a view to achieving a rough equality among the churches.

The goal of equality, which Paul advocates in this passage, has often been rejected as unbiblical or dismissed as utopian (or, even worse, as communist or socialist). But this concept is at the heart of both the jubilee provisions and the idea of *koinonia*. It is presented here by Paul, not as an ideal, but as something that is realistic and achievable. This equality will be approximate rather than exact and dynamic rather than static: the sharing of resources will not be a one-off activity but an ongoing re-equalising of resources in communities practising *koinonia*. But, in a world of gross inequality, such actions within Christian communities could be provocative and attractive, a sign that the coming Kingdom will be a kingdom of compassion, justice and equality.

The word used twice here by Paul (*isotēs*) is a term with a rich classical heritage.[37] It is frequently used in a judicial context and so,

---

[37] There is a helpful discussion of this in Georgi, *Remembering*, 84–91, 154–155.

though rendered 'equality' in most English versions, it can also be translated as 'equity' or 'fairness'.[38] The equalising of resources for which Paul argues here is a matter of justice rather than charity. This concept reminds us that *koinonia* involves rejecting the often sacrosanct principle of private property in favour of holding goods in trust for whomever within the church has need of them. It implies that injustice and inequality will no longer be tolerated among God's people. It encourages honesty, faith and determination to move forward, in spite of practical difficulties and risks, because the cause is just. Tithing may adequately fund a religious institution or channel resources to charitable causes, but it will not effect the equalising of resources – indeed, if we are to believe the testimonies of tithers who have received back more than they gave away, it may even have the opposite effect. Tithing does not have the same transformational potency, nor is it concerned primarily about justice.

Finally, Paul is concerned in these passages with the sharing of resources between churches rather within a single church. New Testament *koinonia* had implications for relationships between churches as well as within them. It seems that, once jubilee principles had produced a rough equality within the church at Jerusalem, Antioch or Corinth, the next challenge was to work through the process again by taking steps to equalise the resources available to the various local churches. Paul's goal of equality in 2 Corinthians relates to the resources enjoyed by several churches rather than just within the local church. His role was not only to raise funds and to ensure that those funds were handled responsibly and administered in a way that was beyond reproach (2 Cor. 8:16–21). It was also to raise awareness of the needs of some churches to receive funds and the opportunities in others to contribute to those needs.

This translocal understanding of *koinonia* could have profound implications for churches today. Within the denominations and networks of churches that comprise the Christian community in Britain are some churches with huge resources and others with very little. What impact might be made on the mission of the church by some attempt at equalising resources among these congregations? The present distribution of resources is, from a mission perspective, both unjust and bizarre, with huge resources gathering interest in

---

[38] Blomberg, *Neither*, 194.

church bank accounts or wasted on expensive new church buildings, while there is minimal investment of resources in the areas of greatest need and greatest opportunity.

If the same question is asked on a global scale, the implications are colossal. What might a watching world make of regular, joyful and substantial transfers of resources from richer to poorer churches along the lines of 2 Corinthians 8 and 9? How would the local community interpret a decision to abandon plans to build an extension to your church building and instead give the half a million pounds already raised to Christians lacking basic amenities in another nation?

The translocal dimension is important also in relation to a further aspect of *koinonia*. We expressed concern in an earlier chapter about the individualistic and privatised ethos that surrounds tithing. Tithing is presented by most advocates as a matter that is between an individual and God. But *koinonia* is all about sharing and community. Decisions about lifestyle, giving and sharing may be personal but they are no longer private. Barnabas, Ananias and Sapphira remained responsible for their resources, but they belonged to a community where needs were shared, financial discussions took place and members held each other accountable. Churches today that decide to explore the implications of *koinonia* will welcome the opportunity to discover a new openness about money and to break the stranglehold that Mammon exerts through the privatisation of this subject.

We need each other's help and discernment if we are to challenge the prevailing values of our consumerist culture and develop liberated lifestyles and counter-cultural communities. The pressures to conform are simply too great for heroic individualism. And we need to escape parochialism and invite the insights and perspectives of the translocal church if we are not simply to endorse each other's prejudices. Sider recognises this:

> We need the help of other brothers and sisters – in our local congregation, in our town or city, and around the world. We need to develop a process for discussing our economic lifestyles with close Christian friends in our congregation. We also need new ways to exchange ideas about the shape of a faithful lifestyle with poor Christians.[39]

---

[39] Ronald Sider, *Rich Christians in an Age of Hunger* (London: Hodder & Stoughton, 1990), 191.

Koinonia, like jubilee, is a very disturbing but utterly biblical paradigm which, for understandable but illegitimate reasons, has been marginalised throughout the Christendom era in favour of the much safer tithe.[40] But if we want to have any good news to share in a post-Christian culture that is weary of safe and predictable Christianity, perhaps it is time to put away the tithing blinkers and take a fresh look at these radical alternatives.

Jubilee, *Koinonia* and Tithing?

Under Christendom, the church became wealthy. As the recipient of state support through tax exemptions and compulsory tithes, it became increasingly difficult for the church to challenge social injustices or to practise the kind of community life described in the New Testament. Simplicity, equality, sharing, contentment, mutual aid, voluntary poverty, holding all things in common and various other aspects of early church life seemed anachronistic and unworkable. But, as we have seen, within dissenting groups such uncomfortable New Testament teachings were rediscovered and attempts made to imitate early church practices. The lifestyle and teachings of Jesus, which had been effectively marginalised in main-stream Christendom, were very influential in these movements. As they studied his teaching and discovered his concern for the poor, his encouragement of simplicity and sharing, and his readiness to challenge injustice, they contrasted what they found with the wealth of the contemporary church and its apparent neglect of justice and of the poor. And some of them dared to challenge the tithe and to operate on different principles.

Christendom operated with a 'hermeneutics of order'. In other words, on all kinds of issues the Bible tended to be interpreted in ways that would not threaten the status quo. From early in the

---

[40] There is not space here to examine the use of the concept of *koinonia* in the first three centuries, but there is evidence that this was used quite extensively. See Swartley & Kraybill, *Building*, 29–35; and Charles Avila, *Ownership: Early Christian Teaching* (Maryknoll, N.Y.: Orbis, 1983), 37–46, 144–146. Avila suggests that *autarkeia* (self-sufficiency) and *koinonia* were the twin goals of ownership according to patristic thought.

Christendom era, it became clear that the Bible would need to be interpreted in the light of new political realities. Kee writes: 'after Constantine, it is the church under the sway of imperial values which now provides the perspective for reading the Bible.'[41] This way of interpreting the Bible became established as orthodox, provided constant reinforcement of the system and diverted possible biblical challenges to it. Liberation theologian, José Miguez Bonino has proposed that we should operate instead with a 'hermeneutics of justice'. He writes:

> If we accept this hermeneutical key for an understanding of the theological determination of priorities, then the question of the Constantinian church has to be turned completely around. The true question is not 'what degree of justice . . . is compatible with the existing order?', but 'what kind of order, which order is compatible with the exercise of justice?'[42]

Not surprisingly, this approach was alien to biblical interpreters in the Christendom era.

Tithing was an ideal tool for the church under Christendom. It provided a practical and efficient way of supporting the state church that appeared to be backed by impeccable biblical authority. Moreover it did not prompt the awkward questions about the just distribution of resources within that society that principles such as jubilee and *koinonia* would have raised. Tithing was not threatening – at least, not to those with power and wealth. But *koinonia*, especially when linked with the concept of equality, was a dangerous idea, and jubilee was a revolutionary paradigm that would have been profoundly disturbing in a hierarchical and fundamentally unjust society.

Although voluntary tithing is now advocated for different reasons and in a different context, it is rooted in the same kind of approach to the Bible that was used under Christendom. Furthermore, this privatised approach to economic discipleship is much more popular with Christians today than the more radical and more threatening models

---

[41] Kee, *Constantine*, 168.
[42] José Miguez Bonino, *Towards a Christian Political Ethics* (Philadelphia: Fortress Press, 1983), 82.

we have examined in this chapter. But tithing is one of the many vestiges of the Christendom era that need to be identified and challenged as inappropriate in post-Christendom churches.

One way of dealing with these vestiges is to submit them to the kind of biblical and historical scrutiny to which we have attempted to submit tithing in this study. Tithing may not operate today in the way that it did when it was a legal requirement, but the advocacy of voluntary tithing is generally based on the same flawed principles of interpretation that justified so many practices that undergirded Christendom. Perhaps it is now time to abandon the 'hermeneutics of order' (and the advocacy of tithing this undergirds) and adopt a 'hermeneutics of justice'? Perhaps it is time to learn from the dissenters, whose hermeneutics and community practices offer an attractive and challenging alternative that might be more appropriate in post-Christendom?

But the question may be asked: is it not possible to embrace the principle of tithing alongside such principles as jubilee and *koinonia*? After all, tithing and jubilee were both components in the Mosaic legislation.

It is certainly possible to do this. Some of those who have explored the principles of jubilee and their implications for today have also endorsed tithing. Yoder interprets Jesus' words to the Pharisees in Matthew 23 as indicating that he did not wish to abolish the tithe, but he warns that tithing can lead to 'easy moral self-satisfaction' and that Jesus 'considered the tithe insufficient'.[43] Tithing might function as a way of making minor adjustments within an approach to giving that is guided by jubilee principles. This seems to have been how the tithe was intended to operate in the Old Testament. Divorced from its jubilee context and applied on its own, however, the principle of tithing, both then and now, is not only ineffective but unjust.

Sider, having explored some of the implications of the jubilee, does not endorse the usual form of tithing but considers the merits of a graduated tithing system, whereby a baseline budget is established on which a tithe is paid but any additional income is subject to a higher rate of giving.[44] This certainly has advantages over the traditional

---

[43] Yoder, *Politics*, 69–70.
[44] Sider, *Rich*, 175–178. See also Blomberg, *Neither*, 194–195.

system of tithing and goes some way towards redressing its inherent inequalities, but many of the criticisms of the tithing system we have considered in previous chapters apply also to graduated tithing. Kraybill, while appreciating Sider's attempt to move beyond 'kindergarten tithing', suggests that it may be preferable to allow the jubilee model to 'graduate us from tithing completely'.[45]

This may well be wiser than attempting to integrate tithing into the more radical approach that we have been exploring. It is surely significant that none of the New Testament writers tried to do this, perhaps realising that this would have caused confusion. If tithing is advocated and practised, even as only one aspect of financial discipleship, it is likely that the 'tithing blinkers' will once more hinder us from seeing clearly the much bigger picture that the principles of jubilee and *koinonia* open up in front of us. Given the wretched history of tithing under Christendom that we are still needing to disavow, perhaps we should be even more reticent about toying with tithing than the early Christians were.

What's wrong with tithing? Many things: the unreliable biblical interpretation on which it is based; the history of oppression and bias against the poor with which tithing has been associated; the dubious theology with which it is often commended; the pastoral difficulties that may arise from its practice; the tendency of churches that advocate tithing to devote most of their income to their own needs; the false sense of security that tithing can bring to those who are still firmly bound by materialism and consumerism; and the difficulty of seeing anything else in the Bible about giving and sharing while we wear the tithing blinkers.

Tithing belongs to the dominant state church tradition and has been for centuries a source of misery, oppression and conflict. Its transmutation in the past century into a model of giving advocated in many churches as the biblical paradigm has not involved adequate engagement with the biblical, historical and ethical issues we have investigated in this study.

Tithing is not an appropriate model for Christians and churches who are concerned about mission in a post-Christendom culture. Tithing is neither good news to the poor nor sufficiently

---

[45] Donald Kraybill, *The Upside Down Kingdom* (London: Marshalls, 1978), 148.

demanding for the rich. Tithing does not address issues of justice within church or society. Tithing tends to channel resources into maintaining church buildings, staff and programmes rather than releasing these into a hungry world. Tithing often results in Christians developing what John Reumann calls 'church tower horizons', where 'they see no further than the church building and are less diligent than non-Christians when it comes to doing what needs to be done in the world that lies beyond them'.[46] Tithing does nothing to challenge the perceptions of those who still believe that 'the church is after our money'.

Not only does the tithing paradigm fail to address issues of justice and questions of lifestyle; the tithing blinkers hinder us from seeing any alternatives. Several critics of tithing, who are aware of its miserable history, inadequate biblical base and its practical deficiencies, nevertheless conclude by commending tithing! Do we lack the courage to challenge this long tradition? Do we still harbour hopes that it might be redeemable? Or is it simply that we cannot identify a viable alternative (except the sporadic and minimal giving evident in churches which do not advocate tithing)?

But, as we have seen, there is an alternative tradition, rooted in both Testaments, and demonstrated by the early churches and in later dissenting movements. Jubilee and *koinonia* are attractive alternative paradigms with solid biblical credentials. They bring good news to the poor and a costly but crucial challenge to the rich. Examples from the New Testament, from the early centuries and from marginalised groups in later centuries show us how they can be put into practice. The challenge we face is not to copy these in a legalistic way but to be creative, sensitive to the situation in which we are living, and determined to make progress towards faithful discipleship in this vital area.

Building communities of justice and compassion; communities that are good news to the poor; communities where issues of lifestyle can be discussed freely; communities where consumerism can be resisted; communities where alternative values can be expressed; communities where creative initiatives can be taken; communities that are no longer trapped by huge financial commitments to

---

[46] John Reumann, *Stewardship and the Economy of God* (Grand Rapids: Eerdmans, 1992), 122.

expensive buildings, staff salaries and the maintenance of church programmes: surely this is more liberating and hopeful than the continued advocacy of tithing?

This will not be easy – but it may just be a component in the formation (or renewal) of churches that are able with integrity to engage in holistic mission in our society. It is important that we do not deceive ourselves. The church in Britain is in serious trouble. Despite much talk of revival, decades of evangelism, church growth courses, church planting initiatives and a range of programmes designed to help churches engage more effectively in mission, there are only sporadic signs of progress. The fact is that the church has declined steadily throughout the past century and continues to lose ground. Most denominations are struggling; some appear to be in meltdown. Short-term responses, typical of the closing years of a century, have not helped. Hopefully, once the millennial celebrations are over, we can settle down to the longer-term and more demanding task of enabling our churches to incarnate and proclaim the good news in ways that connect with contemporary culture.

Tithing is not the sole cause of the problem! Abandoning tithing will not, by itself, reverse the decline, transform the church or revolutionise its mission. But tithing may be a symptom of the underlying problem – the struggle the church faces as it emerges from Christendom and encounters the opportunities and challenges of a very different culture. Setting aside the tithing paradigm and exploring biblical and historical alternatives might do more than simply change the way our churches deal with their finances. It might open up to fresh scrutiny all kinds of assumptions and practices that have accumulated during the Christendom centuries. We might find biblical and historical alternatives in many other areas of life that could enable us to become the kinds of communities that have good news to share in the twenty-first century.

Postscript

Beyond Tithing – What If . . . ?

I have received a number of comments from friends who discovered I was writing a book about tithing, in which I was challenging the legitimacy of this practice. Those whose contact with evangelical and charismatic churches is limited were surprised to hear that tithing is still popular. Some who are members of such churches were equally surprised that anyone should question tithing. A few felt threatened by what they thought I might write and defended their practice as biblical and responsible. Others were intrigued and asked what system I would advocate instead of tithing. Several assumed that I would argue that Christians should give much more than a tithe.

I hope by now it is clear that there are serious problems with the way in which tithing has been advocated and practised over many centuries. I do not believe that tithing can be redeemed and I have no hesitation in advocating the abandonment of tithing – the sooner the better.[1] I realise that this will be deeply threatening to those who have tithed for years and to churches who have taught tithing and are supported through a tithing system. I know church leaders who agree with the argument of this book but who dare not tamper with a system that they have advocated publicly and that funds their premises and programmes (not to mention paying their own salary) so effectively.

---

[1] The argument advanced against tithing in the previous chapters is not presented as if it were the final word on the subject. I find the cumulative evidence in the case against tithing compelling, but I look forward to listening to and learning from those who have different perspectives on tithing.

And I appreciate that abandoning tithing, though this has been liberating for some, can be scary and unsettling. If we don't tithe, what do we do? We have looked at biblical principles such as jubilee and *koinonia*, and we have listened to Christians in the early churches and in dissident movements describing how their communities operated. But, interesting though these perspectives may be, surely all this is rather unsatisfactory if we are searching for a new system of giving and sharing?

But the last thing we need is to replace tithing with another authoritative system. In this postscript, then, I have no intention of introducing or endorsing such a system. Contrary to the assumptions of some of my friends, I am not advocating that tithing be abandoned in order to urge all Christians to give more of their money to God, to the church or to anyone else. I actually believe that some ought to be giving less and receiving more! Nor am I advocating a free-for-all individualistic approach that will inevitably result in a return to undisciplined and meagre giving. I really do not have an alternative system or a hidden agenda that I will suddenly present in the final pages as a replacement for the tithing system. All I want to do here is to ask the question: what if? What if we dared to abandon tithing (or even to suspend it temporarily) in order to explore alternatives? What if we began to dream of different churches, even a different kind of world?

Some of the 'what ifs' have already been hinted at in earlier chapters. Here are a few more to stimulate our creativity as we consider moving beyond tithing. They are not particularly radical; they are simply starting points that are within reach of many local churches. Although I know of no one church that is exploring all of these possibilities, I know of churches that are actively working on several of them. Some are just beginning; others already have years of experience from which we might learn.

What if we were to start talking about money in a new way? What difference would it make if . . .

- we identified consumerism as one of the powerful idols of our time and determined to resist this idol?

- we recognised that excessive privacy and individualism strengthen the grip of this idol on our lives and rejected these cultural hindrances?
- we talked openly and regularly about our finances with trusted friends, breaking the bondage imposed by the taboo on such conversations?
- these conversations explored how we earn our money, our attitudes towards our possessions, our values and priorities, our lifestyle, our decisions about spending and saving?
- we discussed how much to give away and to whom, how to monitor our giving, and when to make changes?
- we helped each other work through the implications of moving into a smaller house or a different neighbourhood?
- we decided that our capital resources as well as our income could be put at the disposal of those in need?
- we considered whether to regard money spent on our own church as subscription payments or institutional support (the equivalent of club fees) rather than giving, since we are really just funding our own pastoral care, meeting place and activities?
- we considered no longer claiming back tax on gifts covenanted for such purposes, since these are not charitable donations but ways of funding benefits for the donors?
- we knew that those with whom we shared our ideas, hopes and fears would be honest but not judgmental, persistent but not intrusive, sensitive but also courageous?
- these friendships and conversations involved mutual accountability, with each participant invited to offer and receive counsel and encouragement?

What if our church community were to support this approach to finances? What if . . .

- we became a church community with counter-cultural reflexes that resisted the idol of consumerism?
- our church provided teaching and training to equip us to think biblically about financial issues and to develop the skills and values required to develop the kinds of friendships in which these can be discussed?
- we studied such biblical principles as jubilee and *koinonia* and asked how these might be worked out creatively and progressively in the local context?

- we undertook a thorough audit of our church premises and found ways to reduce costs and damage the environment less?
- we asked whether we really needed these premises, or at least whether we might be able to share them with another congregation or community group?
- we invited the comments of others before deciding to spend money to improve our facilities – the members of a church in a poorer area, a homeless person, a refugee?
- we asked whether we really needed the staff our church employs – or is thinking of employing – and whether we could reduce our costs by together investing more time in mission and ministry?
- we chose to fund a staff member in a poorer church instead of appointing a new staff member in our church?
- we determined to appoint as church leaders only those who were known as friends of the poor?
- we chose to give away to disaster relief or development projects the hundreds of thousands of pounds in our building fund?
- we differentiated clearly between (a) money given by church members to support our staff, premises and programmes and (b) money given for people and causes beyond the local church?

What if we started to apply some more of these principles to our church life? What if . . .

- we were sufficiently secure in our friendships and open-hearted in our attitudes to begin to address the inequalities in our own church?
- we were to discover ways to begin to redistribute resources among our members, so that those who have more than they need could contribute towards those who have less than they need?
- we were to sell our surplus possessions and give the proceeds to the poor, so that we could say truthfully that there are 'no needy persons among us'?
- we were to pass round a collection bag and invited those who wanted to give to put some money in the bag and those who were in need to take money out?
- we formed common-purse communities to explore more deeply the disciplines of sharing and accountability to help the rest of us move on?
- we encouraged small groups in the church to share their resources in order to release funds for ministry and mission?

- we rediscovered the ministry of the deacon as one who distributed resources for the benefit of the poor?
- we were to work towards becoming a debt-free congregation by helping those in debt to break free and stay free of debt?
- we were to take this a step further and found creative ways to pay off mortgages and to fund major expenses without incurring future debts?

What if we saw financial matters as an important dimension of our mission in a consumerist and debt-ridden culture? What if . . .

- we extended this way of sharing to others in our local community, on the fringe of our church and beyond?
- we became known as a community that took financial issues seriously and was able to offer more than just sympathy (or condemnation) to those in debt?
- we chose to risk being taken for a ride rather than refusing to help others, or being seen as a soft touch rather than hard-nosed?
- we explored ways of sharing our homes with homeless people?
- we invited others to follow the One who releases debtors and calls them to release others?
- we sent church planting teams into pioneer mission situations who would fund themselves by sharing their resources?
- we forged deep links with other churches in different parts of our nation or our world and explored together how to share spiritual and material resources without dependency or paternalism?
- we encouraged one another to campaign and vote for policies that favour the poor in our own nation and globally?

What if . . . ?

- poor people were to realise that the gospel is good news and to recognise that our church incarnates this good news?
- we were to find that this kind of sharing was exciting, liberating and joyful?

What if . . . ?

Appendix 1

Tithing: Humour and Complaint

In the Middle Ages

The York Mystery Plays in the later Middle Ages contained a 'pointed reference to the 10 per cent which Judas Iscariot thought his due. The thirty pieces of silver amounted, in his calculation, to 10 per cent of the value of the box of ointment which ought to have been sold for the benefit of the poor.'[1]

In the Eighteenth Century

The following poem by William Cowper (1731–1800) appeared in 'The Yearly Distress, or Tithing Time at Stock in Essex' (1779).

> The Priest he merry is and blithe
> Three Quarters of the Year
> But Oh! it cuts him like a scythe
> When tithing time draws near
>
> For then the farmers come, jog, jog
> Along the miry road
> Each heart as heavy as a log
> To make their Payments good

---

[1] Christopher Hill, *Economic Problems of the Church* (Oxford: Clarendon Press, 1956), 79.

> Now all unwelcome, at his gates
> The clumsy swains alight
> With rueful faces and bald pates
> He trembles at the sight
>
> And well he may, for well he knows
> Each bumpkin of the clan
> Instead of paying what he owes
> Will cheat him if he can

Poet Thomas Edwards (1739–1810) was invited by a local priest to write a short poem about wheat. He complied:[2]

> Here is a field of white wheat
> Growing slowly
> And a tenth of the field's produce
> Goes to the devil's servant.

In the Nineteenth Century

Doreen Wallace reports the following story:[3] To one poor old Quaker, a bootmaker, the parson said, 'You have not paid your tithe!' The Quaker said, 'No, I am not going to pay thee. I do not attend thy meeting–house, neither have I any use for thy services, therefore I will not pay.' The parson said, 'But it is the law of the land. You could attend if you wanted; my door is always open and my services are at your disposal.' Next morning the parson was surprised to receive a bill for a pair of boots from the Quaker. He hurried to the shop and said, 'There is some little mistake here. I have had no boots.' The Quaker replied, 'No. I know thou hast had no boots, but my doors are always open, my services are at thy disposal, and thou couldst have had a pair of boots if thou hadst desired them!'

---

[2] *The Tithe War* (Hawarden, Deeside: Clwyd Record Office, 1978), 1. The poem was originally written in Welsh.
[3] Doreen Wallace, *The Tithe War* (London: Victor Gollancz, 1934), 149.

An obituary card attached to a tithe cow in Wales in 1894 read as follows:[4]

> In loving memory
> Of the
> BELOVED COW
> Of Mr James Davies, Nant-y-Merddyn, Uchaf
> Llansannan
> Who went a prey to the insatiable greed
> Of the Ecclesiastical Commissioners
> April 25th 1894

In the Twentieth Century

The memoirs of Rev. T. Eurig Davies, a Welsh nonconformist minister, include the following passage:

As children we heard much talk of how the anti-tithe rebels marched from district to district, and from farm to farm when animals and property were sold to meet the demands. At the front of the procession the head of the parish priest would be carried – carved skillfully from a turnip. Pretty effective ways were devised of obstructing the auctioneer and not everyone was pacifist either, as the odd officer, escaping in haste, found to his cost.

A Suffolk farmer, F. S. Fisk, produced the following verses:[5]

Money, oh, money, thy praises I sing;
Thou art my Saviour, my God, and my King!
'Tis for thee that I preach, and for thee that I pray
And make a collection twice each Sabbath Day.

I have candles and all sorts of dresses to buy,
For I wish you to know that my Church is called High!

---

[4] *The Tithe War* (Hawarden, Deeside: Clwyd Record Office, 1978), 9.
[5] Wallace, *Tithe*, 168–169.

I don't mean in structure of steeple or wall,
But so high that the Lord cannot reach it at all.

I have poor in my parish who need some relief;
I preach for their poverty, pray for their grief.
I send my box round to them morning and night,
And hope they'll remember the poor widow's mite.

I gather my knowledge from wisdom's great tree,
And the whole of my Trinity's £, s and d:
Pounds, shillings, and pence are all that I crave,
From my first step on earth to the brink of the grave.

And when I'm laid low and my body's at rest,
Place a box on my grave — 'tis my latest request —
That friends may all see who come for reflection
I can't rest in peace without a collection.

Money's my creed, I won't pray without it;
My heaven is closed against all those who doubt it;
For this is the essence of Tithe Parson's religion:
Come reg'lar to church and be plucked like a pigeon.

My pay may be hundreds or thousands a year;
Double it, treble it, still I am here,
With my box or my bags, collecting your brass —
I can't do as Jesus did, ride on an ass.

I have motors and horses, servants and all;
I'm not going to foot it like Peter and Paul,
Neither like John live on locusts and honey.
So out with your purse and down with your money.

Fools sometimes ask what I do with the money:
They might as well ask what bees do with their honey.
I answer them all with a wink and a nod —
I keep three-thirds myself and give praises to God.

In the cold silent earth I shall soon be laid low
To sleep with the blest that went long ago.
I shall slumber in peace till the great resurrection,
Then be first on my legs to make a collection.

H. McQueen wrote the following poem, entitled 'Tithe':[6]

forgetting we are nomad
we settle, lay our drains
panic, like distress, is best avoided
until the floodbanks burst
then we float the paddocks, rescue stock
the heart enjoys the risk
& for a while
           the unfamiliar landscape
yesterday's pig sty
        tin drum
        dream house
                float down the creek
when the waters recede
            we cuddle back
            to new boundaries
the bishop rises from the hard stone floor
announces a new tithe
                it'll enclose a field
                  rebuild a nave
                  get him to Rome
it'll not do to wait another winter

bureaucrats labour on
like sheep an unimportant but collective
                   weight
we wear lasting tracks in the fabric of
                 events
they converge at the watering places

---

[6] H. McQueen, 'Tithe', *Landfall* 35(2) (1981), 180–181.

honestly it must also be said
the cash is meant to help the poor
                         the sick
                         the ignorant
            defend the realm
usually the system works until the design
                              fault is revealed
who doesn't like to run guns to the rebels

silt cracks in the sun
                    peasants plough
managers calculate
                money comes & money goes
adds a little sherry to the trifle

old tithe
            new tax
                        new tithe
                            old tax
evaporation
            precipitation
                        respiration
        the witches dance around the cauldron

Appendix 2

Select Bibliography

Atkinson, A. G. B. *Tithe Rent-Charge* (London: SPCK, 1921)

Avila, Charles *Ownership: Early Christian Teaching* (Maryknoll, N.Y: Orbis, 1983)

Batey, Richard *Jesus and the Poor* (London: Harper & Row, 1972)

Best, Geoffrey *Temporal Pillars* (Cambridge: CUP, 1964)

Blickle, Peter *Communal Reformation: The Quest for Salvation in Sixteenth-Century Germany* (London: Humanities Press, 1992)

Blomberg, Craig *Neither Poverty Nor Riches: A Biblical Theology of Material Possessions* (Leicester: Apollos, 1999)

Bond, Michael *Dying to Give* (Nottingham: United Reformed Church, East Midlands Province, 1988)

Boyd, Catherine *Tithes and Parishes in Medieval Italy* (Ithaca, N.Y.: Cornell University Press, 1952)

Brigden, Susan 'Tithe Controversy in Reformation London', *Journal of Ecclesiastical History* 32(3) (1981): 285–301

Buck, Laurence 'Opposition to Tithes in the Peasants' Revolt: A Case Study of Nuremberg in 1524', *Sixteenth Century Journal* 4(2) (1973): 11–22

Clapp, Rodney *The Consuming Passion: Christianity and the Consumer Culture* (Downers Grove, Ill.: IVP, 1998)

Clinard, H. Gordon 'Preaching on Stewardship Themes', *Review and Expositor* 70(2) (1973), 197–206

Constable, Giles *Monastic Tithes* (Cambridge: CUP, 1964)

Cosway, A. H. *Guide to the Tithe Act, 1936* (London: Sir Isaac Pitman & Sons, 1937)

Countryman, L. William *The Rich Christian in the Church of the Early Empire: Contradictions and Accommodations* (New York: The Edwin Mellen Press, 1980)

Daniel-Rops, Henri *Cathedral and Crusade* (London: J. M. Dent & Sons, 1957)

Daniel-Rops, Henri *The Church in the Dark Ages* (London: J. M. Dent & Sons, 1959)

Delorme, Roger 'La Mesure de la Dime' *Historia* 443 (1983): 13

De St Croix, G. 'Early Christian Attitudes to Property and Slavery' in Derek Baker (ed.), *Church, Society and Politics*, Studies in Church History 12 (Oxford: Blackwell, 1975)

De Vaux, Roland *Ancient Israel: Its Life and Institutions* (New York, McGraw Hill, 1965)

Evans, Eric *The Contentious Tithe* (London: Routledge & Kegan Paul, 1976)

Evans, Eric *Tithes and the Tithe Commutation Act 1836* (London: Bedford Square Press, 1978)

Flynn, Eileen 'Beware the Tithing Team', *Theology Today* 40 (1983/84): 195–196

Georgi, Dieter *Remembering the Poor* (Nashville: Abingdon, 1965)

Gonzalez, Justo *Faith and Wealth* (San Francisco: Harper & Row, 1990)

Gnuse, Robert *You Shall Not Steal* (Maryknoll, N.Y.: Orbis, 1985)

Hastings, Robert *My Money and God* (Nashville: Broadman, 1961)

Hatch, Edwin *The Growth of Church Institutions* (London: Hodder & Stoughton, 1885)

Hawthorne, G. F. 'Tithe', *New International Dictionary of New Testament Theology* (Carlisle: Paternoster Press, 1976/1986)

Hayden, Roger *The Records of a Church in Christ in Bristol, 1640–1687* (Bristol: Bristol Record Society, 1974)

Hengel, Martin *Property and Riches in the Early Church* (London: SCM Press, 1974)

Hensey, James *Storehouse Tithing; or, Stewardship Up-to-Date* (New York: Fleming H. Revell, 1922)

Herman, Menahem *Tithe as Gift: The Institution in the Pentateuch and in light of Mauss's Prestation Theory* (San Francisco: Mellen Research University Press, 1991)

Hertig, Paul 'The Jubilee Mission of Jesus in the Gospel of Luke: Reversals of Fortune', *Missiology* 26(2) (April 1998): 167–179

Hill, Christopher *Economic Problems of the Church* (Oxford: Clarendon Press, 1956)

Hobbs, Herschel *The Gospel of Giving* (Nashville: Broadman Press, 1954)

Hollis, Allen *The Bible and Money* (New York: Hawthorn Books, 1976)

Jaffee, Martin *Mishnah's Theology of Tithing: A Study of Tractate Maaserot* (Chico, Calif.: Scholars Press, 1981)

Jagersma, H. 'The Tithes in the Old Testament' in Albrektson, B. (et al.), *Remembering All the Way* (Leiden: Brill, 1981)

James, Margaret 'The Political Importance of the Tithes Controversy in the English Revolution', *History* 26 (1941): 1–18

Johnson, Luke *Sharing Possessions* (Philadelphia: Fortress Press, 1981)

Kain, Roger and Prince, Hugh *The Tithe Surveys of England and Wales* (Cambridge: CUP, 1985)

Kauffman, Milo *The Challenge of Christian Stewardship* (Scottdale, Pa.: Herald Press, 1955)

Kendall, R. T. *Tithing* (London: Hodder & Stoughton, 1982)

Kendall, R. T. *The Gift of Giving* (Hodder & Stoughton, 1992)

Kraybill, Donald *The Upside Down Kingdom* (London: Marshalls, 1978; Scottdale, Pa.: Herald Press, 1990)

Kreider, Alan *Journey Towards Holiness* (London: Marshalls, 1986)

Ladurie, Emmanuel and Goy, Joseph *Tithe and Agrarian History for the Fourteenth to the Nineteenth Centuries* (Cambridge: CUP, 1982)

Leavell, Frank *Training in Stewardship* (Nashville: Sunday School Board of the Southern Baptist Convention, 1920)

Little, A. G. 'Personal Tithes', *English Historical Review* 60 (1945): 67–88

Mann, Adrian *No Small Change* (Norwich: The Canterbury Press, 1992)

McConville, J. Gordon *Law and Theology in Deuteronomy* (Sheffield: JSOT, 1984)

McManners, John 'Tithe in Eighteenth-Century France: A Focus for Rural Anticlericalism' in D. Beales and G. Best, *History, Society and the Churches* (Cambridge: CUP, 1985)

McQueen, H. 'Tithe', *Landfall* 35(2) (1981): 180–181

Milgrom, J. *Cult and Conscience: the Asham and the Priestly Doctrine of Repentance* (Leiden: Brill, 1976)

Morris, Robert *The Tithe War* (Oxford: OUP, 1989)

Mullin, Redmond *The Wealth of Christians* (Exeter: Paternoster Press, 1983)

Nelson, Janet 'Making Ends Meet: Wealth and Poverty in the Carolingian Church' in W. J. Shiels and Diana Wood (eds), *Studies in Church History* 24: *The Church and Wealth* (Oxford: Blackwell, 1987)

Nelson, Richard 'Biblical Perspectives on Stewardship' *Lutheran Theological Seminary Bulletin* 70(4) (1990): 3–11

Norrington, David 'Fund-raising: The Methods Used in the Early Church Compared with Those Used in English Churches Today', *Evangelical Quarterly* 70(2) (1998): 115–134

North, Gary *Tithing and the Church* (Tyler, Tex.: Institute for Christian Economics, 1994)

Olford, Stephen *The Grace of Giving* (London: Lakeland, 1972)

Pagolu, Augustine *The Religion of the Patriarchs* (Sheffield: Sheffield Academic Press, 1998)

Pearse, Meic *The Great Restoration* (Carlisle: Paternoster, 1998)

Pilgrim, Walter *Good News to the Poor* (Minneapolis: Augsburg Publishing, 1981)

Rashid, Salim 'Anglican Clergymen and the Tithe Question', *Journal of Religious History* 11(1) (1980): 64–76

Reumann, John *Stewardship and the Economy of God* (Grand Rapids: Eerdmans, 1992

Ringe, Sharon *Jesus, Liberation and the Biblical Jubilee* (Philadelphia: Fortress Press, 1985)

Rusbuldt, Richard *A Workbook on Biblical Stewardship* (Grand Rapids: Eerdmans, 1994)

Salstrand, George *The Story of Stewardship in the United States of America* (Grand Rapids: Baker, 1956)

Scott, Tom and Scribner, Bob (eds) *The German Peasants' War* (New Jersey: Humanities Press, 1991)

Seccombe, David *Possessions and the Poor in Luke-Acts* (Linz: Studien Zum Neuen Testament Und Seiner Umwelt, 1982)

Sider, Ronald *Rich Christians in an Age of Hunger* (London: Hodder & Stoughton, 1990)

Sloan, Robert *The Favorable Year of the Lord* (Austin, Tex.: Schola Press, 1977)

Stagg, Paul 'An Interpretation of Christian Stewardship' in Duke McCall (ed.): *What is the Church?* (Nashville: Broadman Press, 1958)

Swartley, Willard and Kraybill, Donald *Building Communities of Compassion* (Scottdale, Pa.: Herald, 1998)

Tate, Marvin 'Tithing: Legalism or Benchmark?', *Review and Expositor* 70(2) (1973): 153–161

Taylor, Stephen 'Sir Robert Walpole, The Church of England, and the Quakers Tithe Bill of 1736', *Historical Journal* 28(1) (1985): 51–77

Thompson, P. W. *The Whole Tithe* (London: Marshall, Morgan & Scott, 1929)

Tilley, W. Clyde. 'A Biblical Approach to Stewardship', *Review and Expositor* 84(3) (1987): 433–442

Tondeur, Keith *Your Money and Your Life* (London: SPCK, 1996)

Trocmé, André *Jesus and the Nonviolent Revolution* (Scottdale, Pa: Herald Press, 1973)

Vischer, Lukas *Tithing in the Early Church* (Philadelphia: Fortress Press, 1966)

Vogt, Virgil *Treasure in Heaven* (Ann Arbor: Servant Books, 1982)

Wharham, Alan 'Tithes in Country Life', *History Today* 22 (1972): 426–433

Wallace, Doreen *The Tithe War* (London: Victor Gollancz, 1934)

White, Barrington *Association Records of the Particular Baptists of England, Wales and Ireland to 1660* (London: Baptist Historical Society, 1971)

White, Barrington 'The English Particular Baptists and the Great Rebellion, 1640–1660', *Baptist History and Heritage* 9(1) (1974): 16–29

Wilson, Michael *Managing Your Money* (Leicester: IVP, 1994)

Wright, Addison 'The Widow's Mites: Praise or Lament? – A Matter of Context', *Catholic Biblical Quarterly* 44(2) (1982): 256–265

Wright, Christopher *Living as the People of God* (Leicester: IVP, 1983)

Yoder, John Howard *The Politics of Jesus* (Grand Rapids: Eerdmans, 1972; revised edition, Carlisle: Paternoster, 1994)

The Jewish Encyclopedia 12 (New York and London: Funk and Wagnalls, 1905)

The Tithe War (Hawarden, Deeside: Clwyd Record Office, 1978)

Biblical and Extrabiblical Index

Subject and Name Index

Author Index